**" To** **to write** **is to learn** **to have** **ideas. "**

— Robert Frost

# GRAMMAR

## English Fundamentals, *Form B*
### Twelfth Edition

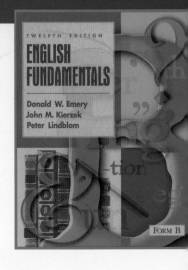

**Donald W. Emery,** Late, *University of Washington*
**John M. Kierzek,** Late, *Oregon State University*
**Peter Lindblom,** *Miami-Dade Community College*

© 2002 • 448 pages • Paper • ISBN 0-205-32972-1

Like its best-selling predecessors, this new edition of *English Fundamentals* offers a solid treatment of grammar and usage that has proven successful in thousands of classrooms.

## *Features*

- **Practice sheets,** one for each lesson, allow students to work at a beginner's level on the principles introduced in the lesson.

- **Exercises** offer more intensive practice on the principles of the lesson. Each lesson contains exercise items that require recognition, identification, and correction.

- **A new Appendix (A)** offers instruction and practice in Sentence Combining.

- As in previous editions, *English Fundamentals* com in **three forms,** giving instructors the option to cove the same material using different exercises from one year to the next.

## *Contents*

### *Book-Specific Supplements*
Answer Key 0-321-09483-2

**ALSO AVAILABLE:**
Emery et al.,
**English Fundamentals, Form 12 A**
© 2001 • 437 pages • Paper •
ISBN 0-205-32239-5

**English Fundamentals, Form 11 C**
© 2000 • 438 pages • Paper •
ISBN 0-205-30903-8

# Sentence Dynamics:
## *An English Skills Workbook*
Fifth Edition

**Constance Immel**

**Florence Sacks,** *both of West Los Angeles College*

© 2002 • 464 pages • Paper • ISBN 0-321-05090-8

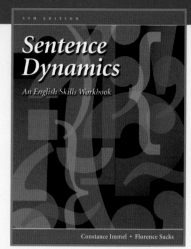

A non-intimidating, easy-to-read workbook format and a wealth of exercises are the hallmarks of this student-friendly text. Comprehensive but not overwhelming, the text's coverage of grammar fundamentals concludes with paragraph-level writing instruction. Practice tests in each chapter — and additional tests in the *Instructor's Manual* — provide plenty of opportunities to assess student progress.

## *New to This Edition*

- **New Organization!** Full treatment of grammar and usage in Chapters 1-9, concluding with instruction on paragraph writing in Chapter 10.

- **Writing Tips throughout** show students how to use grammar effectively in their own writing.

- **Editing Practices** added to each chapter encourage students to practice proofreading skills.

- **New Reading Selections** that focus on the theme "What is an American?" are included in an appendix at the end of the text and can be used for class discussion and writing assignments.

- **Answers to exercises** are included in the *Instructor's Manual.*

## *Contents*

1. Nouns and Pronouns.
2. Verbs.
3. Understanding the Parts of the Sentence.
4. Adjectives and Adverbs.
5. Main Clauses.
6. Subordinate Clauses.
7. Agreement.
8. Commas.
9. Punctuation, Sentence Mechanics, and Usage.
10. Writing a Paragraph.
Additional Readings.
Glossary.
Chart of Irregular Verbs.

### *Book-Specific Supplements*
Instructor's Manual/Test Bank 0-321-05092-4

# SENTENCE TO PARAGRAPH

## Signals: *Choices for Effective Writing*

**George E. Bell,** *Cecil Community College*
**Carolyn Farkas,** *Cecil Community College*

© 2002 • 448 pages • Paper • ISBN 0-205-29830-3

*Signals* is a comprehensive developmental writing text that addresses writing skills at the sentence and paragraph level. The text stresses sentence-level writing skills within the context of paragraph development, focusing on the choices writers make to communicate effectively.

*Coming Fall 2001!*

## Features

- **Connected Discourse Exercises and Grammar in Context.** Students learn grammar in high-interest contexts, then apply grammatical concepts to their own writing.

- **Becoming a Writer.** The text emphasizes the writing process, prewriting strategies, and writing effective paragraphs.

## Contents

**Book-Specific Supplements**
Instructor's Manual 0-321-09479-4

# PARAGRAPH TO ESSAY

## The Write Start with Readings:
### *Paragraphs to Essays*

**Lawrence Checkett,** *St. Charles County Community College*
**Gayle Feng-Checkett,** *St. Charles County Community College*
©2002 • 576 pages • Paper • ISBN 0-321-06118-7

*Coming Fall 2001!*

Clear, simple, and straightforward, *The Write Start with Readings: Paragraphs to Essays* was written and designed with the needs of today's developmental students (many of whom are learning disabled) in mind.

## Features

- **Clear and Easy-to-Read 4-Color Design.** Created with developmental students and learning disabled students in mind, the design is crisp and clear, emphasizing the content and presenting it in a manner that is easy to navigate.

- **Awareness of ESL issues.** Co-author Gayle Feng-Checkett, a certified ESL instructor, has adapted ESL pedagogy to meet the needs of developing writers, whether native or non-native speakers of English.

- **"Read All About It" links** allow students to read the complete essay from which a sentence or paragraph example is taken.

- **Additional Readings.** Each "strategies" chapter in Part Two has two corresponding professional essays in the Additional Readings section, and is followed by a set of questions and writing prompts.

- **Student Essays.** Examples of well-organized academic essays written by students of similar skill level are found throughout the text.

- **The Writer's Resource** provides comprehensive information of and ample practice in basic grammar, punctuation, usage, and spelling.

## Contents

### Book-Specific Supplements
Annotated Instructor's Edition 0-321-6118-5
Instructor's Manual 0-321-06120-9
Test Bank 0-321-06121-7
Companion Website www.ablongman.com/checkett

### Also Available by Checkett/Checkett

**The Write Start with Readings: Sentences to Paragraphs**
© 2002 • 512 pages • Paper • ISBN 0-321-06114-4

# Progressions
## *With Readings*
### Fifth Edition
**Barbara Fine Clouse**

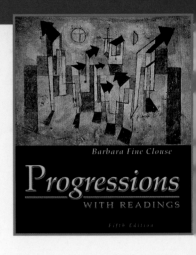

© 2002 • 644 pages • Paper • ISBN 0-205-33375-3

A longtime bestseller, *Progressions* helps students learn the characteristics of effective sentences, paragraphs, and essays, as well as the procedures for writing effectively. Geared toward improving basic writers' competence and confidence, *Progressions* provides abundant support by showing student writers what to do at every stage of the writing process.

## New to This Edition

• "Thinking, Learning, and Writing in College" boxes focus on applications of these skills in other college courses.

• New Organization! Each pattern of development (rhetorical mode) is presented in its own chapter.

• Whole and continuous discourse exercises give students ample practice in recognizing grammatical structures, allowing them to more effectively edit their own work.

## Contents

### *Book-Specific Supplements*
Instructor's Manual 0-321-09451-4
Companion Website
www.ablongman.com/clouse

### *Also Available by Barbara Fine Clouse*
**Conventions and Expectations: A Brief Handbook and Guide to Writing**

A brief, inexpensive rhetoric with ample coverage of grammar and usage.

© 2001 • 320 pages • Spiral Bound • ISBN 0-321-06122-5

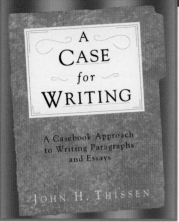

# A Case for Writing: *A Casebook Approach to Writing Paragraphs and Essays*

**John H. Thissen,** Emeritus, *Harold Washington University*

© 2002 • 272 pages • Paper • ISBN 0-321-01571-1

*A Case for Writing* provides a fresh outlook on writing for developmental writers at the paragraph-to-essay level. This unique approach uses brief cases on high-interest topics to teach grammar, paragraphs, and the essay. Throughout the text, the focus is on reading, thinking, responding, and writing.

## Features

- Introductory chapters: "How Writing Works" and "Getting Started" set the stage for productive use of the casebook approach.

- 17 detailed cases vary in difficulty, milieu, and emotional intensity.

- Glossary of useful terms accompanies each individual case.

- "Analyzing the Case" follows each case sorting out the issues and problems of each situation followed by further questions for class analysis.

- Writing assignments and exercises accompany each case—ranging from a sentence or two to a fully developed essay.

- A chapter on Types of College Writing provides instruction and practice in academic writing including essay exams, research, writing about literature, and writing across the curriculum.

- Additional Cases are included in an appendix for further exploration, along with ESL tips.

## Contents

***Book-Specific Supplements***
Instructor's Manual 0-321- 04454-1

# Essay/Bridge Course

## Keys to Successful Writing:
### *Unlocking the Writer Within*

Second Edition

**Marilyn Anderson,** *El Camino College*

© 2002 • 608 pages • Paper • ISBN 0-321-05093-2

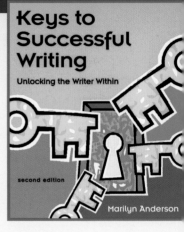

*Keys to Successful Writing, 2/e,* provides a simple heuristic as the foundation for successful college writing. Developed by the author in her classes, the text emphasizes five "keys" to successful writing: purpose, focus, material, structure, and style.

## *New to This Edition*

- Chapter 8, "Writing With Sources," encourages students who are familiar with the stages of the composing process to use interviews and electronic or print sources to strengthen their essays.

- New Part IV offers 20 additional professional essays with questions on content and strategy.

- A New Diagnostic Test and New Editing Exercises in Part V offer opportunities to practice editing skills in context.

- New Service Learning writing options encourage students to get involved in their communities.

- ESL coverage added to handbook provides helpful hint for non-native English speakers.

## *Contents*

### I. EXPLORING THE REALM OF COLLEGE READING AND WRITING.
1. Reading, Thinking, and Writing for College.
2. Defining the Essay and the Composing Process.
3. Discovering through Prewriting.
4. Finding a Thesis and Drafting.
5. Using Body Paragraphs to Develop Essays.
6. Creating Effective Introductions and Conclusions.
7. Revising and Polishing the Essay.
8. Writing with Sources.

### II. EXPLORING DEVELOPMENT OPTIONS: CHOOSING PATTERNS TO FIT PURPOSE.
9. Writing about Events: Narration and Illustration.
10. Observing the World: Description and Definition.
11. Making Connections: Process and Cause/Effect.
12. Showing Relationships: Comparison/Contrast and Division/Classification.
13. Taking a Stand: Argument.

### III. EXPLORING OTHER OPTIONS: A WRITER'S TOOLKIT.
Unit 1: Timed Writing
Unit 2: Portfolios
Unit 3: Application Letters and Résumés
Unit 4: Public Writing

### IV. EXPLORING OTHER WRITERS: A COLLECTION OF READINGS
**College Community:**
"For Equality's Sake, the SAT Should Be Abolished" Julian Weissglass.
"We're Lying: Safe Sex and White Lies in the Time of AIDS" Megan Daum.
"The Path of Books and Bootstraps" Jill Leovy.
**Work Community:**
"Ambition" Perri Klass.
"Zipped Lips" Barbara Ehrenreich.
"Delivering the Goods" Bonnie Jo Campbell.
"The Turning Point" Craig Swanson.
"McDonald's Is Not Our Kind of Place" Amitai Etzioni.
"Darkness at Noon" Harold Krents.
"Facing Down Abusers" Im Jung Kwuon.
**Civic Community:**
"The Declaration of Independence" Thomas Jefferson.
"Gravity's Rainbow" Guy Trebay.
"Offering Euthanasia Can be an Act of Love" Derek Humphry.
"Who Gets to Choose?" Jean Nandi.
"The Character Question" Jason Silverman.
"American Health, Then and Now" Bryan Williams and Sharon Knight.
**Writer's Community:**
" A List of Topics for Writing Practice" Natalie Goldberg.
"We Are, Like, Poets" Jim Frederick.
"Normal Life Too Often Isn't part of the News" Susan Benesch.
**Family Community:**
"Diary of a Child Anorexic" Lori Gottlieb.
"The Meanings of a Word" Gloria Naylor.
"And Then I Went to School" Joseph H. Suina.
"Whose Eyes Are Those, Whose Nose?" Margaret Brown.
**Global Community:**
"The Salsa Zone" Richard Rodriguez.
"The Knife" Richard Selzer.
"When You're Meant to be Together, True Love Conquers All" Kathleen Kelleher.
**Media Community:**
"How To Produce a Trashy TV Talk Show: the Four Secret Ingredients" Kimberly Smith.
"In a Chat Room, You Can Be NE1" Camille Sweeney.
"Normal Life Too Often Isn't Part of the News" Susan Benesch.

### V. EDITING ESSAYS: A CONCISE HANDBOOK.

### *Book-specific Supplements*
Instructor's Manual 0-321-05095-9
Companion Website
  www.ablongman.com/anderson

# The Visual Guide to College Composition with Readings

**Joanna Leake,** *University of New Orleans*

**James Knudsen,** *University of New Orleans*

©2002 • 640 pages • Paper • ISBN 0-321-06099-7

*Coming Fall 2001!*

*The Visual Guide to College Composition* combines a conversational writing style with an emphasis on visual learning to teach the paragraph and essay skills needed for college success.

## Features

- **Numerous Illustrations** engage readers and provide a visual way for them to learn the basics of effective paragraph and essay writing.

- **Grammar Coverage.** The fundamentals of grammar are thoroughly, clearly, and efficiently covered.

- **Special Section on Argument** helps students clearly think their opinions through, avoid logical fallacies, and analyze the argument of others.

- **Proofreading Cards** provide handy summaries and focus on common grammar problems.

- **Q&A Sections** anticipate common questions.

- **Modular Format.** Discrete chapters allow instructors to teach chapters to fit their own style.

## Contents

Part One. The Why and How of Effective Writing.
Part Two. Starting Up.
Part Three. Writing Effective Paragraphs.
Part Four. Writing Effective Essays.
Part Five. Exploring Ways to Develop Ideas.
Part Six. Fighting Fair and Winning an Argument.
Part Seven. Developing Style.
Part Eight. Avoiding the Fatal Four.
Part Nine. Avoiding Other Grammar Problems.
Part Ten. Thinking about Your Writing.
Part Eleven. Writing for Different Purposes.
Part Twelve. Additional Practice.
Part Thirteen. Mastery Tests.
Part Fourteen. Readings.
Part Fifteen. Tips for Second Language Learners.

**Readings:**
"Success Takes Time, Sacrifice and Hard Work" by Tim O'Brien
"Mericans" by Sandra Cisneros

**Description/Narration.**
"How to Enjoy Poetry" by James Dickey

**Process.**
"Life Lessons for Students" by Jeff Herring
"The Story of an Hour" by Kate Chopin
"The Great American Cooling Machine" by Frank Trippert

**Cause/Effect.**
"A Blue Plate Special Town" by Sue Pace

**Cause/Effect/Description.**
"What's Wrong With Playing 'Like a Girl?'" by Dorothea Stillman

**Cause/Effect/Examples.**
"Troublemakers in The Office" by *Time* Magazine

**Classification.**
"Harriet Tubman" by David Ramsey
"The Freedom of Living Alone" by Patricia Leigh Brown
"The Rich Don't Need It All" by Leonard Pitts, Jr.

**Examples.**
"Looking for My Prince Charming" by Shamali Pal

**Narration/Examples.**
"Changing The Rules of The Game" by Dennis Williams
"UFOs A Second Look" by Randy Fitzgerald
"Witch Doctors and The Universality of Healing" by E. Fuller Torrey

**Comparison/Contrast.**
"It's Time to Open The Doors of Our Prisons" by Rufus King
To Come: Pro-Prison Essay Opposing Mr. King

### Book-Specific Supplements

Annotated Instructor's Edition 0-321-06100-4
Instructor's Manual 0-321-06103-9
Test Bank 0-321-06104-7
Companion Website
www.ablongman.com/leake

### Also available by Knudsen/Leake
**The Visual Guide to Writing with Readings**
©2001 • 512 pages • Paper • ISBN 0-321-06098-8

# READING AND WRITING

## Making Sense: *A Guide for Readers and Writers*

**Al Starr,** *Community College of Baltimore County at Essex*
**Donna McKusick,** *Community College of Baltimore County at Essex*

©2002 • 512 pages • Paper • ISBN 0-205-31335-3

*Coming Fall 2001!*

*Making Sense* is a combined developmental English text that integrates reading and writing instruction in every chapter. Designed to appeal to instructors of both reading and writing, the book offers comprehensive coverage of reading skills, vocabulary development, the writing process, and grammar along with readings from across the disciplines.

## Features

- Integrated instruction in developmental reading and writing makes the text perfect for courses that combine both reading and writing instruction, as well as writing courses with a heavy reading component.
- Use of authentic but accessible readings prepares students for college-level studies.

- Emphasis on metacognition helps students understand how they learn and how to successfully apply their individual learning style to other courses.
- Thematic Emphasis. Chapters are organized by a theme (memory, intelligence, stress, etc.) that connects reading/writing skills and helps understanding through consideration of single theme.

## Contents

### Book-Specific Supplements
Instructor's Manual ISBN 0-321-09481-6

# DEVELOPMENTAL READER

## Expectations: *A Readers for Developing Writers*

**Anna Ingalls,** *Southwestern College*
**Dan Moody,** *Southwestern College*

©2002 • 304 pages • Paper • ISBN 0-205-32937-3

*Coming Fall 2001!*

*Expectations: A Reader for Developing Writers* contains a carefully chosen collection of 40 readings for developing writers. Reprinted from magazines, textbooks, newspapers, and other sources, each reading features pre-reading questions, comprehension questions, discussion topics, vocabulary work, writing assignments, and journaling opportunities.

## Features

- **Multicultural Representation.** Readings reflect the multicultural and pluralistic nature of American society, including articles that feature the Japanese-American experience, gender issues in the workplace, disabled athletes, and the experience of an African-American midwife in the South.

- **Strategies for Active Reading.** A short introduction, "Strategies for Active Reading," introduces previewing, audience and purpose, main idea, discovering meaning through context clues, making inferences, evaluating for logic and bias, reviewing, and reflecting on the reading.

- **Thematic organization.** The readings are organized by the following themes: Social and Cultural Issues, Media and Popular Culture, Fitness and Health, Education and Career, Nature and the Outdoors, and Technology and the Future. Within each theme, readings are organized in order of difficulty, with easier readings first.

## Contents

**Book-Specific Supplements**
Instructor's Manual 0-321-09484-0

# Innovative Resources From Longman
## *FOR INSTRUCTORS:*

### Electronic Test Bank for Developmental Writing
Features more than 5,000 questions in all areas of writing, from grammar to paragraphing through essay writing, research, and documentation. Instructors simply choose questions from the electronic test bank, then print out the completed test for distribution OR offer the test online. *Free to adopters.*

ISBN 0-321-08117-X   Also available in a printed version ISBN 0-321-08486-1

### Developmental English Electronic Newsletter
Twice a month during the spring and fall, subscribers receive a free copy of the Longman Developmental English Electronic Newsletter in their e-mailbox. Written by experienced classroom instructors, the newsletter offers teaching tips, classroom activities, book reviews and more. To subscribe, send us an email at: **BasicSkills@ablongman.com.**

### Teaching Online
*Second Edition*
This easy-to-follow guide offers basic definitions, numerous examples, and step-by-step information on finding and using Internet resources.   ISBN 0-321-01957-1

### Teaching Writing to the Non-Native Speaker
This helpful supplement discusses how to teach writing to ESL students, how to respond to ESL writing, and how to manage a multicultural writing classroom.   ISBN 0-673-97452-9

### Diagnostic and Editing Tests
*Third Edition*
This collection of six, 60-item diagnostic tests helps instructors assess students' competence in standard written English for purposes of placement or to gauge progress.

ISBN 0-321-08382-2   TestGen EQ WIN/MAC CD ROM 0-321-08782-8

### Competency Profile Test Bank
*Second Edition*
This series of objective tests covers 10 general areas of English competency. Each test is available in remedial, standard, and advanced versions.

ISBN 0-321-02224-6   TestGen Win ISBN 0-321-02633-0   TestGen Mac ISBN 0-321-02632-2

### CLAST Test Package
*Fourth Edition*
These two, 40-item objective tests evaluate students' readiness for the CLAST exams. Strategies for teaching CLAST preparedness are included.

ISBN 0-321-01950-4   Test Gen EQ WIN ISBN 0-321-01982-2   Mac ISBN 0-321-01983-0

### TASP Test Package
*Third Edition*
These 12 practice pre-tests and post-tests assess the same reading and writing skills covered in the TASP examination.

ISBN 0-321-01959-8   TestGen WIN ISBN 0-321-01985-7   TestGen MAC ISBN 0-321-01984-9

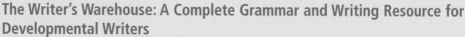

COMING
ECEMBER
2001!

## The Writer's Warehouse: A Complete Grammar and Writing Resource for Developmental Writers

*The Writer's Warehouse* is the first developmental writing program that allows students to actually write on the Web — to save their work in various stages and see a piece of writing through the complete writing process. In addition to full coverage of the writing process, *The Writer's Warehouse* offers full coverage of grammar (including diagnostic tests, whose results help students target areas of weakness), an online writer's journal, a handbook with thousands of interactive grammar exercises, research coverage, a collaborative network, Web-based activities, and multimedia (audio, video, and image-based) writing activities. Instructors receive class reporting through classroom management capabilites. A demo CD will be available in September, 2001. *Available FREE when packaged with any Longman Developmental English text.*

## The Writer's ToolKit Plus

Offers a wealth of tutorials, exercises, and reference materials for writers, including more than 3,000 grammar exercises. It is compatible with either a PC or Macintosh platform, and is flexible enough to be used either occasionally for practice or regularly in class lab sessions. *Available FREE valuepacked with any Longman Developmental Writing text.*

ISBN 0-321-07894-2

## Grammar Coach Software

This interactive tutorial is designed to help students practice the basics of grammar and punctuation through 600 self-grading exercises. *Available FREE when packaged with any Longman Developmental Writing text.*

IBM Only. ISBN 0-205-26509-X

## The English Pages Website

http: //www.ablongman.com/englishpages

Both students and instructors can visit this free, content-rich Website for additional reading selections and writing exercises. Visitors can conduct a simulated Web search, find additional reading and writing exercises, or browse a wide selection of links to various writing and research resources.

## Researching Online

*Fourth Edition*

*Researching Online* gives students step-by-step instructions for performing electronic research. Detailed discussions of Internet tools includes: e-mail, listservs, Usenet newsgroups, IRCs, MU*s, and Gopher, as well as a glossary of Internet terms. *Available FREE when packaged with any Longman text.*

## The Longman Writer's Journal

*by Mimi Markus*

Provides students with their own personal space for writing and contains helpful journal writing strategies, sample journal entries by other students, and many writing prompts and topics to get students writing. *Available FREE valuepacked with any Longman Developmental Writing text.* ISBN 0-321-08639-2

### ESL Worksheets

*Second Edition*

FREE worksheets provide ESL students with extra practice in areas they find the most troublesome. Diagnostic tests, suggested writing topics, and an answer key are included. *Available FREE valuepacked with any Longman Developmental Writing text.*

ISBN 0-321-01955-5

### Eighty Practices

A collection of ten-item exercises that provide additional practice for specific grammatical usage problems, such as comma splices, capitalization, and pronouns. *Available FREE valuepacked with any Longman Developmental Writing text.*

ISBN 0-673-53422-7

### A Guide for Peer Response

*Second Edition*

Offers students forms for peer critiques, general guidelines, and specific forms for different stages in the writing process and for various types of papers. *Available FREE valuepacked with any Longman Developmental Writing text.*

ISBN 0-321-01948-2

### Learning Together

This brief guide to the fundamentals of collaborative learning teaches students how to work effectively in groups. *Available FREE valuepacked with any Longman Developmental Writing text.* ISBN 0-673-46848-8

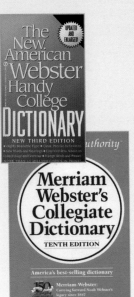

### The New American Webster Handy College Dictionary

A paperback reference text with more than 100,000 entries. Available for a nominal fee with any Longman text.

ISBN 0-451-18166-2

### Merriam Webster's Collegiate Dictionary

This hardcover comprehensive dictionary is available at a significant discount when packaged with any Longman Developmental Writing text.

ISBN 0-87779-709-9

### Longman Editing Exercises (formerly known as A&B Editing Exercises)

54 pages of paragraph editing exercises give students extra practice using grammar skills in the context of longer passages. *FREE when packaged with any Longman Developmental Writing text.*

ISBN 0-205-31792-8

### 100 Things to Write About

This brief book contains over 100 individual writing assignments, on a variety of topics and in a wide range of formats, from expressive to analytical. *FREE when packaged with any Longman Developmental Writing text.* ISBN 0-673-98239-4

## 10 Practices of Highly Effective Students

This study skills supplement includes topics such as time management, test-taking, reading critically, stress, and motivation. *Available FREE valuepacked with any Longman Writing text.*

ISBN 0-205-30769-8

## The Pocket Reader **and** The Brief Pocket Reader

Inexpensive readers containing 80 and 50 readings respectively—organized rhetorically.

Pocket Reader ISBN 0-321-07668-0

Brief Pocket Reader ISBN 0-321-07699-9

## ACT/COMPASS/Write Pass Study Package

Designed to support students and instructors through customized writing study plans. By creating a customized study plan based on diagnostic test results from ACT's Computer-Adaptive Placement Assessment and Support System (COMPASS), this study package targets study and exam preparation and guides the student through the textbook and other writing resources. *Available when bundled with Meyers,* Writing With Confidence *or Meyers,* Composing with Confidence.

# OR FLORIDA ADOPTERS

## Thinking Through the Test:
### *A Study Guide for the Florida College Basic Skills Exit Tests*

*D. J. Henry*

FOR FLORIDA ADOPTIONS ONLY. Features both diagnostic tests to help assess areas that may need improvement and exit tests to help test mastery of skills. To support classroom instruction and prepare for college classes, passages for the items in *Thinking Through the Test* have been taken from textbooks currently used in freshman college classes. The exercises in each chapter are similar to the items on the state tests. *Available FREE valuepacked with any Longman Developmental Writing text.*

   ISBN 0-321-08066-1 (with answers)

   ISBN 0-321-09988-5 (without answers)

## Writing Skills Summary for the Florida State Exit Exam

*D. J. Henry*

FOR FLORIDA ADOPTIONS ONLY. An excellent study tool for students preparing to take Florida College Basic Skills Exit Tests for Writing, this writing grid summarizes all the skills tested on the Exit Exam. *Available FREE valuepacked with any Longman Developmental Writing text.*

ISBN 0-321-08477-2

## The Longman Workshop: Custom Resources in Reading, Writing, and Study Skills

The freedom to build the book you want — and your students need — is exactly what *The Longman Workshop* delivers. Create your own version of a text, or mix and match chapters from several texts. You may also include your own material or material from other publishers, and you may shrink-wrap your *Longman Workshop* custom book with any Longman or Pearson Custom Publishing text for a 10% discount off the package price!

*The Longman Workshop gives you the following advantages —*

- Flexibility: Revise and update your book every term to suit your changing course needs.

- Instructional Support: You will receive desk copies of your custom book and a custom answer key. You'll also have access to all supplements that accompany the traditional textbooks. A special instructor's manual will be available online in September, 2001.

- Cost Savings: Your students pay only for material they use.

- Quick Turnaround: Publishing your text takes only 4-6 weeks from the time we receive your order from your bookstore.

- Combine Your Custom Workbook or Text with a Custom Reader! You can also design your own custom reader using *The Mercury Reader* and shrink-wrap your *custom reader* with your Longman Workshop text to take advantage of the 10% package discount!

*For more information on The Longman Workshop, contact your Longman sales representative, or contact us directly at:*

Project Editor - *The Longman Workshop*
Pearson Custom Publishing
75 Arlington Street, Suite 300
Boston, MA 02116

Phone: 1-800-877-6872 Ext. 2
FAX: 1-617-848-6366
Email: dbase.pub@pearsoncustom.com
Web: www.pearsoncustom.com

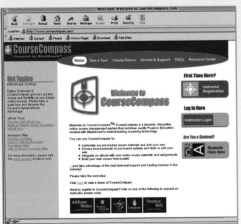

## CourseCompass

**CourseCompass combines the strength of Longman content with state-of-the-art eLearning tools!** This easy-to-use and customizable program enables professors to tailor content and functionality to meet individual course needs. Every CourseCompass course includes a range of pre-loaded content such as testing and assessment question tools, chapter-level objectives, chapter summaries, photos, illustrations, videos, animations, and Web activities—all designed to help students master core course objectives. **For more information, or to see a demo, visit www.ablongman.com/coursecompass, or contact your local Longman sales representative.**

*To order an examination copy of any of the texts in this brochure:*

- Contact your local Allyn & Bacon/Longman sales representative
- Email your request to exam.copies@ablongman.com
- Fax your request to (617) 848-7490
- Visit us on the Web at http://www.ablongman.com
- Phone us at (800) 852-8024

0-321-10166-9

# A CASE FOR WRITING

# A CASE FOR WRITING

## A CASEBOOK APPROACH TO WRITING PARAGRAPHS AND ESSAYS

### John H. Thissen

*Emeritus, Harold Washington College*

Longman

New York    San Francisco    Boston
London    Toronto    Sydney    Tokyo    Singapore    Madrid
Mexico City    Munich    Paris    Cape Town    Hong Kong    Montreal

Vice President and Editor in Chief: Joe Opiela
Senior Acquisitions Editor: Steven Rigolosi
Associate Editor: Barbara Santoro
Marketing Manager: Melanie Craig
Supplements Editor: Donna Campion
Production Manager: Joe Vella
Project Coordination, Text Design, and Electronic Page Makeup: Shepherd, Inc.
Cover Design Manager: John Callahan
Cover Designer: Neil Flewellyn
Manufacturing Buyer: Al Dorsey
Printer and Binder: Maple-Vail Book Manufacturing Group
Cover Printer: Coral Graphic Services, Inc.

For permission to use copyrighted material, grateful acknowledgment is made to the copyright
holders on p. 235, which are hereby made part of this copyright page.

**Library of Congress Cataloging-in-Publication Data**

Thissen, John H.
   A case for writing : a casebook approach to writing paragraphs and essays / by
   John H. Thissen.
     p. cm.
   Includes index.
   ISBN 0-321-01571-1
    1. English language—Paragraphs.  2. English language—Rhetoric.  3. Report writing.
  I. Title

PE1439.T47 2001
808'.042—dc21

                                        2001029053

Please visit our website at http://www.ablongman.com

ISBN 0-321-01571-1

1 2 3 4 5 6 7 8 9 10—MA—04 03 02 01

FOR SHEILA, KATHLEEN, AND JOHN

# BRIEF CONTENTS

# Additional Resources for Writers    153

# DETAILED CONTENTS

# Additional Resources for Writers     153

# PREFACE

This book was written to fill a need—mine. In the three decades that I taught entry-level college composition courses, I used many different textbooks, but I couldn't find the one I really wanted. I was on the hunt for a book that would let students discover that their job in my classroom had some connection with the world outside Room 604. Teaching in a large urban college brought me into contact with busy adults from 18 to 75 whose time, patience, and gullibility were limited. They were willing to concede to their math, computer science, and social science teachers that some classroom efforts had grounding in future tasks. But their notion of what English teachers dispensed was often based on a suspension of disbelief: "You're a nice guy, so I'll go along with this stuff. Besides, the course is required."

I wanted a book that was not merely "relevant"—to use that wonderful horse we all began riding in the sixties—but one that would enable students to see for themselves that writing is something people do because the world runs on it, not because English teachers say so. A **casebook approach** seemed to be a good possibility, so I tried a few case-oriented textbooks and labored to make them useful. I admired the ingenuity of their authors and found myself totally absorbed in the microcosms of communication that individual cases could create. But I also found my developmental students overly challenged by the level of diction and complexity of sentence structure that the available casebooks contained. I liked the idea of using role playing and immersion in a realistic situation, but I found it necessary to do a counterproductive amount of explaining and explicating. No books of this type were suitable for my students. English 100 is not English 101.

Finally, with the encouragement of many, many people, I decided to write one of my own. This text is a compendium of all the useful tricks, stratagems, insights, nuggets, ploys, and methodologies I could assemble for one simple purpose: I want beginning composition students to understand that *all writing is writing for an audience,* and I want them to see this truth manifested in real ways as accomplished by real people. When they see this, they can do it for themselves and continue to get better at it. The casebook approach, if used patiently and creatively, is a valid and effective way for students and teachers to collaborate on writing as it actually takes place in concrete situations.

What will you find in this book and this approach to writing?

Most importantly, **students** will find an attempt to readjust some of the steps they have followed in the past. Instead of concentrating on watching others write, then analyzing what they've done, and, finally, imitating it, students who use *A Case for Writing* will jump right into the "real world" and *become* writers as their world's exigencies force them to write. Each situation becomes the student's situation. The student is the theater owner, the library board member, the animal rights activist, the thoughtful writer of a letter to the editor.

As a **teacher,** your role will be to encourage and facilitate your students' attempts at analyzing situations, role playing, and constructing worlds in which communication takes place. You will oversee the process of writing as it fits these constructs, and you will point out to students that if they can write in such and such a "case," they can write within the cases that their own life will inevitably supply. From your own experience, you will help them find the verbal sets, makeup, props, and syntactic stagecraft necessary to make "artificial" writing believable.

To help you accomplish these tasks, *A Case for Writing* supplies many resources:

- Two **introductory chapters** that set the stage for the productive use of the casebook approach. The first, "How Writing Works," analyzes the writing process and illustrates the major thrust of the course. The second chapter is titled appropriately, **"Getting Started."** Both of these chapters introduce students to the use of cases and what will be expected of them during the course.

- Seventeen fully realized, detailed **cases** to be used as jumping-off points for writing. They vary in difficulty, milieu, and emotional intensity. They range from big-city bus crashes to small-town colleges, from suburban factories to neighborhood theaters. They are peopled by a mixture of characters, multiracial, multiethnic, multifaceted.

- Each case is accompanied by **Key Terms** to be explored and used as appropriate in discussing and writing about the case.

- A section on **Analyzing the Case** follows each case, setting out some of the issues and problems involved in the situation. Further questions for class analysis are also included.

- **Roleplaying.** A section on roleplaying accompanies each of the cases. Students are introduced to this important technique and shown how to move from roleplaying into writing. By inhabiting the minds of others, they discover how people write in realistic situations.

- Writing assignments and various kinds of **exercises** accompany each case. Writing assignments range from a sentence or two to fully developed essays.

- Separate parts on **"Writing Paragraphs"** and **"Writing Essays."** The instruction in these parts is then incorporated into the cases that follow.

- Separate discussions of important **Writing Conventions** in eight chapters, including spelling, punctuation, sentence completeness, pronoun agreement, and consistency in person and tense. Numerous exercises accompany the writing conventions. These treatments are not exhaustive, and it is expected that this book will be supplemented by a standard handbook, either print or electronic.

- Separate treatment of various **methods of development,** including description, example, comparison/contrast, cause and effect, definition, process, and classification. Each method is accompanied by exercises.

- A chapter on **"Types of College Writing."** This chapter includes such areas of academic writing as essay examinations, research, writing about literature, and writing across the curriculum.

- An **appendix** that contains the following:
  1. Additional cases for further exploration. This collection enables an instructor to tailor and adapt the course by substituting different cases for those contained in the individual chapters.
  2. A discussion of the most difficult challenges facing English as a second language (ESL) students, including use of articles, verb forms, and an overview of the general syntactic basis of English.
  3. Two professionally written articles, "Claim Your Domain Name Before the Internet Winter Hits," and "Wood Ghost." These articles are annotated to illustrate how professional writers go about their business. In addition, "Wood Ghost" has a section on vocabulary study.

- A **glossary** of the terms appearing in boldface throughout the book.

- An **instructor's manual** that includes tips on teaching methods and answers to the exercises. A list of additional supplementary materials follows.

# THE TEACHING AND LEARNING PACKAGE

In addition to the instructor's manual described previously (ISBN 0-321-04454-1), many other innovative supplements are available for both instructors and students. All of these supplements are available either free or at greatly reduced prices.

## For Additional Reading and Reference

**The Dictionary Deal.**  Two dictionaries can be shrinkwrapped with this text for a nominal fee. *The New American Webster Handy College Dictionary* is a paperback reference text with more than 100,000 entries. *Merriam Webster's Collegiate Dictionary,* tenth edition, is a hardback reference with a citation file of more than 14.5 million examples of English words drawn from actual use. For more information on how to shrinkwrap a dictionary with this text, please contact your Longman sales representative.

**Penguin Quality Paperback Titles.**  A series of Penguin paperbacks is available at a significant discount when shrinkwrapped with *The User's Guide.* Some titles available are Toni Morrison's *Beloved,* Julie Alvarez's *How the Garcia Girls Lost Their Accents,* Mark Twain's *Huckleberry Finn, Narrative of the Life of Frederick Douglass,* Harriet Beecher Stowe's *Uncle Tom's Cabin,* Dr. Martin Luther King, Jr.'s *Why We Can't Wait,* and plays by Shakespeare, Miller, and Albee. For a complete list of titles or more information, please contact your Longman sales consultant.

***The Pocket Reader,* First Edition.**  This inexpensive volume contains 80 brief readings (one to three pages each) on a variety of themes: writers on writing, nature, women and men, customs and habits, politics, rights and obligations, and coming of age. Also included is an alternate rhetorical table of contents. (ISBN 0-321-07668-0)

***100 Things to Write About.***  This 100-page book contains 100 individual assignments for writing on a variety of topics and in a wide range of formats, from expressive to analytical. Ask your Longman sales representative for a sample copy. (ISBN 0-673-98239-4)

***Newsweek* Alliance.**  Instructors may choose to shrinkwrap a 12-week subscription to *Newsweek* with any Longman text. The price of the subscription is 57 cents per issue (a total of $6.84 for the subscription). Available with the subscription is a free "Interactive Guide to *Newsweek*"—a workbook for students who are using the text. In addition, *Newsweek* provides a wide variety of instructor supplements free to teachers, including maps, Skills Builders, and weekly quizzes. For more information on the *Newsweek* program, please contact your Longman sales representative.

## Electronic and Online Offerings

### The Writer's ToolKit Plus CD-ROM.
This CD-ROM offers a wealth of tutorial, exercise, and reference material for writers. It is compatible with either a PC or Macintosh platform and is flexible enough to be used either occasionally for practice or regularly in class lab sessions. For information on how to bundle this CD-ROM FREE with your text, please contact your Longman sales representative.

### The Longman English Page Web Site.
Both students and instructors can visit our free content-rich web site for additional reading selections and writing exercises. From the Longman English pages, visitors can conduct a simulated web search, learn how to write a resume and cover letter, or try their hand at poetry writing. Stop by and visit us at **http://www.ablongman.com/englishpages.**

### The Longman Electronic Newsletter.
Twice a month during the spring and fall, instructors who have subscribed receive a free copy of the Longman Developmental English Newsletter in their e-mailbox. Written by experienced classroom instructors, the newsletter offers teaching tips, classroom activities, book reviews, and more. To subscribe, visit the Longman Basic Skills web site at **http://www.ablongman.com/basicskills,** or send an e-mail to **Basic Skills@ablongman.com.**

### Daedalus Online.
Longman and The Daedalus Group are proud to offer the next generation of the award-winning Daedalus Integrated Writing Environment. Daedalus Online is an Internet-based collaborative writing environment for students. The program offers prewriting strategies and prompts, computer-mediated conferencing, peer collaboration and review, comprehensive writing support, and secure, 24-hour availability.

For educators, Daedalus Online offers a comprehensive suite of online course management tools for managing an online class, dynamically linking assignments, and facilitating a heuristic approach to writing instruction. For more information, visit **http://www.ablongman.com/daedalus,** or contact your Longman sales representative.

*Teaching Online: Internet Research, Conversation, and Composition,*
**Second Edition.** Ideal for instructors who have never surfed the Internet, this easy-to-follow guide offers basic definitions, numerous examples, and step-by-step information about finding and using Internet sources. Free to adopters. (ISBN 0-321-01957-1)

## For Instructors

**Electronic Text Bank for Writing.** This electronic test bank features more than 5,000 questions in all areas of writing, from grammar to paragraphing, through essay writing, research, and documentation. With this easy-to-use CD-ROM, instructors simply choose questions from the electronic test bank, then print out the completed test for distribution. (ISBN 0-321-08117-X) Printed version also available (0-321-08596-5)

**Competency Profile Test Bank, Second Edition.** This series of 60 objective tests covers ten general areas of English competency, including fragments, comma splices and run-ons, pronouns, commas, and capitalization. Each test is available in remedial, standard, and advanced versions. Available as reproducible sheets or in computerized versions. Free to instructors. (Paper version: ISBN 0-321-02224-6; Computerized IBM: ISBN 0-321-02633-0; Computerized Mac: ISBN 0-321-02632-2)

**Diagnostic and Editing Tests, Third Edition.** This collection of diagnostic tests helps instructors assess students' competence in standard written English for purpose of placement or to guage progress. Available as reproducible sheets or in computerized versions, and free to instructors. (Paper: ISBN 0-321-08382-2; Computerized IBM: ISBN 0-321-08782-8; Computerized Mac: ISBN 0-321-08784-4)

**ESL Worksheets, Third Edition.** These reproducible worksheets provide ESL students with extra practice in areas they find the most troublesome. A diagnostic test and posttest are provided, along with answer keys and suggested topics for writing. Free to adopters. (ISBN 0-321-07765-2)

**80 Practices.** A collection of reproducible, ten-item exercises that provide additional practices for specific grammatical usage problems, such as comma splices, capitalization, and pronouns. Includes an answer key; free to adopters. (ISBN 0-673-53422-7)

**CLAST Test Package, Fourth Edition.** These two 40-item objective tests evaluate students' readiness for the CLAST exams. Strategies for teaching CLAST preparedness are included. Free with any Longman English title. (Reproducible sheets: ISBN 0-321-01950-4; Computerized IBM: ISBN 0-321-01982-2; Computerized Mac: ISBN 0-321-01983-0)

**TASP Test Package, Third Edition.** These 12 practice pretests and posttests assess the same reading and writing skills covered in the TASP examination. Free with any Longman English title. (Reproducible sheets: ISBN 0-321-01959-8; Computerized IBM: ISBN 0-321-01985-7; Computerized Mac: ISBN 0-321-01984-9)

***Teaching Writing to the Non-Native Speaker.*** This booklet examines the issues that arise when nonnative speakers enter the developmental classroom. Free to instructors, it includes profiles of international and permanent ESL students, factors influencing second-language acquisition, and tips on managing a multicultural classroom. (ISBN 0-673-97452-9)

## For Students

***Researching Online,*** **Fifth Edition.** A perfect companion for a new age, this indispensable new supplement helps students navigate the Internet. Adapted from *Teaching Online,* the instructor's Internet guide, *Researching Online* speaks directly to students, giving them detailed, step-by-step instructions for performing electronic searches. Available free when shrinkwrapped with any Longman text. Ask your Longman sales representative for more information. (ISBN 0-321-09277-5)

***Learning Together: An Introduction to Collaborative Theory.*** This brief guide to the fundamentals of collaborative learning teaches students how to work effectively in groups, how to revise with peer response, and how to coauthor a paper or report. Shrinkwrapped free with any Longman Basic Skills text. (ISBN 0-673-97365-4)

***A Guide for Peer Response,*** **Second Edition.** This guide offers students forms for peer critiques, including general guidelines and specific forms for different stages in the writing process. Also appropriate for freshman-level course. Free to adopters. (ISBN 0-321-01948-2)

**[For Students in Florida]** *Thinking Through the Test,* **by D. J. Henry.** This special workbook, prepared specially for students in Florida, offers ample skill and practice exercises to help students prepare for the Florida State Exit Exam. To shrinkwrap this workbook free with your textbook, please contact your Longman sales representative. Also available: Two laminated grids (one for reading, one for writing) that can serve as handy references for students preparing for the Florida State Exit Exam. (ISBN 0-321-08066-1)

**The Longman Writer's Journal** provides students with their own personal space for writing. In addition to helping students with their own writing voice, it offers helpful journal writing strategies, sample journal entries by other students, and many writing prompts to get developing writers started on their voyage to successful writing. Available free when packaged with *A Case for Writing* (ISBN 0-321-08639-2). Ask your Longman sales representative for more details.

## ACKNOWLEDGMENTS

This book owes its existence to many people. First of all, I am indebted to thousands of students at Harold Washington College who have shown me what writing is all about. Over the past 30 years, we have taught each other many things worth knowing, and my students' marks are on every page of this book as surely as my own. My colleagues in the City Colleges of Chicago have been truly generous and wise. It's impossible to thank them all, but I am especially indebted to Raymonda Johnson, Dorothy Clark, Joan McVeigh, Della Burt-Bradley, and all my colleagues in the Department of English, Speech, and Theater and the Department of Foreign Language/English as a Second Language at Harold Washington College. Among the latter, Professor Roger Conner deserves special thanks for developing the material that formed the basis of the ESL section. I was fortunate to have the advice and guidance of Mary Margaret Cunniff, Executive Director of the National Anti-Vivisection Society, for the material on animal rights. I am grateful to Harold Washington's President Nancy DeSombre, a fellow English teacher, for her encouragement and to the City Colleges of Chicago for a sabbatical that allowed me to formulate the proposal and prepare sample chapters for submission to my publisher.

Of course, it has been editors and publishers who caused the book to come to pass, and I have been fortunate in my experiences with each of them. The initial impetus for this project came quite a few years ago from Brenda Sullivan, Mary Jo Southern, and Jain Simmons. The first two had paid me generously for reviewing and criticizing other people's textbooks, and all three suggested that I put up or shut up by writing my own. My eventual publishing efforts at Longman Publishers found me in the very competent hands of Ellen Schatz and Lynn Huddon, both of whom enabled me to grow as an author and to profit from their considerable patience and wisdom. Peggy Francomb of Shepherd, Inc. provided patient editorial oversight, and Deborah Anderson of Photosearch, Inc. acquired the excellent photos which illustrate the cases. Excellent, detailed commentary, advice, and encouragement came from the following reviewers:

Alice Adams, Glendale Community College
Jim Addison, Western Carolina University
Robert Bator, Olive-Harvey College
Pam Bourgeois, CSU Northridge
Kimberly D. Braddock, Blinn College
Bob Brannan, Johnson County Community College
Judith Branzburg, Pasadena City College
Alice Cleveland, College of Marin
John Covolo, Lakeland Community College
Thomas Harford, City College of New York
Lee Jones, DeKalb College–Gwinnett
Peggy Karsten, Ridgewater College
Tina McGaughey, Austin Community College
Kathryn Mincey, Morehead State University
George Otte, CUNY–Baruch
Ann Schlumberger, Pima Community College
Karen Standridge, Pikes Peak Community College
Martha Vertreace, Kennedy-King College
Cynthia Walker, Faulkner University

Finally, I am most grateful to Steven Rigolosi, Senior Acquisitions Editor at Longman Publishers, for guiding me through the book's completion and making it happen.

Several other people deserve profound thanks. Encouragement at times when I most needed it came from Mary Kay Craig, Eugene Thissen, and Joseph Haley, among many others. Extensive review of the manuscript and valuable suggestions were supplied by Prof. John Scheid, Kathleen Thissen, and John Thissen, Jr. Finally, my greatest debt is to my large, supportive, and genuinely interested family and to my many friends who often asked good naturedly when I might "finish the thing" and then wished me well. Above all, my wife Sheila Malone Thissen, and my children Kathleen and John were always there when I needed them. This book is for them.

Comments, advice, and suggestions on how the book might be improved are welcome. E-mail me at thisscase@aol.com. Thank you.

John H. Thissen
Glenview, IL

# An Overview of a Case for Writing

| Chapter | Case | Writing Conventions | Methods of Development |
|---|---|---|---|
| **Part One: Introduction** | | | |
| 1 | Animal Rights | | |
| 2 | Animal Rights, cont'd. | Spelling | |
| **Part Two: Writing Paragraphs** | | | |
| 3 | Writing Paragraphs | | |
| 4 | Adult Film Theater | Sentence Completeness | Description |
| 5 | The Lottery Winner | Pronoun Clarity | Examples |
| 6 | The Cheating Scandal | Letter Writing | Comparison/Contrast |
| 7 | The Bus Crash | Commas | Cause and Effect |
| **Part Three: Writing Essays** | | | |
| 8 | Writing Essays | | |
| 9 | The Company's Child Care Center | Colons, Semicolons | Definition |
| 10 | Transfer to Another College | Quotations | Process |
| 11 | Censorship in the Library | Consistent Tense/ Consistent Person | Classification |
| 12 | Types of College Writing | | |
| **Appendix A Additional Cases for Study** <br> **Appendix B English as a Second Language** <br> **Appendix C Professional Readings for Study** | | | |

# A CASE FOR WRITING

# PART 1

# INTRODUCTION TO WRITING

# CHAPTER 1

# HOW WRITING WORKS

## GETTING STARTED

To get started, ask yourself some questions about your own writing.

- If I write letters to people, do I wonder how they will react to my words? Does this concern lead me to write or not write certain things?

- Have I read materials—articles, memos, etc.—that weren't written with me in mind? If so, how could I tell they were not aimed at me?

- Have I seen an author in a photo or on television and been surprised that his or her appearance didn't match my mental image?

- The first time I heard my tape-recorded voice, was I amazed at how different I sound to other people? Is it possible that my writing gives a different impression than I realize? How can I tell?

- Outside of this school, do I know someone who writes or has written material that is read by more than ten people? One hundred people?

Right now, as you are reading these words, you are probably making some kind of judgment about the person who wrote them and then told you to read them. This is a two-way street. As the author, I also made some judgments about you. Let's see if they were accurate.

You, the reader, may be some years out of high school, or you may be a recent graduate. You probably have a job of some kind, and people may count on you to earn money. Some of these people may be your parents, brothers, and sisters. Or they may be your spouse and children. You don't have time to waste. You have commitments that limit your study time. Although you have decided to study for this course, writing for teachers has never been one of your favorite activities. You do, however, think that writing well is a valuable skill.

Did I come close? If this description applies to you, then I have accomplished one of the major tasks facing any writer. I sized up my audience, and from that point on I have had to choose every word I write to appeal to my audience—to you.

The term **audience,** as used in this book, simply means the intended reader or readers of a piece of writing. The writing may sometimes be read by people other than those the author wrote for, but the author still must write with particular readers in mind.

Being in touch with your audience is the most important thing you will do for yourself as you work your way through this book and this course. The words you write will depend on your ability to "see" and even "become" the person who will read them. If you become skilled at this kind of vision, you will know how to make writing work for you.

The idea behind this book is simple: People have real reasons for writing and they write for real people. Because of this, you can learn to be a better writer by observing how people express themselves differently in differing situations.

If you agree that this statement sounds reasonable, you need to return to it frequently and remind yourself of its meanings. Everything you do in a writing course should be based on this truth. Writing well is not a mysterious process. It is not a collection of secrets known only by writing priests who distribute them to special people. Writing is a way to get things done.

## WHAT DO PEOPLE WRITE?

Don't try to number them, but do a quick inventory of the pieces of writing you have encountered so far today. On a piece of scratch paper start listing them. When you spooned your instant coffee into its cup, your hand was covering a carefully composed label, complete with nutritional components. Your cup itself may have boasted that it was the property of "World's Greatest Mom" or offered some other inspirational message. If the TV was on, its screen periodically offered words, slogans, and ads. Before you arrived at your classroom, you may have encountered some or all of the following: newspaper, bus transfer, train schedule, "WASH ME" on the back of the truck you followed through traffic, billboards, theater marquees, expressive T-shirts, and bumper stickers. Everything you read was written by someone, and you turned out to be part of the audience. What happened when the two of you—the writer and reader—made contact?

People write things because other people read them. Before he became a famous actor, Morgan Freeman played a character on *The Electric Company.* As "Easy Reader," he would roam through the city, eagerly reading everything in sight—neon signs, bus transfers, matchbooks in the gutter, T-shirts, instructions, and advertisements. Occasionally, he would look up at a skywriting airplane leaving a message, and he would smile because he enjoyed learning to read. In fact, when you were younger, it probably seemed to you that things to be read were everywhere. Somebody put them there so someone else could read them. You didn't analyze beyond this simple level. Written words were all around you, just like people, trees, bugs, clouds, and the air itself.

Since then, your understanding of the world around you has become more complex. Adults' lives are increasingly cluttered with words. Think of those automobile commercials on television that end with a screen full of small print, shown for maybe two seconds, warning you that "prices may vary." Think of the frustration caused by the product you bought without noticing the phrase "some assembly required" on its carton. Think of filling out tax forms, even the E-Z version. After a fender-bender accident, your insurance company wants you to fill out a couple of "simple" forms. Is *simple* the word you would use to describe them?

In each case, the words you read were chosen by someone as the right ones to appear in print. If you produce words in response to a situation, you must choose all of them carefully. Because you live in a complex world, you have to learn how to accomplish this task. If the setting of your world is a college, your task is even more complex because you will have to learn to write the way colleges have traditionally expected their students to write (see the section on Academic Writing in Chapter 12). Even so, it is still a matter of sizing up your audience and then acting accordingly.

## How This Book Works

Each chapter has several sections. Most of them begin with a **case** for analysis. You'll read more about cases shortly.

Following the case is a list of **key terms,** the kinds of words you might find useful in writing about the case you've read. For example, the key terms in Chapter 6, "The Cheating Scandal," include words such as *moral relativism, guilt by association,* and *amoral.* You may not be familiar with these terms, but they may be useful as you write about the case. You will need to explore these terms to understand them fully. For this purpose, nothing is more useful than a good, current dictionary. Experienced writers have one with them wherever they do their writing. Your dictionary may be inside a book's covers, inside your computer's memory, or on a web site. It is a valuable tool wherever you use it. As you use your dictionary to explore these key terms, you will find that words start to take on a life of their own.

In addition to the cases, you will find **writing conventions** and **methods of development.** These last two sections are designed to help you work on your skill in writing for various audiences. The writing convention sections which begin in Chapter 2, discuss some area of writing, such as punctuation or consistent tense, with which an audience will expect an educated writer to be familiar. Starting in Chapter 4, the methods of development give you more tools in your writing toolbox, ways that you can give your audience enough to think about as they attempt to understand your ideas.

Remember that you want your readers to take you seriously as a person who knows how an educated writer sounds. You are in an academic setting, so your writing is academic writing. Also, remember that you will need to have access to a **writing handbook** and a current **dictionary.** Your instructor will either require or recommend certain books for you to use along with this text.

Now that you have done a bit of self-examining and gotten yourself thinking about what people do when they write, you are ready to begin exploring this book and its cases. In a typical case, different people are writing for different reasons, and you can find clues to their purpose in the words they use. Get started by jumping into the following case and seeing what kinds of writing situations develop.

As you read the case, put yourself into an active frame of mind. This means:

- Asking questions, raising doubts, noticing your own feelings. When you analyze a case, you have to get yourself into it as realistically as you can.

- Painting pictures in your mind. Cast the players in the drama, using recognizable faces of famous people if it helps.

To help you, there are **exercises** and **assignments** throughout the book. They are here because *writing is a skill.* That means that you get better at it when you practice it. You were not born with the ability to write college-level English. To become a good writer, you must practice writing.

# Case: Animal Rights

Anne McCormick, a sophomore at Carson College in East Carson, Illinois, has been working on a term paper for her Applied Ethics course. She is trying to write about animal rights, and she is running into some problems. Although she is from a small farm town downstate, she has always been a bit uncomfortable with getting to know young animals as individual creatures and then exchanging them for some kind of profit. The profit might be the money brought in by a fattened hog, or it might be the peace of mind that comes from setting a leg trap for the raccoons that have been raiding garbage cans on the back porch. She has talked with her family about these concerns, but she has never been moved to do anything about them. After all, as her parents have pointed out, Anne loves cheeseburgers, shiny shoes, and long-lasting lipstick, so some animal is always making sacrifices for her benefit.

*(Continued)*

*(Continued from previous page)*

The more she works on the term paper, the more she finds herself troubled by what she sees as injustice in the kinds of treatment that animals receive from humans. Walking behind a classmate in a fur jacket causes her to wonder just how dead animals' bodies get turned into coats. At a local campus lunch counter, she pauses a moment over the menu. Then, without saying anything to her friends, she switches from the Sloppy Joe and orders a salad. On the other hand, she is also sympathetic to the arguments she reads explaining that humans are only doing what is right and reasonable in their use of animals. They exist for us, not the other way around. Anne continues to read and to think, but the term paper's deadline is coming up soon.

Meanwhile, she is excited when the college newspaper, *The Carsonian,* runs a notice about an upcoming debate. It will feature speakers from a national animal rights organization and supporters of the position that animals are legitimate resources to be used by the dominant species on the planet—namely, humans. Anne knows she has to be there.

As she enters the auditorium building, she is confronted by two sets of people handing out leaflets and flyers. She takes copies of everything. After she sits down in a row near the front, she looks at the printed material. One group's literature contains graphic images of rabbits being held in clamps and being experimented on by a cosmetics manufacturing company. In another, a hunter smiles at the camera as he holds up the enormous antlers and flopping head of the deer he has just killed. The opposing group's flyers contain an appeal to be reasonable about the issues involved and not to forget that even the Bible identifies humans as the animals who should dominate the earth. Some medical research that will benefit humans depends on use of animals for testing. Both sides of the debate, she realizes, have some powerful, convincing arguments.

The moderator, a senior majoring in business, begins the discussion with an attempt to outline the opposing groups' viewpoints, and he concludes by expressing hope that both sides will "behave themselves." The panelists do, but their cheering sections do not. Throughout the evening, members of the audience shout at the panel, chant slogans, and hold up signs made in haste with magic marker and sheets of poster board. Campus security guards stand at the back of the auditorium, looking uncomfortable. Before the discussion ends, two people have been dragged out of the auditorium, one for trying to splash paint on someone's fur jacket, the other for knocking the paint and the would-be splasher to the floor. As the security guards remove the two, their cheering sections drown out the moderator's pleading. Finally, each of the nervous, frustrated panel members makes a closing statement and the event is over.

Within the next two weeks several things happen on the Carson College campus:

- *The Carsonian* runs a front page story on the debate and an editorial that blames both sides for being unwilling to listen to the other.

- Letters to the editor printed in *The Carsonian* repeat the arguments made during the debate.

- A local chapter of the national animal rights group is formed and begins to recruit members.

- Anne sends her parents a short letter. Included in it is a brief reference to the controversy.

- She turns in her term paper and receives an A from her Applied Ethics teacher. She is pleased with the grade, but she is more pleased that she has figured out where she stands in this bitter controversy.

This case is complicated, isn't it? Notice how many of the actions require written words for their completion. Also notice that nobody writes simply to be writing; they are writing words that other people will read. You will find examples of this throughout the book. Note: It may be useful to read the article "Wood Ghost" in Appendix C as background for your discussion of animal rights.

## Exercise 1-1: Kinds of Writing

Review the case and count the different pieces of writing that were generated. How many did you find? Next, use your imagination to come up with at least two more possible pieces of writing that could have been created in the case. ◆

# AUDIENCE

An audience is not simply a group of readers. As we noted earlier, an audience may be one person, a few people, or a large group of people. As a writer, you need to remember the following:

**Everything written has an audience.**

Understanding what it means to write for an audience is one of the most important ideas for any successful writer. A person composes words so that someone else will read them. This point seems obvious, but it may be forgotten when you're sitting in front of a blank piece of paper or a computer screen. Thinking about the audience for your written words is as important as looking people in the eye when you're talking to them. If you go back over the animal rights debate, you will see that the case includes many audiences. Each of these audiences merits special consideration.

The word *audience,* as used in this book, does not simply mean a group of readers, similar to concert-goers, who happen to be on the receiving end of a writer's performance. An audience may be one person, the college president. It may be all the people who are handed a flyer at the debate. Or it may be the student sitting in the lounge, reading the school newspaper.

What's important about the concept of audience for you as a writer is the realization that everything written has one. The person who composed the words did it so that someone else would read them. This seems obvious, but it is easily forgotten when you're the one sitting there silently in front of that blank piece of paper or computer screen.

## Exercise 1-2: Questions for Discussion

1.  Who is the audience for Anne McCormick's term paper on animal rights? Does it matter if she knows her professor's viewpoint on animal rights?
2.  Who is the audience for the school newspaper's reporter writing about the debate? Is there more than one audience? For example, readers include the editors, other reporters, faculty, and students.
3.  Who is the audience for the homemade signs held up by the opposing demonstrators at the debate? Again, is there more than one audience?
4.  Who might be the audience for a letter to the editor? Is it simply the editor? ◆

# APPROPRIATE LANGUAGE

Observation and practice are especially critical here. To write effectively, you need to put yourself into your readers' shoes and choose the right words for the situation. The best writers pick the words and sentence structures that will get their job done.

These different language or "discourse" approaches are all around you. Look at the big-haired anchorperson who reads serious words from a TelePrompTer on the evening news program. Someone wrote those words so that they would sound appropriate for the situation. A few minutes later, a commercial uses wildly imaginative, funny, and/or silly words to sell you toothpaste. In shifting from news listener to toothpaste buyer, have you become someone different? To the person addressing you, you have. The people preparing the different groups of words for you are addressing you differently. They are relying on their sense of how you react to information and, especially, on what you expect to hear. The levels of language may range from very formal to very informal, from complete sentences to catch phrases, from abstract wisdom to wisecracks.

Now read through the animal rights case again and imagine what might be going through the different writers' minds as they think about how to compose the words that will work best with their particular audiences. As you progress through this book, you will get better at this kind of analysis.

## Exercise 1-3: Types of Language

Discuss the following:

1. If you had to write the opening paragraph of the moderator's speech for the animal rights debate, what kind of words would you use? How about: "Now settle down, kids," or "If you can't behave, you're outa here," or "Let's at least listen to what these jerks have to say"? Why or why not? Should a moderator take sides? What are some other words that could express these ideas appropriately?

2. **Euphemism** is an expression used to make negative concepts sound less negative. Undertakers, for instance, refer to "the loved one" instead of "the body." Is there a euphemistic way to say, "You torture animals for profit," or "You're a fool to put animals ahead of people"? Do euphemisms perform a valuable service for their authors, or do

they just seek to sugarcoat the truth? Think of a euphemistic word or words that you consider dishonest.

3.   Should Anne McCormick's term paper show the difference between other people's ideas and her own? Why does this matter? Can she simply use others' ideas and say they are hers? Is it ever effective to say that your opponents idea might be worthwhile? ◆

## SAMPLE DOCUMENTS

To help you examine the ideas of audience and appropriate language, it is helpful to look at some sample documents. Examine these carefully and ask yourself whether you would have written them this way. Try to read between the lines, and trust your judgment. The accompanying memo on page 13 is from the college's dean, John Kane, to the director of student activities.

### Exercise 1-4: Analysis

Does the language of this memo tell you something about its author and its audience? What clues can you pick up? Could you have written this memo? Why or why not? Which parts might make Q. Sturgess a little nervous? Mr. Sturgess is going to underline certain words and fax a copy of this memo to his assistant. He wants to warn him that the outcome of the debate might make a difference to the assistant. He also wants to be able to cover himself in case something goes wrong. He will mark the memo in pen and then add a polite, two-line note at the bottom of the page, followed by the initials Q.S. The following note is one example of how he might do it. ◆

---

Bill,

This is important. J.K. wants no problems. If you value your job, you will make sure that there aren't any. Right?

Q.S.

---

Now try your own version of this note. Think of a less threatening way to address your assistant and still get your message across. Sign it *Q.S.* ◆

# *Carson College*

*200 College Circle, East Carson, IL / 555-1766 / www.carcoll.edu*

Date:      July 20, 2001
To:        Q. Sturgess, Director of Student Activities
From:      John Kane, Ph.D., Dean of Instruction
Subject:   Animal Rights Discussion

I know you are aware of the college's wish to avoid negative publicity. This upcoming forum could be challenging. I would not have scheduled it, but, since you wanted to, I decided to go along with it. There are fools on both sides of the argument, but you, of course, know which fools I consider the more foolish. I will not look kindly on a performance that makes our side look bad.

Take steps to be sure that your moderator knows what we want. And, just in case, inform Security that they should have extra personnel on hand. I'll want a full report.

Best wishes on this. I'll be watching closely.

cc: President Newsome
    Trustees Finch and Taylor

JK/jt

**Founded 1906**

# TYPES OF WRITING

Writing takes many forms, from essays to business letters and memos. Here is an overview of some different kinds of writing. You will see examples of all of them throughout this book. Chapter 12 will take a detailed look at types of writing that are usually referred to as *academic writing*.

## Letters

These include everything from a note to the postal carrier to a formal letter to your U.S. senator. In this book you will learn to write letters that are fairly formal. Essential information in a typical letter includes information about you as well as a heading, which contains the name, title, and address of the person you are writing.

For examples of a formal letter, see p. 85 in Chapter 6, where the various parts of a letter are labeled for you.

## Memos

A common form of writing, especially in the business world, is the memo, sometimes referred to as an *interoffice memo*. Much of the material in a memo is determined by the **context** or situation in which it's written. If, for example, you are writing to people within a company, college, or association, you will write it the way other people in the same situation write theirs. The idea is not to dazzle people with your skill at memo writing. Rather, you want to use this form because it's practical and it works. Look back at John Kane's memo (p. 13) for an example of a typical memo.

## Reports

In some cases writing a report means using a printed form developed for that purpose. For example, the security guard who writes up a report on a disturbance at an official college event will use a form supplied by the college administration. It will have blanks to be filled in, indicating time, date, other employees on duty at the time, names of witnesses, and other relevant information. Most forms also include a place for a paragraph or two where the report writer explains in his or her own words just what happened.

All kinds of people write reports: police officers, emergency room technicians, salespersons, airline pilots, remodeling estimators, and many others. These reports, like any other piece of writing, have an audience, even when the audience is "the files." Someone who needs to know what they contain can be expected to read them.

In situations where your job is to write a report without a preset format, imagine that the person to whom you are reporting is standing in front of you and asking you questions. Ask them yourself and answer them. What happened? What are the details, the numbers, the names, the times, the possible consequences? If your judgment is expected, give it; otherwise, simply tell the reader what happened. Don't "editorialize" by using words that indicate your feelings unless you make it clear that you are doing so.

## Flyers

Flyers can include posters, handouts, leaflets, pamphlets, notices, and similar items. All of them share the same basic nature of written communication. They combine words in ways that will affect certain readers, and they call on you to use your visual and artistic judgment in laying the material out on the page. This is increasingly true of web pages, where the audience expects to find words used carefully and clearly.

The use of pictures, drawings, different typefaces, and visual layouts involves skills that are not part of this course. It may be that you are more gifted at this than you realize. It's also possible that you will be able to develop this kind of skill because of the sophisticated, easy-to-use desktop publishing and web site development programs that are available.

All of the types of writing listed here can, of course, be shared on the Internet through web pages. Computer technology may be challenging and rapidly changing, but words still must be put together in ways that will communicate with an audience.

## Articles

*Article* is a general term that covers several different kinds of writing. The usual image of an article is something written by a reporter or correspondent for a newspaper, magazine, or web site. The people who write articles for a living are successful only if they have a clear vision of their audiences. If a magazine doesn't find its readers, it quickly goes out of business. Bikers, 4-H club members, and rugby players expect that reading material on their special interests will sound as if it has been written by someone who is an expert and who shares their tastes.

Beginning journalists are taught to follow the rule of the "five *W*s" when writing an article. They are who? what? when? where? and why? By adding an *H* (how?) to the *W*s, you have a simple, easy-to-memorize device to help you write a complete account of an event or occurrence. The skillful article writer uses these elements without making them overly obvious to an audience.

Who?
What?
When?
Where?
Why?
How?

Consider, for example, the use of the five *W*s in the accompanying article on page 17 by a local newspaper publisher who wants readers to send in material.

## E-Mail

For many people, their largest output of written words takes place online. As more people around the world have access to computers, e-mail is becoming one of the primary ways that written communication takes place. The ease with which e-mail can be composed and the relaxed way people express themselves in it are having a strong effect on the practice of writing. At the moment, it's difficult to know exactly how online expression will affect us in the long run, but it's likely to have both positive and negative effects. On the one hand—provided we learn to use a keyboard—computer-based communication allows us express ourselves spontaneously and instantly, sending our ideas anywhere in the world just about as quickly as we can think of them. On the other hand, this ease of expression may cause us to be less concerned with turning out the best written words we can compose. Electronic mail messages don't seem to us to be as permanent as words printed on paper. Of course e-mail can be saved in the computer's memory, but we get used to the fact that anything can be erased or thrown into the cyber trash can with the flick of a mouse. As a result, we may tend to be sloppier and less concerned with precise, clear words. As in speaking, we always know that we can clarify what we just said as soon as we know our audience is a bit puzzled. Like any other skill, writing improves with practice, so be sure to use even the writing you do online as an opportunity to keep sharpening this skill. (Note: See Internet Job Search in Appendix A for more on this subject.)

# HOW TO TURN A BLANK SCREEN INTO A WELL-WRITTEN NEWS STORY.

It's easy to recognize a good news story. It's timely, well-organized, and worthy of people's attention.

But how can you tell if your news is 'newsworthy'? Any local event or social action that is open to the public, and which either affects a number of people or needs high attendance to be successful, is deserving of coverage in your Pioneer Press paper. Here are examples of newsworthy items:

- Fund-raising events and attractions such as plays, concerts, sporting events, art showings, and community fairs
- Public service projects sponsored by your organization, restoration of a public building or landmark, or conferences or workshops
- Public meetings featuring an interesting speaker and/or open discussion on a particular issue.

How do you prepare your news release? Your release should be typed double-spaced on white 8½ x 11-inch paper. At the top right hand corner of the page, type the name of your organization, its address, your name, address and phone number. Beneath that you are welcome to indicate your preferred date of publication.

Please do not write a headline. Our editors will do that.

The first sentence of a new story is called "the lead" and should be very straightforward, containing the five key points: the five "W's" of who, what, when, where and why.

It isn't necessary to cram all five into the first sentence of your release but, by all means, have them all covered by the end of the second or third.

The "Who" in the lead is you, your organization. Use the formal title of the organization in your first reference. Check your spelling and, when referring to a person, use first and last name. Our style does not allow for courtesy titles (Mrs., Miss, Mr. etc.) except for medical doctors, dentists and members of the clergy.

"What" of your story is the event you wish to publicize. Be specific, so that the editor and the reader have no question as to what's happening.

"When" is especially crucial. Be sure to include time, day of the week, and date, in that order. (The rummage sale will be held at 10 a.m. Saturday, August 31.)

"Where" should include the name of the meeting place, street address and town.

"Why" allows you to indicate the purpose of your event. If it will benefit a specific charity, please let the public know that.

You will find that by following the above tips, your news story should get the kind of response from readers that you desire.

## PIONEER PRESS
### YOUR LOCAL SOURCE

## Exercise 1-5: Writing Assignments

Your audience for this assignment is your instructor and your fellow students.

1.   Briefly explain what brought you to this class. Give some personal history if it will help you make your expression more interesting.
2.   If you use word processing on a computer, do you think it has improved your writing? Why or why not?
3.   Describe something you read in the past week that was probably not written with you in mind. How could you tell? Was it interesting or worth reading anyway?
4.   Do you still need to convince yourself that writing well is a valuable skill? What would make it easier to convince yourself (or someone else)? ◆

In the next chapter you will begin to work your way through the steps a good writer follows in communicating with an audience.

### Visit the Longman Englishpages!

For additional readings, practice exercises, Internet links, and activities, visit us online at
**http://www.ablongman.com/englishpages**

# CHAPTER 2

# GETTING STARTED/ THE WRITING PROCESS

## TAKING IT STEP BY STEP

In Chapter 1, we talked about the audience, and we discussed different types of writing. Now it's time to show exactly how good writing is done.

Good writers go through a set of activities to make their work the best it can be. On rare occasions, they simply write down the words as if they were inspired, but usually they must consciously work their way through, step by step. First, they consider who their audience is and how best to communicate with this audience. Then, if possible, they role-play to get inside their readers' heads and decide what should be said. Third, they sketch out their ideas in an outline. Then, they write, beginning with a rough draft and followed by as many more drafts and versions as are necessary. Finally, they review what they have written, polish it, and proofread it.

---

### Steps Taken by Effective Writers

- They think of who their audience is and how best to communicate with this audience. When role playing helps to do this, they use it.
- Based on role playing, they try to get inside the readers' heads and decide what should be said. Their overall main idea (topic sentence/thesis) should be expressed in one sentence.

*(Continued)*

---

---

*(Continued from previous page)*

- They sketch out their ideas in an outline.
- They write, beginning with a rough draft.
- They review what they have written, revise it to make it better, and polish and proofread it carefully.

---

This is where the real work of becoming a good writer begins. Writers cannot afford to simply get something down on paper and leave it at that. They must begin to revise, to find better ways to say things, to show their readers that they know who they are.

## ANALYZING THE AUDIENCE

### Role Playing

If you had to write a letter to convince that dean of student services that the subject of animal rights should be discussed on campus, would you know how to begin? One way to develop your writing skills is through the use of **role playing.** This means putting yourself inside the minds and hearts of various people involved in real situations, such as the kind described in these cases, trying to determine how to write for particular audiences. You think like the participants so that you can express yourself the way you think they would. As much as possible, you become these people, not to show your skill as an actor, but to figure out what they would write for their particular audiences. In writing, you have to be able to trust your judgments and trust your ability to get them right often enough to keep communicating.

Role *playing* does not imply phoniness or fakery. It is not simply play, any more than soldiers training in war games are playing. Role playing is not the same as acting. There are similarities, however. In role playing, you share with actors their ability to "become" someone else and to do what their character would do in a given situation. You observe people and their actions to see what motivates them to do the things they do. You imagine how they will react to the things you say, and you observe them as closely as necessary to see if they react the way you expected. Your job is to imagine how you would react if the written words were directed at you. Then by putting yourself in someone else's place, you can sharpen your ability to pick just the right words and expressions. Here are some pointers to keep in mind as you role-play:

- Don't worry about obvious differences between you and the person you are temporarily becoming. If it's a young woman, so are you. If it's a college president, so are you. If it's an outspoken champion of some point of view, so are you—at least while you're role-playing.

- Don't misplace your sense of humor. Be patient with yourself and your fellow students as you try to get into this method of studying and creating. You can learn on your own, but you will learn much better by collaborating with others who are trying to do the same thing.

- Try assuming different roles. Put your ego aside for the time and be willing to be criticized by others. Equally important, be willing to criticize and make suggestions to others, even if your judgment tells you that you are criticizing people who write better than you do. They may write better than you, but you can do something for them that they cannot do as well for themselves: You can get outside of their writing and look at it as an outsider. They (and you, when you're on the receiving end of criticism) may find it difficult to be totally objective about their words. They're too close to what they wrote to judge it objectively.

- Remember that criticism doesn't have to be negative. Constructive, positive criticism is truly golden. Again, keep your sense of humor handy and use it often.

## Exercise 2-1: Discussion Questions

Review the animal rights case in Chapter 1. This time, however, picture the following people and answer the questions indicated.

A.  The Applied Ethics teacher who grades Anne McCormick's term paper, but who didn't attend the debate.
B.  A sophomore reporter for the school newspaper, who hopes to be editor-in-chief by senior year.
C.  The statewide coordinator of the animal rights organization, who will have to let the national executives of the organization in Washington, D.C., know how things turned out at Carson College.

Answer these questions:

1.  What do these people have in common?
2.  Which of the three might have the most trouble communicating with the other two? Why? (Beware of stereotypes.)
3.  With which of the three would you find it easiest to communicate? Why? Now read through a sample script and see how a couple of people might try to get inside each other's minds.  ◆

## Exercise 2-2: Sample Script

The reporter from the school paper is interviewing the director of campus security. Take one of these parts and act it out with a partner. When you reach the last words, keep the dialogue going. Try to get into each other's minds by really listening to each other's words.

**Security:**    Go ahead. You wanted to meet with me.
**Reporter:**    Right. Thanks for giving me your time. May I please see a copy of the report you turned in to the administration?

| | |
|---|---|
| **Security:** | I'm not sure we can do that. What do you want it for anyway? |
| **Reporter:** | I just want to use it as part of the background for the story I'm writing. I'm trying to find out whether people on both sides of the debate were treated equally by the college—by you people. |
| **Security:** | What would make you think that they weren't? If you've got something you're trying to say, just say it. |
| **Reporter:** | I'm sorry. I think I got us off to a bad start. I'm not implying anything about your honesty. OK, now tell me why you think things started to get out of hand the other night. Whose fault was it? |
| **Security:** | Is this on or off the record? I'll want to see your article before it gets printed. |
| **Reporter:** | Have you heard of a free press? We can't allow you or anyone to infringe on our rights by censoring us. But don't worry. I'm not out to do anything but get at the truth and communicate it to our readers. So, let me ask you: Did you feel that both sides were equally to blame for the disturbance at the meeting? |
| **Security:** | Well, not exactly. As a matter of fact . . . |

You take it from here. Try to explore each other's motivation. Are you both just doing your job? How much do you trust each other, and how does this show up in the words you use with each other?   ◆

As you can see, conversation is much easier than writing. When you are speaking, you have the luxury of being able to repeat yourself. If someone's facial expression tells you that you are being misunderstood, you can fix things. "No, that's not what I meant. What I really meant was . . . ." And, depending on your interpersonal skills, you will continue to act and react, speak, and listen. You nod your head as the other person talks, and you may wave your hands around for emphasis when it's your turn. All in all, conversation is a complicated activity that seems simple because we do so much of it.

For most people, writing is harder than speaking. Your audience/listener is not there in front of you when the communication takes place. You don't get the immediate feedback of a raised eyebrow, smile, cold stare, or nervous cough. None of those little signals you've learned to recognize are there—the signals that indicate everything from boredom to passion, prejudice to acceptance, agreement to deep puzzlement.

Your challenge as a writer is to imagine the reaction your audience might have, based on your ability to get inside their minds. You need to do some serious thinking about your potential readers. You need to really listen and not simply think of what you will say next. How you proceed will vary depending on whether you are writing for one person or more.

Keep reminding yourself that your written words might mean one thing to you and be taken in a totally different way by your audience. Here are a few actual headlines that newspapers have used for stories and feature articles. Aren't you glad you didn't write them?

Something Went Wrong in Jet Crash, Experts Say

Iraqi Head Seeks Arms

Panda Mating Fails; Veterinarian Takes Over

Teacher Strikes Idle Kids

Plane Too Close to Ground, Crash Probe Told

Juvenile Court to Try Shooting Defendant

Stolen Painting Found by Tree

War Dims Hope for Peace

Couple Slain; Police Suspect Homicide

New Study of Obesity Looks for Larger Test Group

Typhoon Rips through Cemetery; Hundreds Dead

## Exercise 2-3: Role Playing

Pick five of these poorly written headlines and rewrite them so that you're sure the audience will not misunderstand them. Put yourself inside the minds of the unlucky headline writers and say what they really meant to say. Use as few words as possible, but make sense. ◆

## Learning from Models

You've already seen the memo from the dean to the director of student activities. Now look at two versions of this letter from the students' public speaking organization that proposed having the animal rights debate in the first place.

# *Carson College Forensics Society*

*306 Student Union Building / Carson College / 295 College Circle / East Carson, IL*
*Phone: 555-1283 / Fax: 555-1284 / e-mail: carforsoc@carcoll.edu*

January 25, 2001
John Kane, Ph.D.
Dean of Instruction
Carson College

Dear Dean Kane,

The Carson College Forensics Society would like to sponsor a debate on the subject of "Animal Rights." Our mission, as you know, is to encourage open and free discussion of important subjects and ideas. We think our fellow students need to learn to see both sides of an argument and to be tolerant of other people's points of view, even if the view happens to be stupid.

We propose to set up a debate between some strong, outspoken people on both sides of this important topic. Will you please give us your encouragement in this? We will work with Mr. Sturgess in the Office of Student Activities, but we want you to be the one who makes the debate a success and gets the appropriate credit for it. Of course, if you have anyone you particularly want to take part in the debate, we will make sure that they are invited. We want to keep you happy.

Thanks again for being a really great Dean. We want Carson College to be proud of its own Forensics Society.

Sincerely,

Charles Lee
President-Elect

c: Mr. Sturgess, Student Activities

CL/jt

Now consider a second version of this letter.

---

## *Carson College Forensics Society*

*306 Student Union Building / Carson College / 295 College Circle / East Carson, IL*
*Phone: 555-1283 / Fax: 555-1284 / e-mail: carforsoc@carcoll.edu*

January 25, 2001

John Kane, Ph.D.
Dean of Instruction
Carson College

Dear Dean Kane,

The Carson College Forensics Society would like to sponsor a debate on the subject of "Animal Rights." Our mission, as you know, is to encourage open and free discussion of important subjects and ideas.

With the cooperation of Mr. Sturgess and the Office of Student Activities, we propose to set up a debate between some strong, outspoken people on both sides of this important topic. We hope you will encourage us in this project. And, of course, we hope you will attend the debate.

Any suggestions or ideas you may have on this important subject will be most welcome.

Sincerely,

Charles Lee
President-Elect

c: Mr. Sturgess, Student Activities

CL/jt

## Exercise 2-4: Discussion Questions

1.  Which of these two letters is more aware of its audience? What does the first letter show about how Charles Lee wants to influence Dean Kane? Is this a wise thing for Mr. Lee to be doing? Why or why not?
2.  What warning signals might Dean Kane pick up in the first letter? Is there anything in the second letter that might make him suspicious?

Mr. Lee is writing on behalf of the Forensics Society. Do any of his words—in either letter—suggest that he might be expressing his personal beliefs and not those of his group? ◆

# ORGANIZING MATERIAL

Our emphasis so far has been on writing as an interaction between the writer and reader. Equally important is the way a writer lines up ideas before putting them down on paper.

Think for a moment of the limitation that written language has simply because it is written. Its words must be put one after another in a linear way—that is, in a line, one after another, from left to right. This means that you won't ever read the end of a sentence before you've read its beginning. You're forced to be patient and to pick up the pieces of information one at a time, just as the writer has laid them out. In recent years, thanks to TV commercials, music videos, and electronic games, you have become accustomed to getting a lot of different kinds of information in a simultaneous rather than linear way. You can absorb huge amounts of visual, musical, rhythmic, and verbal information all at once. But when you write or read, you have to take things a chunk at a time.

In speaking, you have the ability to say, "Oh, I almost forgot . . . ," and go back to pick up a fumbled idea. As a writer, you need to do some revising so that you can have it just right the first time you present it to an audience. This means you must do most of the work for your audience members and not expect them to organize things as they read them. If it's important enough to them, they will try to figure out what you are trying to say, but you can't count on that happening. If your writing is confusing, your readers will become confused and simply drift away. Even worse, they may resent you because they resent your disorganization. You need a plan.

## Rough Outlines

You'll discover many ways to organize your ideas. For example, you can:

- Show how events or ideas happen in a certain order.

- Organize your ideas so that your strongest, most persuasive one is left for last.

- Describe something or someone in a logical way, not simply jumping around from one detail to another at random.

- Use one or more of the other **methods of development** mentioned in Chapter 1 and explained throughout the rest of the chapters.

However you organize your writing, it's important that your audience gets the impression you have given your material some serious thought rather than simply jotting it down as it occurred to you. You should have a main focus or point that you're trying to get across to your reader. In paragraphs this main point is called a **topic sentence** (see Chapter 3), and in longer pieces of writing that include a number of paragraphs, it's called a **thesis** (see Chapter 8). For now, simply use your common sense in trying to pull your ideas together in a way that seems clear and useful. You will examine topic sentences and theses in more detail as you proceed through the cases.

Take a look at this box and refer to it frequently throughout the course.

[The main idea I want to convey is **that**] _____

_____

_____

## Exercise 2-5: Main Idea

1.  Come up with a possible main idea about animal rights, and then express it in one sentence. Write the sentence in the box and put it at the top of your working draft. For example: "*The main idea I want to convey is that* we should have an animal rights organization here at Carson College." The word *that* guarantees that you will have to write a complete idea after it. Experiment by writing more than one possi-

ble main idea. When you cross out the first nine words, you are left with a complete sentence.

2.  Then, with one eye firmly on this main, unifying idea, list some of the things that could help you make your point. Write them all down at first. You can always cross things out later or combine some ideas with others. What's important is to move your thoughts from your head to the paper.

3.  Experiment with a simple paragraph, part of a letter. Suppose you are a Carson College student who wishes to start a local chapter of the national animal rights organization and your audience is the Director of Student Activities, Mr. Sturgess. Let's say you write this sentence on your scratch paper (or word processing screen):

    The main idea I want to convey is **that** getting a local chapter of this organization would benefit the student body.

Now you need some ideas that can help you get this point across. Here are some. Just jot them down without worrying about sentence structure and punctuation for the time being.

Animals don't deserve to be tortured

Methods of research which don't require abuse of animals

Shows that Carson is a humane, forward-looking college

Promotes free exchange of ideas

Can work against those who profit at the expense of our fellow animals

Provide an outlet for idealism of students

Reform the fur and cosmetics industries

Get even with people who disagree with us

Add a couple of your own. Cross out one or more of the ones listed if they are not going to help establish your point/thesis.

_____

_____

Maybe the famous five *W*s (and *H*) would be useful here. As you ask who? what? and so on, watch for some kind of worthwhile idea to begin to make itself clearer. Notice how some of your ideas overlap with others. Also, some ideas that are jotted quickly may be irrelevant. That's OK. This will happen when you let yourself write without censoring your words. The time for being more reasonable and hardheaded comes after the initial, "anything goes" stage of writing.

But, for now at least, you have enough to make a temporary, rough, or "scratch" outline, such as:

Reasons for having a local chapter of animal rights protection organization here on campus

it's educational, what a college is for

subject important(?) to future of Carson's students

gives us a chance to stand up for animal rights

This gives you enough to get started on. As you write, you will make changes, but you can work with this outline. ◆

## Exercise 2-6: Topic Sentence

Which of these examples results in a complete sentence?

1.    [The main idea I want to convey is that] the animal rights debate is going to become more bitter during the next few years.
2.    [The main idea I want to convey is that] increasing arguments in the animal rights debate.

Produce another possible main idea for a piece of writing. Start off with *The main idea I want to convey is* **that**. . . ." Complete the sentence. Then cross out the first nine words and you'll see that what's left is the statement of your main idea or thesis. ◆

## Adding Materials

The scratch outline is still general and not very interesting. It will turn into the raw material for a good piece of writing because of the **supporting material** you add. Supporting material means information you use to back up the statement you are making in your topic sentence or thesis. Your readers want evidence, facts, mental pictures, and images. It's up to you to supply the supporting material that makes your ideas convincing and clear. For example, you might include a statistic on the number of colleges that already have a chapter of this organization. Other vivid details could include the close connection between common consumer products, such as cosmetics and fur, and use of animals in research and production.

## Exercise 2-7: Rough Outlines

Try adding ideas to the rough outline. A couple have already been supplied for you.

Reasons for having a local chapter of animal rights protection organization here on campus
It's educational, what a college is for
Pamphlets and other literature available free

_____

_____

subject important to future of Carson's students

_____

_____

Career choice based on knowledge of offending industries
gives us a chance to stand up for animal rights

_____

_____

_____ ◆

## Writing a Rough Draft

After you have developed rough outlines, you will write a **rough draft** of the piece you are working on. Think of a rough draft as the first part of a conversation you are carrying on with your audience. Get your ideas out there, put them on paper, and make them sound as effective as you can. Some guidelines:

- Don't let uncertainty about punctuation, spelling, or sentence structure interrupt the flow of your ideas.

- If you have an incomplete idea, jot down what you have and get it outside of your head where you can work with it.

- Don't be afraid to revise your rough outline. The very act of looking for one way to say something will often help you discover an even better one.

- After you've created your first draft, reread it to assume the role of the reader.

Question what you see. Does the writing get off the point? And just exactly what is the point, anyway? Has it been set out clearly somewhere toward the beginning of the work?

Here's an example of a rough draft based on the rough outline:

(Rough Draft)
After attending last month's debate, I am convinced that there are several reasons why having a local chapter of the animal rights protection organization right here at Carson College would benefit our student body. For one thing, it would be educational, and that is what college is for. We could receive and distribute literature here on campus, and we could write papers about animal rights for our classes. Like other college activities, it could be important for our future. We could learn to accept the kinds of people we will meet in our future lives and learn how to deal with their opposing viewpoints. We might also learn which potential employers to avoid because they exploit animals. Most of all, having a chapter of the organization here at Carson would enable us to stand up for what is right. Animals don't have the power to do this for themselves. Their lives, like those of every living thing, are valuable. Abusing animals harms the animals, but it harms those people who abuse them even more. So, I say let's have a local chapter of the animal rights organization here at Carson.

## Exercise 2-8: Rough Drafts

Whether or not you agree with this example, you will admit that it is a pretty good start toward a finished paragraph (more on paragraphs in Chapter 3). Sure, there is some repetition, and some of the ideas are rather vague and generalized, but it makes a point and sticks to it.

Now try one of your own. Take a different point/thesis, and write a rough draft of a paragraph. You might find this useful: ~~The main idea I want to convey is~~ **that the lessons we could learn from the national animal rights organization would be valuable.** Use some of the ideas you have already included in your rough outline, rearranging them to fit this new point/thesis. ◆

## Rereading and Revising

Here are some suggestions to help get your writing closer and closer to what will communicate best to your audience. Follow them as you write versions of the paper that are less and less "rough."

- Read your writing out loud. This is the best way to catch yourself repeating the same words too frequently. You may discover that you have started several sentences exactly the same way, which can be distracting or monotonous to readers.

- Look for general terms that might be made more specific. Give examples of your ideas, naming names and giving physical characteristics where possible. Don't say "representatives of an organization"; give the names of the organization and the people's names. Don't say that "refreshments" will be served; list pop and pizza.

- Add connectors and transitions between sentences and paragraphs. Words like *however, also, in addition, finally, first of all, therefore, for instance, for example,* and *in conclusion* can be useful. Your readers may not see the relationship between two of your ideas unless you use a word or two to make it clear.

- Whenever you think it's acceptable, use words that relate to your reader's senses. Put sights, sounds, flavors, odors, and textures on the page: humming fluorescent bulbs, screeching tires, sweat on your nose, waterfalls that make the ground vibrate beneath your Reeboks. You probably have some vivid memories of certain things you write about, complete with a mental gallery containing images of your experiences, such as how each of the people sitting around that particular table last Thanksgiving Day looked and sounded. Make use of details like these in developing others for your writing.

## Exercise 2-9: Support

Once again, return to the animal rights case in Chapter 1 and reread it. Then try the following: Write another version of the paragraph you have been working on. This time make use of the advice provided this far in this chapter. Include details and ideas in your writing that you would appreciate having a writer present to you. Make it real and make it interesting. ◆

# POLISHING AND PROOFREADING

Writing should be revised as an ongoing process. At some point practicality tells you that you've done as much as you are going to do. It's time to submit the words to their audience. Before reaching this point, however, you must polish and proofread. Respect for your audience demands that you take a final look at your product. This is when you pick up on the little things that could detract from your effectiveness.

**Polishing** means making final adjustments to your words to get them the way you want them. Polishing for a writer is what using different grades of sandpaper is for a furniture maker. **Proofreading** is more mechanical and cold-blooded. You must check the physical words and letters on your paper or monitor to make sure you wrote the correct ones.

Here are some examples of polishing:

- Noticing whether your pronouns ("they," "their," "hers") clearly point to the persons they represent. If you have referred to two different people by name (Jack and Fred) and then refer to "him," you know who he is, but will your reader? (See more on this in Chapter 5, Pronoun Clarity)

- Substituting a strong, interesting verb for the bland word *is* wherever you can. Don't distort your sentences to do this, but try it in a few places before you consider your job done. Example: Not, "The breeze *is* strong," but "The breeze touches each piece of grass."

- Making sure that your opening and closing sentences are as well written as you can possibly make them.

- Looking for consistency. Did you shift from one tense to another? Did you shift your point of view by addressing the reader as "you" and then jumping to discussion of "he or she"? (See more on this in Chapter 11.)

- Check for **clichés.** These are expressions that have been overused because they were originally very good. The first person who said "last but not least" was a writing hero. Now the expression—and thousands like it—show a lack of originality and a willingness to take the easy way out (Oops, another cliché).

## Exercise 2-10: Polishing

Take a look at this possible rough draft.

(Rough Draft)
   [1]After attending last month's debate, I am convinced that there are several reasons why having a local chapter of the animal rights protection organization right here at Carson College would benefit our student body. [2]For one thing, it would be educational, and that is what college is for. [3]We

could receive and distribute literature here on campus, and we could write papers about animal rights for our classes. [4]Like other college activities, it could be important for our future. [5]We could learn to accept the kinds of people we will meet in our future lives and learn how to deal with their opposing viewpoints.

[6]We might also learn which potential employers to avoid because they exploit animals. [7]Most of all, having a chapter of the organization here at Carson would enable us to stand up for what is right. [8]Animals don't have the power to do this for themselves. [9]Their lives, like those of every living thing, are valuable. [10]Abusing animals harms the animals, but it harms those people who abuse them even more. [11]So, I say let's have a local chapter of the animal rights organization here at Carson.

Now deliberately change something that will detract from the quality of the paragraph. Don't worry. This is simply to show yourself things that might go wrong and demonstrate how to avoid them. For example:

1.  In sentence 2, take out the words *that is,* and replace them with *these are.* Now the sentence has to be fixed. How?
2.  In sentence 6, take out the verb *exploit* and replace it with *are not nice to.* Should *exploit* be put back, or is there an even better word to use in its place?
3.  After sentence 11, insert this sentence: "I guess it couldn't hurt." Do you want to remove it? Why?
4.  At the end of sentence 5, add the words, "because it takes all kinds." Is this a cliché? If so, should it be removed? ◆

Proofreading means looking at the physical words as they appear on your page or monitor and checking them for accuracy. It is the final task. You've done the best you can, and now it's time to take a last look at what you've written and let it go. Does it say exactly what you think it says? Some hints:

•   Read **only** what is on the paper or computer monitor. Do not read what is in your head. This is the most basic advice for proofreaders, but it is the most difficult to follow. You will still be composing mental sentences as you read the ones in front of you, and you will inevitably miss some mistakes. Everyone does, but the best writers don't miss very many.

•   Make your proofreading a physical activity: Put your finger on each word, slide your (capped) pen along under each line, move your lips and whisper your words to yourself. On a computer screen, move the cursor or mouse slowly along the lines. Don't let yourself worry too much about more revision at this point. Now the writing is a product in front of you. Imagine that someone else wrote it and you are simply reading their words looking for errors and typos.

• Try to allow some time between the end of your writing and the beginning of your proofreading, a day or two if possible. This allows you to be somewhat removed from the words you have been writing. You have a better chance of catching small, careless errors. Also, it may help to proofread in a different physical location. For example, if you write at the kitchen table, proofread in the library. A simple change of setting will help you see the page in a fresh light.

• If you work on a computer or word processor, don't rely totally on your spell-checking program. If you wrote *an* when you meant *and,* the computer won't know that. *Their* and *there* or *too* and *to* look equally good to the spell checker, but only one of them is correct in each situation.

## Exercise 2-11: Proofreading

1. Get a copy of your school newspaper and find at least two typographical errors. Keep looking. They're there.
2. Look at the owner's manual for one of your home appliances. Now that you're familiar with this appliance, try rewriting a couple of sentences in it to make them clearer to potential new customers.
3. Find at least two clichés within one paragraph in your town's major newspaper. Hint: The sports pages and the food sections may provide many more than you need. ◆

## Exercise 2-12: Proofreading Practice

Read through the following selections and make any needed changes. A computerized spell-check program will not catch some errors, so read carefully.

1. *(From the album notes of a Chieftans' CD)* The Chieftans are Ireland's foremost cultural ambassadors. They have proudly taken the traditional music of Irenlad, a music forged in the modest homes of the people

throughout the centuries, to audiences everywhere since the group was formed in Dublin in 1963. they have performed thousands of concerts all over the world, winning freinds and new converts to the music wherever they have gone. As Paddy Moloney's biographer Bill Meek notes, they have in the process amassed an impressive list of "firsts": "first Irish folk ensemble to be named *Melody Maker* 'Group of Year,' first band to play in the Capital Building of the United States, first musicians in history to perform on the Great Wall of China, first Irish group win an Oscar."

2.   *(From the label on a bottle of cough suppressant)* Do not exceed recommended dosage. If nervousness, sleeplessnes, or dizzziness occur, discontinue use and consult an doctor. A persistint cough may be a signs of a serious condition. If cough or other symptom persist, do not improve within 7 days, tend to recur, or are accompanied by fever, rash, or persistent headache, conslut a physician. As with any drug, if you are pregnant or nursing a baby, seeke the advise of a health professional before using this product.

3.   *(From the introduction to a college dictionary)* The goal of the Third Edition is to to provide the user with comprehension and appreciation of the language in a readable manner. Keeping the kneads of the contemporary user in mind, we have presented the central and often the most frequently sought meaning of a word frist. The definitions are worded in concise, lucid prose without the specialized terms and abreviations that make most dictioneries forbidding and confusing.

4.   *(From a biography of Sinclair Lewis, Nobel Prize-winning American writer)* He retruned to New Haven in september, and at this point he began to lose interest in his diary. The entries for the remaining months of 1905 are few, and there is not diary at all for 1906. Except for the summer of 1906, when his parents perserved some of his correspondence, it is impossible now to reconstruct the details of his daily affairs until November 12, 1907, when he took up his dairy again; he maintained it, thereafter, until his graduation from Yale in June 1908. We know exactly, however, the direction in which he was moving, and we know where he arrived. In his third year at yale he was the outspoken dissident.

5.   *(From the Chicago Sun-Times sports pages [8/8/00, p. 95])* Julie Krone began riding a pony bareback as a barefooted 5-year-old. She kept right on riding—and winning—and on Monday became the first women inducted into the National Racing Hall of Fame in Saratoga

Springs. N.Y. "I wish I could put every one you here on a racehorse at the eighth pole, so you could have the same feeling that I did," Krone said. "I got to do something I love so much every day. And today I know for sure that life doesnt get any better." Krone was intorduced by the man who trained her. He told of the day Krone showed up in Maryland with fore cardboard boxes tied with a rope. "Her luggage," he said. ◆

## Exercise 2-13: Clichés

Here is a list of clichés. Finish it off and add another ten if you're in the mood. (Don't use *in the mood*).

1. Look out for number one.
2. Keep your eye on the ball.
3. Better late than never.
4. When the going gets tough the tough get going.
5. Go the extra mile.
6. _____
7. _____
8. _____
9. _____
10. _____ ◆

# GETTING AND REACTING TO FEEDBACK

You can learn on your own, but you will learn much better by **collaborating** with others who are trying to do the same thing. Collaborating is a word that means "working together," and it describes one of the best ways to sharpen your skills as a writer. When you are working with other writing students, you can try out your material on a sympathetic audience. You can help others by helping them see and hear what their words are really like. Likewise, they can tell you if something misfired when you tried to get it across. It's only practice for writing outside of your classroom, but it is valuable practice because the audience is practicing and learning the same things you are. You will get valuable feedback from your teacher, certainly, but some of the best comes from your fellow would-be writers.

## Exercise 2-14: Getting Feedback

Trade the rough draft of your paragraph on animal rights with another student and read each others' papers. For the time being, don't worry about fine points, such as variety in sentence structure, perfect punctuation, and word choice. Instead, look to see if the paper you are critiquing does the following:

1. It states a clear main point/thesis.
2. It follows a plan in using material to support the main point/thesis.
3. It sticks to the main point/thesis. ◆

# WRITING CONVENTION: SPELLING

One meaning of *convention* is "a standard, accepted way of doing something." For example, a convention for most of us in the United States is to eat our dinner with knives, forks, and spoons. That's certainly not the only way to do it—in fact more of the world's people eat with chopsticks or fingers than with our type of utensils. Each method has advantages and disadvantages, and within certain cultures, each one is conventional. Successful writing is conventional too, in the sense that it meets your audience's expectations. That means you don't distract them by drawing unnecessary attention to your unconventional spelling, punctuation, vocabulary, and sentence structure. Conventional doesn't mean dull. It doesn't mean unimaginative. It simply means that you know how the game is played and you can operate within the limits upon which players agree.

To help you do this, the chapters in this book provide you an overview of writing conventions. Spelling is the first of the writing conventions that you will explore. Remember that you should be using this book in conjunction with one of the standard writing handbooks on the market. The sections on writing conventions contained here are not a substitute for a more complete study of them. Your teacher can help you find this material, either in books or possibly in the form of interactive computer programs.

Spelling is truly a *writing* convention. We don't spell—or punctuate, for that matter—when we speak to each other, and we get along just fine without doing so. But the minute we put words down on paper or a computer screen, our spelling becomes the business of our readers. They expect us to get it right.

Why is spelling in English so difficult? It isn't difficult in all languages. Spanish, for instance, is easy on its spellers. If you know how to pronounce a word in

Spanish, you know how to spell it, and vice versa. That's not true in English. Why? Back in 1066, when the French sailed across the English Channel and conquered the English, the two languages began battling each other, just as their speakers fought. Because the French were winning the wars, the rulers of England spoke French. Meanwhile, out on the streets of England, people were speaking a language that we would recognize as English.

As time passed, the French rulers tried to learn the local language, and the locals tried to learn what their new rulers were saying. When either side tried to spell what they thought the other was saying, the result was a hodgepodge of bad pronunciations translated into a bad choice of letters. Thus, we have inherited a collection of words that is very rich and flexible, but one that has come down to us with a tradition of often haphazard spelling. Even Shakespeare spelled his own name several different ways. If you try to reason and to analyze your way toward the spelling of a modern English word, you will often find yourself faced with this loose, confusing tradition.

What do you do?

1.   You acknowledge that life isn't fair and that, in spite of all this, you still need to present your written words spelled perfectly to your audiences. Fortunately, you live in an age of computerized spell checkers. These digital wizards, which you can be sure were used in the preparation of this book, will help solve some—but not all—of your problems.

2.   In addition to computers, your English handbook probably has a list of "the 300 most frequently misspelled words," as well as some rules for memorizing them. You know, "The Princi*pal* is your pal," "*i* before *e,* except after *c,*" and so on. In addition, your instructor can supply you with spelling exercises and refer you to one of the computerized learning labs that most schools now have. There you will find software programs and lessons that will help you train yourself to become a better speller.

3.   You must make friends with your dictionary. Good dictionaries are inexpensive and full of useful information, including correct spelling. You know the catch-22: If you already knew how to spell it you wouldn't have to look it up, but if you don't know how to spell it, you can't look it up. That's not entirely true; you can learn to make educated guesses, and eventually you will find that your success rate will increase. It's a long, hard haul, but it may be that knowing the background of the problem will take some of the mystery out of English spelling. An added benefit of looking up words is that you find many others you didn't know before in the process, and your vocabulary continues to grow painlessly.

## Exercise 2-15: Spelling

1.  List four pairs of words that might be incorrect in your writing and still not be caught by a computer's spell checker. Examples: no/know, here/hear.
2.  Make a list containing at least ten words you use even though you are not always completely sure of their spelling.
3.  Examine your dictionary's explanation of how it divides words into syllables. Does this help you spell words more logically? ◆

# THE NEXT STEP

In Chapter 1 you were introduced to the activities you will be performing in the process of becoming more skillful in the use of written language. You saw the approach that you will be expected to take to gain mastery of this important skill. Chapter 2 has given you some of the tools and techniques you will need to continue fine-tuning your writing. It also introduced the first of the writing conventions you will need to master, namely, spelling.

Beginning with the next chapter and continuing to the end of the book, you will apply the ideas and methods you have learned. Your writing will become more ambitious as you proceed. Chapter 3 will use the case method to help you write paragraphs like the ones you have seen so far. Beginning with Chapter 8, you will be combining from three to five paragraphs into longer compositions known as essays. By the end of the course, you will have learned to write paragraphs and essays in ways that are expected of a college student.

## Exercise 2-16: Writing Assignments

1.  Write a brief essay that explains in your own words what the case approach to writing skill is all about. In this one rare instance, your audience is yourself.
2.  Sketch out a case that you are familiar with—or make one up—in which at least three different pieces of writing have to be produced by different participants. Look at this book's table of contents for some ideas. Also look in the Appendix, for more examples.

3.  Describe a piece of writing that you are glad you *don't* have to write. Explain the situation and why you would find it difficult to produce this piece of writing. What might your potential audience have to do with your reluctance? For example, if you were a junior executive attending an emergency meeting where it was decided that your company would be firing large numbers of employees, would you like to be the one who was ordered to come up with a letter to all the employees explaining this move?

4.  Analyze a piece of writing that looks as if it was done in a big hurry. Give evidence of this. Do the ideas get jumbled together without transitional words? Are words left out? Does the writing get off the main point? Give examples. ◆

### Visit the Longman Englishpages!

For additional readings, practice exercises, Internet links, and activities, visit us online at
**http://www.ablongman.com/englishpages**

# PART 2

# WRITING
# PARAGRAPHS

# Chapter 3

# Writing Effective Paragraphs

## Making Sense through Paragraphs

Everything we have discussed about writing so far has reminded you that your words are written for someone to read. Moreover, your goal is that people will read your words exactly the way you want them to be read. You build up a series of words, one after another, and they convey a series of ideas in groups (sentences, paragraphs, essays, books). This chapter will help you write good paragraphs, one of the most valuable skills an educated person can acquire. You will also be writing them as you work through the next eight chapters.

A **paragraph** is a collection of sentences grouped together for effective communication. Paragraphs are visibly separated from other paragraphs because of spacing on the page and often because the first line is **indented.** This means that it starts a few spaces (usually five) in from the left margin. Most importantly, the sentences are placed together, separate from other paragraphs, because they *belong* together. They make up a unit, which expresses one basic part of what the author is trying to say to the audience. One sentence, frequently the first one, sums up the overall idea of the paragraph and is called the *topic sentence.* The rest of the paragraph's sentences work together to get the topic sentence's idea across effectively.

Let's examine paragraphs by starting with some commonsense facts about words. Even as children, when we speak or write words, we string them together in groups, usually more than three at a time. The "Me Tarzan" type of language doesn't get much done. These groups of words represent groups of ideas. When we string words together to express ideas, we follow certain accepted rules and customs, and then our audience understands what we're saying. In our writing, these accepted practices mean that we can create sentences, which range from easy, little ones to overly complicated ones. Here are two sentences:

1.  My name is John. (four words)

2.  Well, since, for some strange reason, you seem to want to know, although it's probably none of your business, or anyone else's for that matter, what my name is, I may as well tell you—since you'd probably find out sooner or, for that matter, later—that my name, believe it or not, is John. (fifty-five words)

Sentence number 1 obviously is a better sentence than number 2, but they're both strings of words, and they both follow the writing method that the English language sets up for us. Part of your job is to know how to string these ideas (words) together in the ways that make the best sentences for your audience. You should spend your life writing more sentences like number 1 than number 2. But that's only part of what this book is about. As we've seen, sentences are gathered together into paragraphs, and then paragraphs can be gathered together into collections of paragraphs, sometimes called *essays.* We'll talk more about essays beginning with Chapter 8.

## Writing Good Paragraphs

Keep these points in mind as you work with paragraphs:

*   As you have seen, writing is not the same as speaking. Not many people naturally speak in paragraphs, certainly not in ordinary conversation. Speaking informally lets you make statements, jump to another idea, switch ideas in midsentence, and even say things like, "Oh, I forgot to mention . . . " However, in writing sentences or paragraphs, you are expected to put everything together so that the person reading them will get the ideas with no unnecessary distractions.

*   Since expressing yourself in paragraphs is not a natural way to talk, it is true that writing things down in paragraph form is somewhat artificial. It takes some time to put a paragraph together, and the result is something "made up," but so are other worthwhile endeavors. A song lyric, a magazine cover, a stained glass window, and a play-action call at the line of

scrimmage are all made up. Artificial does not have to mean phony. It can mean taking the time and effort to create something worthwhile. You need to write and rewrite until you get your paragraphs the way you want them.

Let's take a moment to study the following typical paragraphs and see how they are put together. Note the obvious fact that they are groups of sentences, but try to see why they are effective groups. Then you will practice rewriting them on your own.

## Model Paragraphs

1.   Watching movies in my own home is much more enjoyable than putting up with the conditions I usually find in a theater. At home, nobody sits behind my slip-covered couch and kicks the back of it during the car chase scene. Also, I almost never find my shoes sticking to the floor in front of me. When I wish to watch in silence, I do not need to turn and say "Shhhh," and if I do, I am not risking a bloody nose. Since my living room has no aisles, no kids can run up and down them during the love scenes. Best of all, I can eat

all the popcorn I want without paying $4.25 for a "medium buttered." (six sentences)

2.    Terrorism and cowardice go hand in hand. Granted, the people who carried out an attack such as the bombing of the Oklahoma City Federal Building a few years ago needed strong nerves and a willingness to risk their own lives. For instance, they had to transport highly dangerous materials into an area swarming with the ordinary people they were about to kill. The terrorists hoped that the mutilated bodies of their victims would soon enough be making the statement that they were afraid to make themselves. But, if the bombers were truly courageous, they would stand up in public and let their message take its chances as part of the democratic process. Striking down innocent, defenseless people with a cloud of exploding fertilizer is not the noble, heroic action they want it to be. In fact, the odor of fertilizer is an appropriate symbol for the terrorists' state of mind. (seven sentences)

3.    I still like this college, but after a semester here I'm ready to suggest some improvements. For one thing, there should be fewer students in beginning classes. This would allow them to get more personal attention from the teachers. I would also like to see more support given to the Titans, regardless of their win/loss record. Could members of the campus security staff be instructed to smile at least once a month? Fewer badly designed posters masking-taped to the student lounge walls would be welcome. And, above all, stop saving money on heating bills, especially in the English classrooms. (seven sentences)

You may not agree with what these paragraphs say, but if you agree that they are fairly good ones, it's because they do what an effective paragraph is meant to do.

## QUALITIES OF A GOOD PARAGRAPH

•    It hangs together, trying to makes one point at a time. This point is usually contained in the first sentence (topic sentence). The topic sentence expresses the main idea that the paragraph is trying to get across to the reader, no more and no less. Each paragraph sticks to its one main idea and shows the audience how this one idea can be developed and explained. Notice the first sentence in paragraph 2, for example. Everything else that follows this one is supposed to help explain how "Terrorism and cowardice go hand in hand."

    It is not always necessary to have the topic sentence come first in the paragraph. Another possibility, as you will see, is having it follow an opening sentence that gets you thinking; then the topic sentence helps you focus on what the paragraph is trying to convey. In fact, sometimes the topic sentence can be the last sentence in a paragraph. This way it can reassure you that your impression of the paragraph's main idea is accurate. Every sentence should grow out of the idea contained in the topic sentence, regardless of where the topic sentence is placed.

- It writes for an audience of people who have senses and feelings, not just intellects. This means that, wherever possible, details help the reader see, hear, touch, feel, and even smell, so that the meaning is memorable and clear. Notice the second sentence in paragraph 1, for example, where the reader can almost feel it in the small of her own back.

- It is specific, particular, detailed. It doesn't generalize. If something can be called by a particular name, it is. If examples can be given, they are. If details are important, they are included. Notice "Titans," in paragraph 3, for example, instead of "our team."

- It communicates in a style that suits the audience—teacher, classmate, whoever. As part of a college assignment, this means clear, well-written, error-free sentences, generally free of slang and colloquial language (no "gonna" and "cuz"). It's not just conversational English; it's academic writing, the kind that is expected in a college assignment.

- It works hard to communicate the main idea of its topic sentence. If necessary, it uses different techniques or methods of development to do this. Paragraph 3, for instance, gives examples to get its point across. (See the list of methods of development in the next section.)

- It uses words and phrases to show the audience how its ideas stick together and how they work together to illustrate the topic sentence. This means using **transitional expressions** to signal the connection among various sentences. In paragraph 2, notice how the following words help keep the audience on track: *granted, for instance, but, in fact.*

## Exercise 3-1: Paragraphs

1.  Add a couple more details to paragraph 1. Don't overdo it. When does enough become too much? Would a very detailed description of the feeling of having butter and salt from popcorn under your fingernails really add anything to the paragraph?

2.    Rewrite paragraph 2, introducing a comment about free speech and see if the paragraph still sticks to the original topic sentence. If the new sentence seems distracting, remove it. Maybe it would fit in a different paragraph.

3.    Rewrite paragraph 3, using your own experience and details. Be specific. Don't be afraid to use your sense of humor. ◆

# PARAGRAPH DEVELOPMENT

What you want to say in a paragraph has started out in your mind. You have an incomplete idea that you are trying to get across, although you may alter it as you keep working on it. As you write things down, you clarify your idea for yourself. Your audience, however, is not inside your head. What the audience reads is whatever you give them, so there must be enough information to make sure they truly get the idea expressed in your paragraph's topic sentence. This book gives you quite a few ways of fleshing out your ideas. You have already seen the so-called five *W*s (who? what? where? when? why? and how?), and by now you may have used them. Perhaps you want to look ahead briefly and preview some other methods of development presented in upcoming chapters:

- Chapter 4 (p. 55), Description
- Chapter 5 (p. 67), Examples
- Chapter 6 (p. 79), Comparison/Contrast
- Chapter 7 (p. 91), Cause and Effect
- Chapter 9 (p. 111), Definition
- Chapter 10 (p. 121), Process
- Chapter 11 (p. 133), Classification

## Exercise 3-2: Analyzing Paragraphs

1.    Take another look at the sample paragraphs. Now write down what you consider to be the topic sentence in each paragraph.

(1) _____

(2) _____

(3) _____

2.  Look at the list of methods of development and write down what you consider the main method used to develop each paragraph. (The third one has been done for you.)

    (1) _____

    (2) _____

    (3)  Examples _____  ◆

## Exercise 3-3: Methods of Development

Choose one of the topic sentences in Exercise 3-2 and write a short paragraph using a *different* method of development. Here a model is provided for you, using the third sample paragraph's topic sentence. The new paragraph is developed by using cause and effect as a method of development, instead of using examples.

**I still like this college, but, after a semester here, I am ready to suggest some improvements.** Spending three months here has made me an expert on several problems which need solving. For instance, shivering in a frigid classroom has taught me how stingy the school is when it comes to heating costs. And having the same long faced security guard pass me in the hallway each day has given me the suspicion that he isn't paid enough to make him enjoy his work. Most important, I see how having a good English teacher has helped me improve my ability to write like a college student.

What do you think? Did you prefer the original version that used examples to develop the topic sentence? Or is this one, using cause and effect, better? In fact, the possible ways a paragraph can be developed are almost limitless. You can also combine more than one method in your writing. (The one you just read uses examples of causes and effects.) You can and should do whatever works, provided your main goal is to communicate. The word *pragmatic* is a good one here. A pragmatic approach means doing what it takes to get the job done. You have to keep experimenting and practicing, knowing that you will continue to become more skillful, whatever methods you use.

Now you try another version on your own. Take one of the original sample paragraphs and decide which method was used to develop it. Then try to develop the topic sentence's idea by using a different method. ◆

# WRITING CONVENTION: CLEAR AND UNIFIED PARAGRAPHS

As we have noted, writing usually differs from speaking by being more artificial and carefully put together. When you speak to someone, you can communicate emphasis by raising your voice or even smacking one fist into the palm of your other hand. If you shrug your shoulders and let your voice trail off into silence, that means something. You can't do these things in writing, so you have to be more conscious of leaving clues for the reader to follow in making sense of your ideas. Here are four ways to do this:

1.  Leave out anything that doesn't help to develop the idea behind the topic sentence. Any inappropriate detail or remark, even if you think it's pretty clever, has the possibility of distracting your audience and detracting from their understanding of your paragraph's point.
2.  Don't be afraid to repeat a term if it will make it clear to your audience what is important. In the sample paragraph 2, notice how some form of the word *terror* is used three times.
3.  Use transitional words as signposts of how your ideas connect with each other. Here is a sampling of some common ones: *for example, because of this, in addition, on the other hand, first of all, finally, in spite of this.*
4.  Be logical and careful with your pronouns. You'll read more about this in Chapter 5.

## Exercise 3-4: Transitions

Insert transitions in the appropriate places in the following paragraph. Take them from this list or, if you prefer, substitute some of your own: *at first, for example, finally, as,* and *then.*

_____ Anne McCormick discovered, animal rights is a subject that inspires strong emotions. _____, she feared that the topic of her term paper would be dull, but the more she found herself involved in the debate the more she realized that people felt passionately about it. _____, the amount of shouting and grandstanding that went on in the auditorium was frightening, even to the veteran security guards. _____, when she read the materials handed out by people on both sides, she was shocked by the graphic photographs and name calling. _____, listening to the level of rhetoric that continued in the student lounge and classrooms convinced her that this was a battle that would not be settled soon.  ◆

## Exercise 3-5: Further Practice

Reread the animal rights case in Chapter 1. Then take one of the following topic sentences and write a short paragraph by adding four sentences to it. Use any method of development that you think will work. Your audience is your classmates.

### Sample Topic Sentences

1.  The bitter controversy over animals' rights at Carson College teaches us a valuable lesson (or valuable lessons).
2.  Wearing a fur coat is an immoral act.
3.  There is nothing wrong with wearing a fur coat.
4.  Animals have the same rights that humans have.
5.  The rights of humans are more important than the rights of animals.
6.  People who worry about animals' rights should be more concerned about other people's rights.
7.  People who don't care about animals' rights are immoral and selfish.
8.  It is difficult to arrive at the truth in the debate over animals' rights.  ◆

## Exercise 3-6: Writing Assignment

Write another short paragraph (no more than five sentences) based on your reading of the animal rights case or your own thoughts on the matter. This time create your own topic sentence. Reread the material on developing an outline in Chapter 2. Your audience is your classmates.  ◆

### Visit the Longman Englishpages!

For additional readings, practice exercises, Internet links, and activities, visit us online at
**http://www.ablongman.com/englishpages**

# CHAPTER 4

# SENTENCE COMPLETENESS/ DESCRIPTION

 **CASE: ADULT FILM THEATER**

Small, neighborhood movie theaters have found it more and more difficult to compete with home VCRs, DVD players, and the large multiplex theaters in malls and shopping centers. The Mystic Theater in Seattle's Madison Park neighborhood is such a theater. It had been closed for more than a year, when the new owner, Ali Sharif, bought it. Mr. Sharif hoped he might make a go of it by showing second-run films and classics as double features. In addition, he charged $2.50 for admission, became active in the local chamber of commerce, advertised heavily, and even put extra butter on everyone's popcorn. For a while business looked promising, and he had a number of regular customers. He still lost money.

He was convinced he was not going to be able to continue losing money long enough to compete successfully with the big theaters and home VCRs, so he seriously considered an offer he had recently received. It came in the mail, following a phone conversation. Charley Sturm, who described himself as a "developer," sent Mr. Sharif the letter outlining his plan for converting the Mystic into an adult theater and bookstore. The offering price he suggested in "ballpark" figures was tempting since it

*(Continued)*

*(Continued from previous page)*

would allow Mr. Sharif to clean up his debts and even make a small profit. What should he do?

He talked it over with a couple of his fellow members of the Madison Park Chamber of Commerce and asked their advice. He thought he was speaking in confidence, but almost immediately, word leaked out and there was an uproar.

The situation developed quickly:

- The head of the chamber of commerce sent a letter to Mr. Sharif demanding that he refuse the offer and assuring him that his friends and colleagues in the neighborhood would help him succeed—without offering details about how this might happen. A copy of this letter, stapled to a cover letter, was sent to all members of the chamber.

- Mr. Sturm made several late-night phone calls to Mr. Sharif and followed them up with another letter in which he raised his offer and declared it to be "final."

- The president of the local elementary school's PTA brought up the possible sale in a speech at a meeting of her organization, and the group unanimously voted to lobby against the new theater.

- First the neighborhood newspaper and then the *Seattle Clarion* sent reporters to cover the story. Mr. Sturm was unavailable for comment, but Mr. Sharif agreed to be interviewed.

- The Civil Liberties Association of Seattle (CLAS) informed Mr. Sturm that it would support his efforts if he encountered any unfair or illegal obstacles.

- Members of a local church congregation circulated a letter to other Madison Park churches asking them to join in picketing the Mystic if it opened as an adult theater/bookstore.

Mr. Sharif decided he had no other choice so he took Mr. Sturm's offer. Six months later the Mystic reopened as Kupid's Kastle, which its advertising

insisted "caters to couples." The rebirth had its problems, including picketing, graffiti, and numerous visits from the city's Office of Inspection and Permits.

Two years later the theater was once again out of business, and at this date it stands empty. On the marquee, large black letters announce:

THEAT R
FOR S LE

## Analyzing the Case

There is a cynical saying that "No good deed goes unpunished." This means that people sometimes obtain negative results by doing what they thought was the right thing to do. Did the would-be theater owner deserve to succeed originally because he was trying to make a contribution to his neighborhood? Whatever his motivation, he got caught in a situation where the words written by various people helped to cause his downfall. For example, did the letter from Mr. Sturm to Mr. Sharif, describing the wonderful opportunity to make money on porno films, use the kind of terminology that might be offensive to Mr. Sharif? Did Mr. Sturm describe it in "neutral" terms, as a business venture, or did he suggest that the current owner might desire to exploit and corrupt the people of the community? Was the language crude, obscene, sexist? Probably not. Was there any hypocrisy in the way community groups wrote about their outrage over something so horrible happening in their corner of the world? Learning to find people's real motivation hidden inside the words they write is a lifelong job.

## Key Terms

boycott
censorship
community standards
competitive
entrepreneurship
eroticism
first amendment rights
obscenity
offensive
pornography

Explore the meaning of these terms, using your dictionary where possible. Discuss them with your teacher and classmates. Do any of them have current meanings that differ from their dictionary definitions?

## Exercise 4-1: Questions for Discussion

1. People talk about small towns where everybody minds everybody's business. Is that also true of communities and neighborhoods in larger cities? For example, do most people care what is happening a few blocks from their homes as long as it doesn't affect their daily lives? Who knows what NIMBY stands for?

2. Have the limits of "public decency" become so stretched that it doesn't really matter what is shown on movie screens since viewers can see the same or stronger at home on television? Or, have people simply become more tolerant and sophisticated?

3. Were the rights of Mr. Sharif unfairly limited? Did he have a right to anything that the civil law allowed, or should such concepts as "higher laws" have controlled the situation?

4. Where do you stand on the issue of censorship? Are there limits to what can be made available to the general population? How about the rights of children to surf the Internet without limits? What about parents' use of the so-called "V-chip" to monitor and limit their children's TV viewing?

5. Are some forms of expression more powerful and potentially dangerous than others? Or can they all be equally strong and forceful? For instance, should people be more concerned over what they consider offensive material in movies than they are about printed words? What

about song lyrics? An old saying suggests that "Nobody was ever ruined by a book," meaning that a person's moral downfall can't be caused simply by an offensive piece of writing. But what about someone who is "addicted" to pornography in any medium? At its deepest level, this question asks whether some types of expression are evil in themselves or whether the evil depends on how individual people react to them. ◆

## Exercise 4-2: Writing Your Reaction

Write a short paragraph. First choose one of the following topic sentences. Then add two sentences to it. Your audience is your classmates.

1.   Mr. Sharif made more than one mistake.
2.   I know how I feel about censorship.
3.   Defining obscenity is difficult.
4.   My community's standards have changed (or should change?) when it comes to pornography. ◆

## Role Playing

Put yourself into the minds and lives of some of the following people involved in this case. For example:

•   Mr. Sharif

•   A thirty-something mother who is active in the local elementary school PTA and who fears that having her children walk home from school past Kupid's Kastle could be dangerous.

•   A local business owner (dry cleaning, maybe?) who is going to call his political party's precinct captain and ask him put pressure on Mr. Sturm by sending lots of city inspectors to examine every inch of the theater's wiring, plumbing, and stairways. He thinks they can find more violations than the owner can fix.

## Exercise 4-3: Role Playing

Imagine these three people sitting in a booth in the Madison Park Diner, having a cup of coffee together a year after Mr. Sharif had sold the theater, but before it had gone out of business. Could they possibly listen to each other calmly? Or would they feel they had to protect themselves no matter what? Write down one sentence that each of them would like the other two to believe and understand. One possibility has been suggested, but you can substitute your own if you wish.

1.   Mr. Sharif:

_____

_____

_____

2.   PTA mother:  <u>I'm really not a prude or in favor of censorship, but I was afraid that</u> <u>this kind of theater would attract the wrong kind of people to our neighborhood.</u>
(Or your version for her) _____

_____

_____

3.   Business owner:

_____

_____

_____ ◆

## Exercise 4-4: Writing Assignment

1.   Write a short paragraph in which you give several examples of media activity (films, music videos, etc.) that some people think should be censored.
2.   Write a short paragraph that makes a point about some people's rights being in conflict with those of others.
3.   Write a short paragraph that makes a prediction about the state of censorship in America ten years from now.  ◆

# WRITING CONVENTION: SENTENCE COMPLETENESS

Written sentences are more formal than spoken ones. Keep reminding yourself of this as you write. Almost no one writes exactly the way he or she speaks. Because of hand gestures, eye contact, and the kind of feedback you get from the people you're talking to, you can get away with spoken half-sentences and still make your point. You can also start an idea one way and shift gears in midsentence, without worrying about whether you are understood. Your listener's smile or nodding head assure you that you have communicated. Your listener may even complete your sentence for you, depending on how well you know each other.

Writing is a different story. Since you don't have that physical feedback and reassurance from your readers, you must take great care to present your ideas as clearly as possible. In English this means writing *complete sentences.* These complete sentences have certain characteristics:

1. They have at least one group of words that includes a *subject* and a *complete verb.* Such a group is called a *clause.* This grouping can make grammatical sense by itself. That means that we could put a period at the end of the group and start a new sentence if we wished.
2. Following the verb there may be an object or some other group of words that say something about the subject. A group of words that hangs together because of their meaning but doesn't include a subject and a complete verb is called a *phrase.*
3. Other groups of words in the sentence (both clauses and phrases) might not make sense by themselves, but they do if they are joined to the kind of grouping described in number 1.

Let's look at some examples.

A.   The man puts butter on the popcorn.
B.   When the man puts butter on the popcorn.
C.   The man putting butter on the popcorn.
D.   The popcorn.

You can sense that items B, C, and D aren't sentences. Look back at the qualities of complete sentences to see why. Item A has a subject (*man*) and a complete verb (*puts*). It even has some other words (*the, butter, on*). But most important of all, it makes grammatical sense by itself, and we can put a period at the end of it if we decide that we're finished with it. "Making sense by itself" doesn't mean that we don't need other sentences to help fill out our whole picture. Naturally, there will be other sentences before and after this one. What we are saying is that this set of seven words can stand alone as a complete sentence, among other complete sentences.

That's not true of items B, C, and D, is it? Why not? You can tell that item B is not complete because the word *when* begins it. Something is missing or not yet expressed. Item C, while it has almost the same structure as item A, doesn't have a complete verb.

What very short word between *man* and *putting* will turn the whole works into a sentence? You got it. As to item D, the words *the popcorn* carry meaning by being together, but they certainly are not enough for a sentence. They make up a brief phrase.

## Exercises 4-5: Sentence Completeness

A.   Decide which of the following would-be sentences are complete. Remember: Look for at least one grouping of a subject and complete verb, and ask yourself whether or not the words make grammatical sense by themselves. If it's not *c*omplete, it's called a *frag-ment*, so put *C* or *F* in the blank. Also, put a period at the end of those you mark *C*.

_____   1.   Rodney, thinking that he was finally alone

_____   2.   Above all, she wanted to make some serious money

_____   3.   Whenever the band would play and the team would march onto the field

_____   4.   Knowing that good things come in small packages, the baggage handler put it in his pocket

_____   5.   Perhaps, she would say, when we look back on this happy time

_____   6.   Good films entertain

_____   7.   The sweatshirt was marked down for quick sale

_____   8.   Because of the lack of customers

_____   9.   In the long history of Madison Park, nothing quite this interesting has ever happened

_____  10.   Whereas, this enterprise is for the good of the neighborhood

B.   In this exercise, indicate the complete sentences with a *C* and a period. Mark the fragments with an *F.* Then put a comma at the end of any fragment and add enough words to turn that fragment into complete a sentence. For example:

_F_   Fearing he might lose his cool,  the teacher took a deep breath.

_____   1.   Because mothers think they know best

_____

_____   2.   The quarterback handed the ball off to the running back

_____

_____   3.   Never thinking that he might drop it

_____

_____   4.   Blue Demons is a strange name for a team

_____

_____   5.   The Oscar winner, being recognized as the best

_____

C.   Now, try it yourself. Write an incomplete sentence in the first blank, and then write a complete one in the second blank. Some topics are provided for you.

   1.   (topic: the Internet) Incomplete:

_____

Complete: _____

_____

   2.   (topic: a recent movie) Incomplete:

_____

Complete: _____

_____

   3.   (topic: Prayer in public schools) Incomplete:

_____

Complete: _____

_____

   4.   (topic: Diet soft drinks) Incomplete:

_____

Complete: _____

_____

_____

   5.   (topic: Social Security/Medicare) Incomplete:

_____

Complete: _____

_____

_____

(Note: ESL students, check Appendix B for tips on adjective clauses. You will find more on sentence completeness in your handbook.) ◆

# METHOD OF DEVELOPMENT: DESCRIPTION

All of the various methods of development (sometimes referred to as _modes of development_) in this book are meant to be of practical use to you as a writer. They are not intended to be used simply for their own sake or to show off. No good writer says,

"Hey, I think I feel a pretty good comparison/contrast coming on, and I'll impress my reader with it." By continuing to write and to practice your skill as a writer, you will find that these methods are most helpful when you have trouble organizing or fleshing out the ideas you need to express.

One of the most basic methods is simple physical description. If you are writing about something that can be experienced by human senses, describe it so that your audience will know what the experience is. Let them see it, taste it, touch it, hear it, smell it, and take hold of it with more than simply their intellects. Read this paragraph:

> The young man sat at his scrubbed kitchen table, writing home to his father. The scratch of a blue Bic on plain, white stationery was drowned out by the sounds of a radio blasting reggae through the cracked plaster walls of his apartment. During the radio's commercial breaks, he might have heard the buzz of his overworked refrigerator and smelled the faint aroma of an aging cheeseburger that made its way through the broken rubber seal on the door. Even here on the third floor, there were traces of the traffic noises out on Wellington Street, the barking dogs, the unending car alarms that nobody bothered to disarm. But as he wrote, the only things he could see and hear were his dad's round face and his lined mouth saying softly, "Come on home, Son. Your mother and I miss you."

What is this paragraph about? Is it about car alarms, cheeseburgers, and reggae? Or is it about growing up, loneliness, and family ties? The first three things are **concrete** and the second three are **abstract,** but they are all real. Description tends to be physical and concrete. That is, it refers to particular, specific objects. But description can be used to get at the abstract ideas you want to communicate, the ideas that are more general and universal. (By the way, which sentence in this paragraph is the topic sentence?)

In using description to enrich your ideas and to make them real to your audience, you need to be aware of the following:

- Follow some kind of order. If you describe a visual scene, you paint the overall picture first and then put in the more particular details. Maybe move from left to right, from distant to near, from top to bottom. If you jump around at random, the effect is comparable to that of a handheld video camera, bouncing jerkily through the forest.

- Don't overdo the details. In the sample paragraph, are there too many sights and sounds? If the author began to describe each of the various kinds of beeping and sirens noises that the typical car alarm makes, you would find yourself bored or distracted before you got to the final image and the main idea.

## Exercise 4-6: Description

1.  List three visual details that might have been seen in the lobby of the Mystic Theater (or in the lobby of Kupid's Kastle):

    _____

    _____

    _____

2.  Now finish the following sentence that expresses a general impression about the atmosphere of this theater lobby. ~~The point I want to convey is~~ **that** _____

    _____

    _____

3.  Now write the paragraph, using your original details, or others if you prefer. _____

    _____

    _____

    _____

    _____

    _____

    _____◆

## Exercise 4-7: Practice with Description

1.  In one or two sentences, describe the physical appearance of this textbook, so that it could be identified if lost. One catch: Don't use the title or author's name.
2.  Choose a celebrity that most people know well. Your job is to describe this person for one of the few people who might not know the celebrity. This person would be shown several pictures of similar appearing people, including one of the celebrity. After reading your paragraph, it will be clear which one is a photo of the celebrity.

3. Describe a room you remember from childhood. Use physical details to let the reader know how you feel about this room. Do you remember the wallpaper? What did you see from the window? ◆

### Visit the Longman Englishpages!

For additional readings, practice exercises, Internet links, and activities, visit us online at
**http://www.ablongman.com/englishpages**

# CHAPTER 5

# PRONOUN CLARITY/
# USING EXAMPLES

 **CASE: THE LOTTERY WINNER**

Your state's lottery has reached a new high, an amazing $200 million. Someone is about to win more money than they can imagine, and, as the television jingle says, "It might as well be you."

You go to your local convenience store. You buy a ticket. You win.

· · · · · · ·

Wait a minute. Take a deep breath. You don't win, but someone does, someone who will not spend the money as wisely and generously as you think you would have. His name is Rex Powers. Life, as usual, isn't fair.

How does this frustrating but exciting series of events play out?

First of all, a complicated system is in place at the state level to manage and promote the lottery. This bureau was set up originally because the citizens and legislators of the state decided it was a good idea. Lots of debating and name calling took place before the state lottery agency was set up, and the whole idea still causes arguments. Newspapers in big cities and small towns all over the state carried editorials and passionate letters to the editor. Politicians, pastors, and professors gave speeches, pro and con. People living in small towns just across the state line licked their

*(Continued)*

*(Continued from previous page)*

chops at the thought of crossing over to buy tickets. Finally, the state acted to create a lottery.

Whatever its ultimate worth may be, it seems to be a short-term success, at least if it's judged by the number of people who buy tickets. That $200 million prize didn't come out of tax funds.

As a citizen you are vaguely aware of the claims that the revenue is benefiting schools and paying important bills for the state. But, like most people, what you are most aware of is the fact that every so often someone wins a large pile of cash. You've found yourself chuckling as you've watched the televised interviews with the big winners who insist that they might just keep their jobs at Wal-Mart and the post office and that they really haven't thought about what they might do with the money. Right.

Before winning the money, Rex Powers had read articles, news stories, and advertisements, all designed to get him to buy tickets. And now, the minute he wins, the flow of words continues. Eventually, he will receive

more than 400 letters and propositions from people who have learned of his good fortune.

- Every newspaper in the state runs a story on the prize. Mr. Powers' hometown paper accompanies its front-page story with several photos showing a typical day in the life of "Our Winner."

- Two short letters are sent from the lottery bureau in the state capital. They confirm information already passed on in phone calls. One letter informs Mr. Powers that he is, indeed, the big winner and that he will be receiving a check for $833,333, minus taxes, every month for the next 20 years. The other letter tells the owners of the Happy Gas & Food Mart at 37th and Pine that they will receive a $2 million check for having sold the winning ticket— also before taxes, of course. The winners will be flown to the capital. There they will be presented with 3-by-6-foot cardboard checks on the steps of the capitol building.

- The state's lottery director writes a memo to his staff with a copy to the Secretary of State. It congratulates everyone, himself included, and says this mighty payout shows that "the people of this great state have embraced our great lottery and all that it stands for."

- Mr. Powers receives a registered letter from Phoenix, Arizona, informing him that the sender is positive they are related. The letter from Mrs. Wendell Powers, a possible cousin, congratulates him and speaks of happy times they had at family gatherings when they were both kids. She looks forward to getting together again. She mentions also that she has learned a great deal about real estate investing in the years since they lost touch with each other.

- The president of his neighborhood bank, Crosstown Federal, sends him a personal letter of congratulations and assures him of his willingness to provide any help he may need "during the exciting years that lie ahead."

- His high school principal sends Powers the first of eight letters he will eventually receive from various people connected with the school. The principal congratulates him and then, "incidentally,"

*(Continued)*

*(Continued from previous page)*

wonders if he is aware that the marching band he once played in has had to limit its playing to home games because of the advanced age of its bus. Another letter, this one from the senior class president, calls him "a distinguished alumnus" and asks him to address the students at this year's graduation exercises. Not bad for a guy who graduated 397th in a class of 450.

- Mr. Powers himself sends some letters. One of them, to his Aunt Millie in New Orleans, thanks her for all her support and encouragement when he was a teenager. It invites her and Uncle Arthur to visit him soon, if their health will allow it. He will, of course, pay their air fare.

- Two days after hearing of his good fortune, Mr. Powers sits down and writes a short statement. The intended audience is himself and, possibly, very close friends. In it he writes what he hopes all this money will do for him and how it will change his life. He lists some of the things he might buy, the gifts he might give, and the investments he might make. After finishing it, he decides not to show it to anyone else.

Other letters, proposals, and propositions continue to come to him and to the person he hires as his agent over the next four years.

Does he, as the stories proclaim, live happily ever after?

## Analyzing the Case

Admit it. You've thought about what you might do if you won an enormous pot of money. In some versions of this fantasy you are a saintly, generous philanthropist, loved by all your grateful relatives and friends as you scatter BMWs and houses like confetti. In others, you take the money and just have as much fun with it as your greed and imagination will allow. If one Rolls-Royce in your garage is good, then five would be five times as good.

Notice again that, just as in all the cases you've seen so far, different kinds of writing are produced by different people for different purposes and different audiences. People's motives play a major part in the way they write. How much sincerity and honesty are present in the various items that are written as a result of Mr. Powers's lucky break? How much of a writer's real motivation can be found in his or her words? Is this a situation that brings out the best or the worst in people?

## Key Terms

actual odds
altruism
deferred payout
fantasize
luck
philanthropy
probability
revenue
small print
truth in advertising

Explore the meaning of these terms, using your dictionary where possible. Discuss them with your teacher and classmates. Do any of them have current meanings that differ from their dictionary definitions?

## Exercise 5-1: Questions for In-Class Writing or Discussion

1.  Big-time state lotteries are clearly here to stay. From your own experience, is this a good thing? Was the previous question asked in too simplistic a manner?
2.  Think of someone who deserves to be a big lottery winner. You'd be happy to think of this person getting all that money. Sorry, it must be someone other than you, your relatives, or your close friends. You can propose an actual winner or an imaginary one whose characteristics make him or her truly worthy in your eyes.
3.  Is a lottery unfair, as its critics suggest, because it encourages people who can least afford it to waste their money? Or is it a harmless outlet for people's desires to dream and take chances?
4.  There are a couple of old sayings: "Be careful what you wish for. You may get it" and "Money can't buy happiness." Are these ideas relevant in this case, or are they simply the thoughts of losers?
5.  Most people are intelligent enough to understand the concept of nearly impossible odds. They know that they probably won't be struck by

meteorites or eaten by tigers. And yet some of these same people think they have a chance of winning "the big one" if they simply buy one ticket. Maybe you're one of these people. What makes them do it? ◆

## Role Playing

Put yourself inside the lottery winner case. If your own personal experiences help you, use them. Have you won, or do you know someone who has?

Remember that writing effectively always means writing *for someone* and having a clear image of who that audience is. Knowing your audience, whether it consists of one person or many, means that you can make good judgments about word choice, about the kind of language you should use, and about what might work best in a particular case. Try once again to get inside some of the characters involved in this case. If you are getting better at role playing, can you help your classmates to improve as well? Relax and enjoy the process.

To understand this case, get inside the minds and take on the passions of some of the people listed here. Once again, if you have time, take another look at the material on audiences in Chapter 1 and on role playing in Chapter 2.

- One of Mr. Powers' fellow workers. He or she has known him for several years and wonders what this will do to him.

- A scam artist who thinks he or she might make a quick buck by proposing a way for the lottery winner to invest his money. As you take on this role, be a real villain. How are you going to take advantage of this opportunity to exploit Mr. Powers? Rub your hands together in glee as you think of the possibilities.

- A local church leader who is convinced that people squander their money on lottery tickets to the disadvantage of their families.

- An old high school buddy who learns of Rex's big score and debates about whether or not to send him a letter of congratulations.

- One of the assistants to the state lottery director. It is her job to find new ways to publicize and promote the lottery—and the lottery director.

- John W. King (1917–1996). As Governor of New Hampshire in 1963, he instituted the first successful state lottery since 1894. The surprising revenues raised by New Hampshire's lottery inspired the modern state lottery movement.

# Exercise 5-2: Role Playing

1. Stage an imaginary conversation between two or three of the people listed here. Give them names and make up believable backgrounds for them. Have them ask each other about their own reactions to the particular case and to the larger questions it raises. Try to be as specific and detailed as possible. Be imaginative; don't be afraid of the humorous, embarrassing, and possibly unexpected details that may come out in such a conversation. Have at least one observer take notes and ask questions of one or the other to keep the conversation going.

2. Interview Rex Powers. Ask him questions that will get him to reveal more about himself and his plans than he might intend. For example, ask him what he thinks other people in his position might do with the money and whether he thinks that would be right.

3. Stage a short meeting between Mr. Powers and his boss. Try it out a couple of ways. In one Powers says basically, "Take this job and" you know the rest. Or he may be charming and cordial, saying how much he will miss working there. How does the boss react in each case?

4. Two neighbors, living on either side of Power's house, meet on the sidewalk. They speculate on what he will do now. They are a bit annoyed to discover that he hasn't shared any plans with either of them. What else motivates the way they discuss him and his future? ◆

# Exercise 5-3: Writing Assignments

1. Here's what it says in small print on the back of an Illinois state lottery ticket:

---

**To Claim Your Prize**

Present this ticket to any lottery agent. Validated winning tickets valued through $600 are eligible for INSTANT PAYOFF. Validated winning tickets higher than $600 will be paid by check after claim is filed. IMPORTANT:

*(Continued)*

---

---

*(Continued from previous page)*

This ticket only valid for date(s) shown. Winners must claim prize within one year of the drawing. All tickets, transactions and winners are subject to Directives of the Director of the Illinois State lottery, the Rules and Regulations of the State Lottery, and State Law, and tickets are only offered for sale in accordance with same. Tickets are void and will not be paid if stolen, unissued, illegible, mutilated, altered, counterfeit in whole or in part, missregistered, defective, incomplete, printed or produced in error, printed in duplicate, or if ticket fails any of the Lottery's confidential validation tests. Liability for void tickets, if any, limited to replacement of ticket. Not responsible for lost or stolen tickets.

---

It sounds legalistic and tough, doesn't it? Could you say the same thing in a way that sounds much more personal and casual? Try it, for instance, taking a group of fifth-graders as your audience. Notice the kinds of verbal problems you run into when you try to take the edge off of legal writing.

2. You are an unscrupulous person, passing yourself off as a distant and needy relative of Mr. Powers. In a letter, you explain why sending you some of his money would be the humane thing for him to do and that you would certainly do the same if your positions were reversed. Does your letter sound believable?

3. The state lottery director wants to say a few words when presenting the jumbo checks on the steps of the state capitol building. Reporters and television crews will be present, so this will be a nice moment for the director. As assistant director you have been told to prepare a short speech for your boss to deliver. Do just the opening and closing paragraphs and remember to make the lottery bureau (and your boss) look good.

4. Write at least the opening paragraph of an editorial for your school paper in which you take a position on the question of whether or not lotteries are a good thing. Consider your audience; does it contain a large number of people who buy lottery tickets?

5. Invent a role and a situation related to this case that call for a particular piece of writing, and then write it. Use your imagination and

explore some of the less obvious persons who have been touched by the lottery. ◆

# WRITING CONVENTION: PRONOUN CLARITY

Pronouns, which we use in place of nouns, save us a great deal of trouble, but they also cause problems of their own. By taking the place of nouns, they keep us from writing silliness such as "Fred turned the corner of Fred's block and discovered, to Fred's alarm, that Fred was being followed." Using *his* and *he* will keep this sentence from sounding ridiculous. But look at another one: "Fred and George seemed equally matched, but, after a mighty struggle, the best player won, and we applauded him." The sentence is perfectly clear to its writer who knows who *him* represents. The reader, however, is confused. The secret to clear, effective use of pronouns is to do what this whole course reminds you to do: Put yourself in the place of your audience. Remind yourself of what your readers know and don't know. If *they* might not know who the best man was in your original sentence, revise it. (Note: Imagine how hard it would be to write that last sentence you just read without the pronouns *they, who, your,* and *it.*) Some conventional uses of pronouns are just that—conventional. We do it that way because we all (or most of us, anyway) agree to do it that way. Other uses are based on avoiding confusion, misreading, and distraction.

The fundamental fact about a pronoun is that *it takes the place of a noun.* Therefore:

1.  There must be a noun for which it takes the place. This is called its **antecedent.** "John knows he is cool." (The antecedent of *he* is *John.*)
2.  The pronoun must be as similar as possible to the noun it replaces. This is called **agreement,** and it means that if the antecedent is singular, the pronoun must be singular. If the antecedent is female, then the pronoun must also be female. "Kathy knows she is just as cool." (*She* is a feminine pronoun that agrees with Kathy.)

Your handbook should explain all the different kinds of pronouns and the rules and exceptions that govern their use.

One question regarding pronouns that has been discussed a great deal in recent years is the sexist nature of certain pronoun conventions. Take this sentence: "*Everyone* (singular antecedent) at this school knows that *he* (agrees with singular antecedent) is attending the country's finest college." Twenty-five years ago not many people would have expressed concern about this sentence. Now most people would agree that, although it is grammatically correct, it is sexist. It implies that everyone is a male. But grammarians would point out that since everyONE is singular, the pronoun that agrees with it must also be singular. Here are some possible ways to solve this problem:

1.  Everyone at this school knows that *he or she* is attending the country's finest college. (Comment: *he or she* sounds rather awkward, especially if it is repeated often in following sentences.)
2.  Everyone at this school knows that *they* are attending the country's finest college. (Comment: Strictly speaking, *they* is a plural pronoun, so it doesn't agree with *everyone,* which is singular. In fact, this use of *they* is common in speaking and will probably be considered perfectly acceptable in writing eventually.)
3.  The students at this school know that *they* are attending the country's finest college. (Comment: Making the antecedent plural (students) solves the problem of using *they.* Sometimes this is the most practical way to handle this dilemma.)

Whichever solution you use, you need to be conscious of the fact that English, like many languages, can be used in sexist ways and that your audience deserves respect.

## Exercise 5-4: Pronoun Clarity

Rewrite the following. The first one has been done for you.

1.  The first state to have a modern lottery was New Hampshire in 1963. There was one previously in 1894, but they discontinued it. (Who's *they?*)
    There was one previously in 1894, but it was discontinued.
2.  The lottery caused confusion in another state because it wasn't prepared properly. (What's *it?*) _____
    _____
3.  I am urging every mother to write to his or her senator to protest the bill. _____
    _____
4.  She dropped a crystal vase on the glass coffee table and broke it.
    _____
    _____

5.   Every American knows that he is part of a long, colorful history.

_____

_____   ◆

# METHOD OF DEVELOPMENT: EXAMPLES

One of the most effective ways to illustrate an idea is to give examples. This immediately begins to nail down the idea for your audience. The more particular examples
they can connect with a general idea, the more it seems real to them. This is why
poems and song lyrics about abstract ideas like "love" and "desire" talk about skin,
blood, sweat, and rose petals. Giving an example is good psychology. Someone reading a statement you have just made is saying, "for instance?" If at that very moment
you have written "for example," your idea is reinforced in the reader's mind.

Take another look at the sample paragraphs presented in Chapter 3. One of them
provides examples of why it's better to watch a movie in your own living room, and
another gives examples of the way a school could be improved. These main ideas
might make sense without the examples, but the paragraphs would be far less
effective.

Examples should be carefully chosen. Not just any example will work. What if
that paragraph about watching movies at home included this sentence: "Another reason I prefer it is because my Uncle Jim from Boise also preferred it"? The audience
would be puzzled. It may be a good personal reason for the author, but readers would
not connect with it. Again, role playing can help you anticipate how readers will
respond to what you write.

## Exercise 5-5: Examples

Begin with one of the following topic sentences and add _at least_ two good
examples.

1.   Blockbuster movies have kept Hollywood rich, but some of the best
     films are smaller, independent ones. For example, . . .
2.   I know that if I won the lottery, I would do only generous things with
     my money. For example, . . .
3.   I know that if most people won the lottery they would do selfish, dan-
     gerous things with their money. For example, . . .
4.   Some things have to be learned the hard way. For example, . . .

5.   Some very encouraging trends have surfaced recently in America. For
     example, . . . ◆

## Exercise 5-6: Writing Assignments

Note: For all of these assignments, your audience is your classmates and
teacher.

1.   Write an essay (three to five paragraphs) that outlines your feelings
     about lotteries and what their success tells us about human nature.
     Base it on a thesis statement that pulls your ideas together in one
     sentence.
2.   Write an essay about celebrities who are considered role models. Give
     examples that prove the point you wish to make about them.
3.   Find a magazine or newspaper article that gives examples of some-
     thing as part of its development. Then briefly summarize the article
     and show how the examples helped it. ◆

**Visit the Longman Englishpages!**

For additional readings, practice exercises, Internet links, and activities, visit us online at
**http://www.ablongman.com/englishpages**

# CHAPTER 6

# WRITING LETTERS/ COMPARISON AND CONTRAST

 ## CASE: THE CHEATING SCANDAL

It was May, and the end of the school year was approaching. The seniors at Blanchard High School could hardly wait to get out and to get on with their lives. Five seniors were especially excited because suddenly they knew they would be getting much better chemistry grades than they had expected. In a couple of cases, this could even affect their college eligibility. Their good fortune occurred because one of them just happened to look in the large wastebasket outside the teachers' lounge and find a crumpled-up copy of Mrs. Gershwin's final exam.

This enterprising student shared the news with six of her friends. Four of them asked for copies. The other two said they would have to think about it. While the exam sheet didn't contain the answers, it did enable the lucky five to know which answers to look up in their underused chemistry textbooks.

Final exam week came and went. Mrs. Gershwin had a moment or two of head scratching as she averaged the final grades. Some students had certainly made a remarkable comeback. "That's seniors for you," she remarked to herself.

*(Continued)*

*(Continued from previous page)*

Then, eight days before graduation, there was a mighty uproar. One of the students who had been approached but had declined to share in the conspiracy wrote an anonymous letter to Mrs. Gershwin and the senior class counselor in which he told most of the story but didn't name names. The vice principal sent a memo to Mrs. Gershwin, directing her to reexamine her grade book and her exam results. If she found anything suspicious, she was to tell him immediately. She, of course, found that several students had done unexpectedly well, and she even found that their examination booklets contained suspiciously similar answers to several questions. She passed this on to the vice principal, but she said she couldn't be absolutely sure and reminded him that people are innocent until proven guilty.

The vice principal lost no time in contacting the three suspects who appeared most guilty and informing them that they and their parents would be expected to appear in the principal's office on the following Monday. Their graduation, he explained, was in jeopardy. By Monday, after a very long weekend, one of the three had decided to tell the truth about the other four and to try to involve the whistle blower as well. She was convinced she knew who it was.

The fallout from Monday's hearing was complicated:

- A letter from the principal informed the original five that they would receive blank diplomas at the graduation ceremonies and would be required to retake chemistry during the summer.

- The father of one of the five wrote a letter to the editor of the local paper, with copies to the principal and the board of education, complaining about "the lack of due process" given to his son and assuring everyone that "this sorry event is not yet over."

- The student who had informed on the others was himself named in an anonymous letter to the parents of the disciplined students and referred to as a "squealer," a "loser," and someone who "is going to get it."

- One of the five wrote a letter to the admissions office of the college she had been planning to attend. She assured the staff there

that she would still attend in the fall and that they should not believe everything they might hear. The puzzled admissions counselor had no idea what she was referring to but placed the letter into her file anyway.

- Mrs. Gershwin received a letter from the vice principal reminding her of the importance of exam security and expressing hope that there would be no future occurrences of such carelessness.

- As it turned out, one of the accused students was falsely accused. He had gotten a tutor, studied hard, and raised his chemistry average from failing to excellent within two months. At the hearing he tried to explain this but was met with disbelief. The "evidence" against him was too strong. A letter from his tutor finally convinced the school's administration that they might be risking a lawsuit if they denied him a diploma. To this day, some people, including some classmates, think he was probably involved but admire his guts in successfully fighting the system.

> •   At the beginning of the following school year, the new senior class president gave a speech at a school assembly. She promised that her class would be honorable and would never harm the reputation of the school in any way.

## Analyzing the Case

"Everybody does it" is an expression that has been used by young and old people in various situations for thousands of years. As it usually does, the question this time comes down to this: Even if "everybody" does it, is it the right thing to do? The students who cheated on the chemistry exam did something that is increasingly widespread in secondary and higher education. They did it because they thought they could get away with it and because the advantages seemed to outweigh the possible disadvantages. The school system reacted in ways that were predictable.

Most students and teachers can readily identify with this situation. As life gets more complicated, so does cheating. For instance, the Internet is now a major source of bootleg term papers, peddled at high prices and accompanied by lots of small print that releases the producers from any responsibility for wrongdoing. The practice of cheating alarms some people and causes others simply to change the subject. It makes people uncomfortable, whether or not they cheat. But good writing should be about what is true, so what is the truth about cheating? And where do you stand on it?

## Key Terms

amoral
character
circumstantial evidence
guilt by association
honor code
integrity
moral relativism
opportunistic
peer pressure
rationalization

Explore the meaning of these terms, using your dictionary where possible. Discuss them with your teacher and classmates. Do any of them have current meanings that differ from their dictionary definitions?

## Exercise 6-1: Questions for Discussion

1. Was Mrs. Gershwin, the chemistry teacher, in any way "at fault" for what happened? Is it the same to say that she was partly responsible and that she was partly at fault?

2. Is it true that the actions taken by the guilty students may come back to haunt them later in their lives? What form could this "haunting" take?

3. Should something that a person has done early in life be held against that person later in adulthood? Why or why not? Think, for example, of political candidates whose early drug use is considered in judging them worthy or unworthy of election to office.

4. How should schools and other institutions handle the problem of cheating? How far should an institution go in imposing its standards on an individual?

5. Does the act of cheating cause harm to the person who cheats, even if no one else finds out about it? If "everyone does it," does this mean that the amount of cheating in schools is increasing, or that it has always been widespread? ◆

## Exercise 6-2: Writing Assignments

Write a three-sentence paragraph, using one of the following as a starting point for your ideas.

1. "Cheaters never win, and winners never cheat."
2. "Nice guys finish last."
3. "Everybody does it."

## Role Playing

It may be easier for you to get inside this case than some of the others in this book. It's almost certain that you have been made aware of the practice of cheating at some point in your school career. ◆

### Exercise 6-3: Role Playing

Put yourself inside the minds of the following people. Try to see the world the way they see it.

- The vice principal, whose job includes taking disciplinary action according to school policies. This means dealing with students and teachers, such as Mrs. Gershwin.
- Mrs. Gershwin, a veteran teacher, who possibly should have known better than to dispose of an exam carelessly.
- A member of the school board who is thinking of introducing a "no tolerance" policy. Students found guilty of cheating would be expelled.
- A student who had a chance to participate in the cheating ring but didn't. This person had already decided to work harder and to get enough help to pass chemistry on his own. After seeing what happened, he wonders if he did the right thing.

Now sit these four down together for a strictly "off the record" discussion of what happened and what it means. Might they agree on any issues? Would it be fair to quiz any of the school officials about their own youthful practices? ◆

### Exercise 6-4: Writing Assignments

Write a short paragraph (four to five sentences) on one of the following. Remember that these topics are not yet topic sentences. It's your job to turn one of them into a complete sentence that can then be the basis of a paragraph. For example, number 1 might be turned into "The point I want to convey is that (W)idespread cheating is not limited to schools."

1.   The role of peer pressure in cheating, both in and out of school.
2.   The effectiveness of "honor codes" in controlling school cheating.
3.   The meaning of "conscience."

# WRITING CONVENTION: WRITING LETTERS

One of the most common formats for written expression is the letter. You will find it used throughout this book, and it is useful in understanding this case. Even informal notes to friends, relatives, the delivery person, and mail carrier have some characteristics in common with more formal letters. Recall the sample letters from the Carson College forensics group inviting the college dean to their animal rights debate (Chapter 2). Despite what you might think about the personality of the letter writer, you

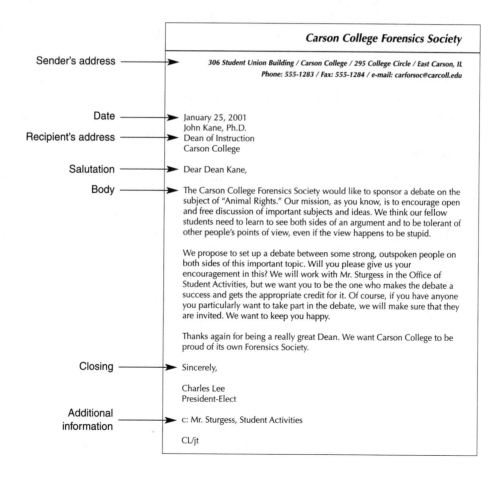

Sender's address

**Carson College Forensics Society**

*306 Student Union Building / Carson College / 295 College Circle / East Carson, IL*
*Phone: 555-1283 / Fax: 555-1284 / e-mail: carforsoc@carcoll.edu*

Date → January 25, 2001

John Kane, Ph.D.
Recipient's address → Dean of Instruction
Carson College

Salutation → Dear Dean Kane,

Body → The Carson College Forensics Society would like to sponsor a debate on the subject of "Animal Rights." Our mission, as you know, is to encourage open and free discussion of important subjects and ideas. We think our fellow students need to learn to see both sides of an argument and to be tolerant of other people's points of view, even if the view happens to be stupid.

We propose to set up a debate between some strong, outspoken people on both sides of this important topic. Will you please give us your encouragement in this? We will work with Mr. Sturgess in the Office of Student Activities, but we want you to be the one who makes the debate a success and gets the appropriate credit for it. Of course, if you have anyone you particularly want to take part in the debate, we will make sure that they are invited. We want to keep you happy.

Thanks again for being a really great Dean. We want Carson College to be proud of its own Forensics Society.

Closing → Sincerely,

Charles Lee
President-Elect

Additional information → c: Mr. Sturgess, Student Activities

CL/jt

have to admit he did know the correct format for letter writing. This format includes the following:

- The sender's address and, usually, phone number. This section may also include designations for fax and e-mail.

- The date. Spell out the month.

- The recipient's address. Depending on the letter, this may include a name, professional title, company or agency name, street address, city, state, and zip code.

- A salutation, for example: Dear Mr. Smith, Dear Warden Smythe, Dear Sir, Dear Madam or Sir, To Whom It May Concern.

- The body of the letter. Note that this letter uses one of the widely accepted formats, called *block style:* single spaced text, with double spacing between paragraphs. In another of the most common formats, the first line of each paragraph is indented (moved in) five spaces. Whichever style you use, be consistent.

- A closing word or phrase, for example, *Sincerely* (almost always appropriate), *Cordially,* or *Very Truly Yours,* followed by the sender's name with the signature directly above it. The closing and signature in block style are up against the left margin (flush left). Some letter writers put these items in the middle of the page.

- Depending on the level of formality, there may be such items as "c" or "cc" (indicating one or more people who receive a copy) and "enc" (indicating something enclosed with the letter). Some letters also include the initials of the sender followed by those of the person who prepared it, such as a secretary or assistant. ◆

## Exercise 6-5: Writing Letters

Prepare one of the following letters. The first has been completed as an example.

1.   Write the letter from the principal to one of the students informing her that she will be receiving a blank diploma.
2.   Write a letter from Ms. Grover's mother to Principal Johnson. Mrs. Grover's message is that she still thinks her daughter was treated

## *John W. Kelly High School / District 306*

*18th and Main, Worthington, SD 82409 / 555-4499 / jkellyhs.edu*

April 30, 2001

Ms. Jill Grover
303 S. 22nd Avenue
Worthington SD, 82409

Dear Ms. Grover,

Acting on the authority of the Board of District 306, I hereby officially inform you that you will not be allowed to graduate with the rest of your class. After due process, it was determined that you and several of your classmates cheated on your final examination in Chemistry. If you wish to do so, you will be allowed to attend the graduation ceremony, but you will not receive an official diploma. Instead you will be required to retake your chemistry class during the summer. Upon successful completion of the course, you will be awarded a diploma.

With every good wish for your continued educational efforts, I remain

Sincerely,

*J.R. Johnson*

J. R. Johnson, Ed.D.
Principal

c. Board of Trustees
JRJ/djc

unfairly. Also claim that, even though no one else will say so, the high school isn't nearly as good as it was when the mother attended.

3. You are the parent of another one of the students accused of cheating. Make up a name and address for the local newspaper and send its editor a letter protesting that your child has been treated unfairly. Use your imagination to include realistic details. ◆

You will find more on letter format, including samples, throughout this book and in your writing handbook. You are also discovering the shortcomings of written words. Some times, the fewer words put on paper—or at least the fewer actually delivered to their audience—the better. Former U.S. President Harry Truman had a powerful temper, but over the years he developed a practice of writing furious letters to people who had somehow offended him (for example, when they suggested that his daughter, a would-be opera singer, had little talent). He would put all of his anger into these letters. Then he would put them into the top, left-hand drawer of his desk and let them sit there for 24 to 48 hours. Fortunately, he rarely sent the letters, but he got to be very good at writing them. Writing for an audience ends when the readers receive their intended words. Then it's up to the audience to begin working on the words.

# METHOD OF DEVELOPMENT: COMPARISON AND CONTRAST

An excellent way of developing a paragraph is to show how things are similar to each other and/or how they are different from each other. "Things" in this sense can include ideas, people, qualities—anything—in unlimited numbers. Making comparisons is a fundamental part of human nature almost from birth: "My mom is nicer than yours," "My lunch box is better than yours," and so on to adulthood and "Our space satellite is better than yours." The human ability to see connections among things is what gives rise to similes and metaphors in our language. Not just poets, but all of us might say that a friend has—using a cliché—a heart of gold and that our landlord has eyes as cold as ice. So we point out how things are like or unlike each other. Use of contrast comes from our realization that showing what something is not is one of the best ways to clarify what it is.

> **Simile:** an expression that compares one thing to another by pointing out that they are similar. "A life without love *is like* a day without sunshine."

**Metaphor:** an expression that compares one thing to another without actually pointing out that they are similar. "A life without love is cloudy and storm-filled."

Your imagination will help you to use comparison and contrast in your writing, and practice will show you how to use this method effectively. Consider this model paragraph:

One way to understand America today is to look at our country before the invention of automobiles and the development of the interstate highway system. In the nineteenth century most people were born, raised, and buried within a hundred mile radius. Now we live in a time when families are scattered; parents, siblings, and relatives live thousands of miles apart. However, despite being scattered, we are more likely to get together with distant relatives than we would have at the turn of the nineteenth century. We think nothing of piling in the car and driving from St. Louis to Seattle, while once we might have lived in isolation from our relatives who were on "the other side of the mountains."

As you can see, the paragraph discusses the ways in which two groups of people living in different eras contrast with each other.

## Exercise 6-6: Comparison/Contrast

1. Add one more sentence to the model paragraph that contrasts these two groups of people. Maybe say something about local accents or forms of amusement when people lived more isolated, regional lives.
2. Write a short paragraph that uses comparison rather than contrast. Show how two people are similar, or two teams, or two films, or two fast-food specialties. ◆

## Exercise 6-7: A Personal Approach

Place yourself at a particular point in your past, indicating your age at the time. Then point out some of the ways you have changed for the better, comparing your present state with the past. For instance, what do you know now that you didn't? How does your emotional maturity show itself in action compared with things you might have done at the earlier age. Give some interesting details, not just general statements. Your audience is your classmates and teacher.

### Visit the Longman Englishpages!

For additional readings, practice exercises, Internet links, and activities, visit us online at
**http://www.ablongman.com/englishpages**

# CHAPTER 7

# COMMAS/CAUSE AND EFFECT

 **CASE: THE BUS CRASH**

The #406 Bus is traveling south on Clark Street, carrying more than 50 passengers and heading for Chicago's downtown Loop district. Suddenly, near Diversey Avenue, a brightly colored truck lurches out of a driveway in reverse. The inexperienced driver had rented it to move his belongings from his apartment to one nearer to the Chicago Cubs' Wrigley Field. He slams it into the right side of the bus, crushing the front door, as the bus driver attempts to swerve away from him.

There is disagreement about some of the things that happen next.

- All agree that there is a great deal of confusion, panic, and screaming. The bus driver gets on his radio immediately. He contacts his supervisors and asks them to begin emergency procedures. He then attempts to calm the passengers and to find out the amount of damage and injury that has occurred.

- Two people push their way to the rear exit, stumble down the stairway, and disappear into the crowd that has almost immediately begun to gather. As they leave, some of the more street-smart passengers instinctively pat themselves to make sure their wallets and purses are still there.

*(Continued)*

91

*(Continued from previous page)*

- At least one person boards the bus, smears himself with some available blood, and begins to moan.

- An attorney, whose secretary has been monitoring the police radio scanner, grabs his briefcase and leaves his office on Oakdale Street in a hurry. Since he is only two blocks from the scene of the accident, he arrives about the same time as the police.

- In less than seven minutes from the time of impact, two police cars arrive on the scene. Another arrives one minute later, followed immediately by an ambulance and a squad of paramedics. The transit company's own investigative unit arrives shortly after.

- Traffic is detoured around the scene, but a "gapers' block" of curious drivers soon causes the police to slap the hoods of slow moving cars and tell people to "Move it!"

- Of the eight people taken to nearby St. Joseph's Hospital, only four are kept for more than one night. The others are observed, bandaged, and sent home.

- Everyone who claims to have been on the bus gives information to the police and to bus company personnel. They are all asked if they thought the driver was at fault.

- Within minutes of the accident, a Channel Six TV van arrives carrying a camera operator, sound person, technician, and reporter. All the people on the bus and on the sidewalk are anxious to tell their version of what happened and, possibly, to appear on the *Ten O'clock News*. The reporter interviews five people, but only the first policeman on the scene will make the news broadcast. Back at the TV station, a news writer pulls the story together and gets it ready for an anchorperson to read.

Over the next two weeks a lot of writing takes place:

- Police officers, paramedics, and transit personnel, including the bus driver, fill out reports.

- Injured (and allegedly injured) passengers fill out forms and reports for insurance companies.

- The driver of the truck gives his version of the mishap to his own insurance company and to the truck rental company.

- A passenger, Thelma Jackson, writes to her family in St. Louis. Although she was physically unhurt, she continues to have disturbing dreams about the accident.

- The *Chicago Globe* publishes an editorial on the dangers of inexperienced drivers and the truck rental business.

- Omero Sanchez, a passenger, is asked by his supervisor to bring a note from his doctor that explains why it was necessary to miss three days of work. His doctor writes the note and Mr. Sanchez submits it.

Ninety minutes after the accident, there is no sign that it ever happened, and traffic on Clark Street is back to normal.

## Analyzing the Case

Could all of this really happen? If you have ever lived in a large city, you know that it does happen fairly regularly. A situation like this one brings out the best and worst in people, ranging from the conscientious bus driver to the phony passenger who hopes to collect some insurance money. Could this event have been prevented, or is it statistically bound to happen because of the crowded conditions of big cities? How much of the writing that takes place because of this accident is routine, and how much is personal or unique to the individuals who write it? For example, does Mr. Sanchez's doctor put much of his own feeling into the letter intended for the work supervisor? As you analyze this case and try to imagine more of the details for yourself, compare your task to that of the first police officer who appeared on the scene and attempted to sort things out under difficult and troubling conditions. When you begin to write about the case, your analytical skills will be useful to you.

## Key Terms

collision
congestion
fraudulent
inadvertent
inevitability
liability
mass transit
opportunistic
uninsured
urban

Explore the meaning of these terms, using your dictionary where possible. Discuss them with your teacher and classmates. Do any of them have current meanings that differ from their dictionary definitions?

## Exercise 7-1: Questions for Discussion

1.  Is someone at fault in this case? What exactly does "being at fault" mean, and how important are a person's intentions in determining whether he or she is "guilty"?
2.  Society is set up in systematic ways. How do these manifestations of "the system" show up in this case? Look for rules, organizations, and obligations, and list some specific examples of them, such as the eager lawyer and the bright yellow paint on the rental truck.
3.  Have you imagined how you might react in an emergency, life-threatening situation? Do you feel confident that your reactions would

be calm and possibly even heroic? Have you ever had a chance to find out how you would react?

4.   Do the advantages of city life make up for their corresponding disadvantages? Have you always had this opinion? Back up your position with some hard facts.

5.   In reading this case, did you find that it sounded realistic to you, or did you find yourself thinking that it was fantastic and unbelievable? Which details seemed the most real and which ones—if any—seemed the most unlikely? ◆

## Role Playing

Put yourself inside the bus crash case. If your own personal experiences help you, use them. Remember that writing effectively always means writing *for someone* and having a clear image of who that audience is. Knowing your audience, whether it consists of one person or many, means that you can make good judgments about word choice, about the kind of language you should use, and about what might work best in a particular case. Try to identify with some of the following people:

• Catherine Lindskog is a 26-year-old community college student. She had just paid her fare and turned to look for a seat when the crash sent her into the laps of a mother and daughter sitting by the front exit. Cushioned by them from serious injury, she spent only 45 minutes being observed at St. Joseph's Hospital before being released. The mother and daughter were unhurt.

• Alan Sunday, Esq., is an unethical "ambulance-chasing" lawyer, and sometimes he even good-naturedly admits that he is. He was handing his card to passengers alongside the bus within fifteen minutes of the crash.

• The unfortunate driver of the moving truck, Charles Hopson, wishes he had listened to his parents and hired a moving company.

• Dolores McGann, a recent journalism school graduate, is a general-assignment reporter for the *Chicago Globe*. It's her job to gather information and file a story on the crash, even though she knows that most of the information she collects will be left out of the story when it's printed.

• Jeanette Moreau is one of the people who pretended to be on the bus in order to make a fraudulent insurance claim. Under a grant of immunity from you, she will be allowed to tell the truth during the upcoming exercise.

- Anthony J. Esquivel, the bus driver, has had an excellent record. In 22 years with the transit company, this is the first time he has been involved in a major accident.

Are you finding it a little easier to role-play? Do you find that your classmates are less self-conscious about doing this than they were in earlier cases?

## Exercise 7-2: Role Playing

1.  Stage an imaginary conversation between two or three of the people listed previously. Have them ask each other about their own reactions to the crash and to the larger questions it raises. Add details to make up believable backgrounds for them. Try to be as specific and detailed as possible. Be imaginative; don't be afraid of the humorous, embarrassing, and possibly unexpected details that may come out in such a conversation.

2.  Interview the truck driver, Mr. Hopson. Try to find out what happened. Don't accept the answer, "I don't know." Use your detective skills by asking indirect questions. For example, don't ask, "Didn't you see the bus?" Instead, ask, "What was on your mind as you backed out of the driveway?"

3.  Stage a conversation between two people sitting in the back row of the bus. Aside from minor bruises, neither of them is seriously hurt. They've been asked to remain in their seats until the paramedics arrive. Since they are strangers, what do they say to each other?

4.  Two weeks after the accident, one of the passengers finds Attorney Sunday's business card in a coat pocket and calls him. How does their conversation go? ◆

## Exercise 7-3: Writing Assignments

1.  A *Chicago Globe* reporter files a story on the accident. She attempts to get the basic information into the first few sentences. Remember the five *W*s. After that she adds details that fill out the overall picture. Write her first paragraph and add a couple of details.

2.  Mr. Sanchez writes a short memo to his supervisor, explaining his absence from work. He attaches the note from his doctor. Write either the note or the memo.

3.   The unlucky Mr. Hopson writes a letter to his brother, who is away at college. The second paragraph of the letter attempts a humorous, light-hearted summary of the accident. Sitting at his computer, Hopson reads over this paragraph and then deletes it. His second version of the crash is much more serious. Write *both* versions.

4.   An employee of Channel Six writes seven sentences to be read by the *Ten O'clock News* anchorperson. The first sentence introduces the story. The next five are to be read while videotape of the accident is shown. After sentence four, a brief videotaped comment by the first police officer to arrive on the scene is inserted. The final sentence switches from the crash to the weather report. Have you watched enough newscasts to write this seven-sentence composition?

5.   Invent a role and a situation related to this case that call for a particular piece of writing, and then write it. Use your imagination and explore some of the less obvious persons who have been touched by the bus crash. ◆

# WRITING CONVENTION: PUNCTUATION / COMMAS

## When to Use Commas

Like other punctuation symbols, commas are added to sentences so that readers are more likely to understand our meaning. Like some punctuation symbols, they signal the things we do with our voices when we speak. A question mark, for example, signals the rising of the voice we sometimes insert at the end of a question. A period goes where we would drop our voice and pause if we were ending a complete spoken idea. Commas, the most frequently used punctuation marks, perform many tasks, indicating pauses and pointing out the "sounds" of our written voice. Here are some examples:

1.   If you weren't on the bus, why are you bleeding?
2.   Have the paramedics been called, Jennifer?
3.   The accident took place at a crowded, noisy intersection.
4.   "The person at fault, as a matter of fact, was you."
5.   The TV van arrived with a camera, sound equipment, and a reporter.
6.   Let the record show that the accident occurred on Tuesday, January 23, 2001.

Read these sentences over carefully as they appear on the page. Then read each of them aloud, slowly, and maybe even a bit more dramatically than you ordinarily would. Notice, for instance, the way you leave your voice up in the air at the end of the word "bus" in #1. That's to show that the most important part of the sentence hasn't been spoken yet. In #2, see what would happen if you omitted the pause before "Jennifer." In #3 the pause between "crowded" and "noisy" shows that these two words are equally important in what they say about "intersection," and they shouldn't simply be run together. Number 4 would sound robotic if you didn't set off the short interruption ("as a matter of fact") with pauses and a slight drop of the voice. The commas in #5 help us keep the items in a series (three or more items ) from running together in a confusing way. And finally #6 uses its commas in a conventional way to keep numbers, dates, and other information (addresses, for example) from blurring together.

Now read the sentences again, and see for yourself that the commas perform functions that you already do automatically when you speak, by pausing, changing pace, and varying your vocal tone.

## Exercise 7-4: Commas

Insert commas where they belong in the following sentences.

1. The bus driver fortunately for us was able to keep his wits about him.
2. An "ambulance chaser" is an unprofessional money-grubbing lawyer.
3. Because he didn't look before he backed out the truck's driver caused an accident.
4. Pain suffering panic and chaos were present on that bus.
5. The worst thing you could have done Sheila was to give your name to that lawyer.
6. Is it a fact that on January 15 1997 you rented a one-ton van? ◆

## When Not to Use Commas

Commas are handy for expressing the sorts of pauses we insert with our voices in speaking, but it is possible to overuse them or to use them incorrectly. The first example is fairly simple. A comma may be omitted after an introductory group of words that begin with a preposition, if

(a) the group is short—generally no more than four words—and
(b) there is no danger of misleading your reader.

Look at these examples:

> As for me give me liberty or give me death.
>
> In both cases the judge recommended the death penalty.
>
> On the whole I'd rather be in Philadelphia.

They're clear enough without introductory commas, although you could use the commas if you wished, and some people would. However, in the next examples, you can see that omitting the commas could lead the reader to misread the sentences.

> In the end, results were mixed. ("end results?")
>
> On the whole, pizza without sausage is unsatisfying. ("whole pizza?")
>
> At the ladder's top, rungs were missing or broken. ("top rungs?")

The second example is less straightforward. Sometimes a sentence will contain a group of descriptive words that could be left in or revised out, and the results might be equally effective. For example:

> Susan Montgomery, *who lives in the apartment next to ours,* has become a good friend of mine. (nonrestrictive)
>
> The woman *who lives in the apartment next to ours* has become a good friend of mine. (restrictive)

Look closely at these two sentences. In the first the italicized words could be omitted and the reader would still know who our new friend is. It's Susan Montgomery. In the second sentence, however, we need those italicized words to identify the person about whom we're talking. What woman? Another way to explain this is to say that in the first sentence the italicized words are **nonrestrictive,** and in the second sentence they are **restrictive.** Perhaps an easier way to remember this distinction is to use the words "essential" and "nonessential" in place of restrictive and nonrestrictive. The writing convention is that we put commas around nonessential (nonrestrictive) groups of words and leave off the commas around essential (restrictive) groups. Look at some more examples.

> Michael Jordan, who set records that might not be broken, had a great career.
>
> The player who set records that might not be broken had a great career.
>
> A '57 Chevy, which has six coats of metallic paint, is my favorite possession.
>
> The car that has six coats of metallic paint is my favorite possession.

## Exercise 7-5: Using Commas

Insert commas in the following sentences if they are needed.

1. The only thing that we have to fear is fear itself.
2. To my way of thinking your whole idea is crazy.
3. Along the way home seemed to be only a distant dream.
4. The bus driver who had never before had an accident spoke calmly to the police.
5. Dolores McGann who has been with the *Globe* for only a year is becoming a fine reporter. ◆

## Exercise 7-6: Practice with Commas

Insert commas, periods, and capital letters in these paragraphs wherever necessary.

except for man and his dogs which really are no match for it the bobcat has no serious enemies if tracked the cat may vault into a tree and wait in ambush or it may loop back appearing behind its hunter reversing the predator-prey relationship such is the stuff of myth and fact fable and truth both literal and figurative which tell of bobcats.

they are largely but not exclusively nocturnal they get their name from their bobbed [cut-off] tail and their ear tufts help them gather sounds they use their whiskers as a navigational device when stalking and females are much more combative than males when defending their territory their eyes glow in the dark because bobcats are eerie, phantom like creatures—and also because light hits a reflective layer behind the retina which bounces the light back and gives the eyes' rods a second chance to absorb the dim nighttime rays. ◆

(Note: For some assistance with this exercise, see "Wood Ghost" in Appendix C.)

# METHOD OF DEVELOPMENT: CAUSE AND EFFECT

Discovering causes and their effects is another way to develop ideas in writing. We learn about cause and effect as early as infancy. Lying in our cribs, we see that people seem to pay attention to us when we cry. So we try it again. We cry, and, sure enough, they come and feed us, hold us, sing to us. All kinds of good things happen. We get the point: One thing (crying) causes another (attention), and we're launched on to a lifetime of causes and effects. It's fundamental to human experience. It's the basis of everything from rocket science and macroeconomics to baking pies and growing petunias.

Sometimes we're mistaken. We say it didn't rain today because we brought our umbrella with us. Or it did rain today because we washed our car. A black cat walked in front of us and we promptly lost our credit card. This kind of cause and effect mistake has a fancy Latin name, *post hoc, ergo propter hoc,* which simply means *after this, therefore because of this.* In other words, if it rained after I planned a picnic, then the rain must have been caused by my plans. Try to avoid this error in logic as you develop your paragraphs using cause and effect.

Try to be as logical as possible in using cause and effect. Ask yourself whether your writing should start with something that causes an effect and then discuss the effect, or should you start with an effect and analyze what its causes were? Use as many concrete and specific details as possible to keep your audience's attention.

Here are examples of these two approaches to the cause/effect relationship between advertising and a consumer's buying habits. When using either approach, remember to include concrete and specific details to keep your audience's attention.

1.   (From cause to effect) As you push your shopping cart past the toothpaste section, several things are happening. For one, a bouncy jingle you have running through your head as you scan down the shelf reminds you that you want "happy, happy teeth." You also have an image of that beautiful couple in the TV commercial who seemed to have more than just dental health on their minds as they smiled at each other. And finally, your fear of offending others with your dragonlike breath brings you to the particular brand that promised yours will soon be "kissing sweet." All of these advertising messages work flawlessly as your hand reaches, not for your usual brand, but for the shiny green box next to it.

2.   (From effect to cause) At the supermarket checkout counter you notice that you have bought a different brand of toothpaste, in a shiny green box, without really knowing why. Then you remember the bouncy jingle you have had running through your head, reminding you of your need for "happy, happy teeth." You recall the beautiful couple in the TV commercial who seemed to have more than just dental health on their minds as they smiled at each other. And finally you admit to yourself that your fear of offending others with your dragonlike breath has led you to buy a product which promises to make yours "kissing sweet." The product's advertising messages have worked flawlessly.

## Exercise 7-7: Cause and Effect

Write a paragraph based on one of the following ideas.

1.  People learning something as a child that enables them to succeed later in life
2.  Someone's advice causing a person to act in a certain way during a crisis
3.  A televised criminal act inspiring a copycat crime
4.  One person's vote having an impact on the outcome of an election
5.  Substance abuse ruining someone's life ◆

### Visit the Longman Englishpages!

For additional readings, practice exercises, Internet links, and activities, visit us online at
**http://www.ablongman.com/englishpages**

# PART 3

# WRITING ESSAYS

# CHAPTER 8

# WRITING EFFECTIVE ESSAYS

## FROM SENTENCES TO PARAGRAPHS TO ESSAYS

Up to now, you've concentrated on writing individual sentences, which you have then combined into paragraphs. The concept of having a main idea that you develop for your reader is just as basic to writing **essays** as it is for paragraphs. Think of an essay as the outgrowth of an opening paragraph. You let your audience know where you are going in the opening section of your essay, and then you proceed to follow through on your promise by adding as many paragraphs as it takes. When you've said enough, you tie it all together and you stop. Then it's up to the written words to do your communicating for you.

Sentence = group of words

Paragraph = group of sentences

Essay = group of paragraphs

Typical college essays are written by combining a number of paragraphs around a main idea or point. The point/main idea, sometimes referred to as a **thesis,** makes a statement in an **introductory paragraph.** If possible, this paragraph also gives the audience an idea of how the paper will work itself out.

Following this introduction are one or more **body** paragraphs that develop the thesis. These paragraphs each add something to the idea expressed in the introduction. They relate to the main point and help the audience to understand it. They follow

each other in some logical order that shows that the author had an **organizational plan** in mind. They may use different methods to develop the main idea, such as examples, definitions, stories, argumentative proofs, comparisons, descriptions, the five *W*s, and whatever else might be helpful. The last paragraph, called the **conclusion,** wraps things up for the audience. Often just a couple of sentences, this final paragraph reminds readers of the main idea and provides a signal that what the thesis promised has been delivered.

Despite all their trappings and terminology, good college essays are an exercise in common sense.

First tell the audience what you are going to tell them.

Then tell them.

Finally, remind them of what you just told them.

This does not mean that you oversimplify things, talk down to your audience, or give the impression that you don't respect them. It does mean you stick to your main point and do whatever you can to make sure it gets across.

# ORGANIZATION

Writing an essay in college, or anywhere else for that matter, works best if your audience feels confident about their ability to understand what you're saying to them. They want to know they are getting your point, and if that happens, it's because you took the trouble to make the ideas flow along clearly and interestingly. Generally speaking, it's a lot harder to write well than to read well, and it's your job to do as much of the work for them as you can.

Three of the major methods of organizing material are called (1) spatial, (2) chronological, and (3) emphatic.

- **Spatial** organization works well when the subject material has physical dimensions of some kind, such as a battlefield, a piece of machinery, or a scenic view.

- **Chronological** organization (from *chronos,* the Greek word for time) follows a time sequence. Some sort of process, series of events, or history can give a plan of development to the piece of writing. This could be about anything from the history of the universe to the construction of a sand castle.

- **Emphatic** order is the most common. This is writing that shares with the audience your sense of what is important, more important, and most important among your various ideas. Generally speaking, it is good psychology to save your most important, strongest, most emphatic material for last. Build up to it. Don't give away your best stuff too early and cause your paragraph or essay to fade out weakly.

## Exercise 8-1: Organization

Indicate which of the three methods of organization described previously might be most effective in writing an essay on the following. Write down your first choice. If you think that another of the three might also be used, indicate that in parentheses.

1. How to raise chinchillas _____
2. Qualities of an effective leader _____
3. Mistakes made by beginners_____
4. A perfectly composed photograph _____
5. Gaining financial security _____ ◆

# OUTLINES

In Chapter 2 you worked your way through a rough outline for a paragraph on the animal rights debate. You began by trying to capture the various ideas you might want to say on this topic. You arranged your ideas and rejected any that didn't seem to fit. You were trying to pull things together so that you could get one main idea (topic sentence) across to your readers. This form became a paragraph.

Now you need to be sure that the same organizing principles are at work in writing an essay. You still want to get a unified, limited idea across, but, instead of using individual sentences to do it, you will use whole paragraphs, one after another. Instead of just a rough outline, you will want a more finished, craftsman-like plan.

Here is an example of a standard outline format used to organize an academic essay:

**Thesis:** [~~The point I want to convey is that~~] The Internet has a far-reaching influence on our lives.

    I Introduction

   II Business

      A. Online commerce

         1. Web site transactions

         2. Advertising

      B. Stocks and speculation

  III Political

      A. Polling

      B. Political web sites

  IV Interpersonal

      A. Interest groups

      B. E-mail

      C. Surfing addiction

   V Conclusion

As this example shows, an outline gives you an overall plan to follow in getting your thesis across to your audience. In looking at the sample outline, you may see some changes you would make if it were yours. You might also wish to add more details. If you added headings under section II, A,1, for instance, that part of the outline might look like this:

        II  Business

            A.  Online Commerce

                1.  Web site transactions

                    a.  Credit card buying

                    b.  Barter

                2.  Advertising

            B.  Stocks and speculation

In this outline format, there are a couple of rules. First, notice that you never have just one heading at any level. That means that you don't have I unless you have at least II, and you don't have A unless you have at least B, and so on. Also, notice that it's customary to alternate between numbers and letters as you move into more and more detailed headings (II, B, 2, b).

Developing an outline is intended to help you write. It is not a goal in itself, nor is it a guarantee that you will write a good essay, but it can be extremely helpful. ◆

### Exercise 8-2: Outlining

Using the model provided previously, create the outline for an essay based on the following thesis:

[~~The point I want to convey is **that**~~] For several reasons I think newspapers are better than television at reporting the news.

Don't worry. You don't have to actually write the essay. Your task is to take this thesis and figure out how it might be developed and fleshed out in an outline that could be turned into an essay. Look back at the material on organization for some ideas on how to proceed. ◆

## WRITING CONVENTION: TRANSITIONS

Once again you want to make it as easy as possible for your audience to follow the development of your ideas. In writing paragraphs, you used transitional expressions (*however, in addition, furthermore, although, first of all, finally*) to glue your sentences together. Now you want to be sure to do the same with your essay's paragraphs. You know what the connection between two paragraphs is, but it might not be obvious to your readers unless you include a transitional expression to show the connection. When you begin paragraph IV of the five-paragraph essay outlined previously, you might write, "Most importantly, in addition to commercial and political influences on our lives, the Internet has changed the way we interact with others in our social lives." Then you could go on to discuss the material in that paragraph and feel confident that the audience would see how it all fit together.

## Exercise 8-3: Transitions

Go back to the sample outline. Now invent a sentence that could be used as the opening sentence of paragraph III (Political). ◆

In the chapters that follow, you will continue to write paragraphs, but you will also be joining them together and organizing them into essays.

### Visit the Longman Englishpages!

For additional readings, practice exercises, Internet links, and activities, visit us online at
**http://www.ablongman.com/englishpages**

# CHAPTER 9

# SEMICOLONS AND COLONS/DEFINITIONS

 ## CASE: THE COMPANY'S CHILD CARE CENTER

"Reverse commuting" is what brings many of Scheid Packaging Corporation's employees to its plant located in what used to be a cornfield. In the past, the typical commuter was a suburbanite coming to a job in a city's central or downtown area. Now, more and more workers, like those at Scheid, are traveling miles from the inner city to a suburban plant or factory. If they can't drive, they take a couple of trains and buses, transferring more than once on bitter February mornings. They are willing to sacrifice several hours of their day to get to a good job, but they spend much of the day worrying about what is happening to the young children they've been forced to leave at home. Will the sitter show up? How much of a burden is this on my children's grandmother? Is my older child really old enough to care for the younger ones? Questions like these make for serious, non-productive distractions.

Like many companies, Scheid Packaging has recognized this as a problem that is not simply humanitarian. It affects the financial bottom line and shows up in absenteeism, workplace accidents, and the loss of good, solid workers who feel they have to choose between their paychecks and their children's well-being.

*(Continued)*

*(Continued from previous page)*

The company decided to do something about it. Following the example of other companies, including their major competitor, Scheid Packaging began planning the steps necessary to set up a child care program for its employees' young children.

- The assistant director of human resources was directed to make a detailed proposal and given a three-week deadline to submit it. Her task was to write a document that would explain what the company would be doing. To do this, she used the five *W*s (who, what, where, when, why, and how; see Chapter 2). She immediately wrote down the questions that needed answering. For example, would employees have to pay for the service, or would it be a fringe benefit? If so, would this be fair to employees without children? She then tried to compress the major issues into one brief paragraph that would be the introduction to her proposal.

- When she had finished the first draft of her proposal (one week before her boss's deadline), she showed it to several of her staff members. She attached a short memo, asking them to read the draft and come to a meeting armed with suggestions and ideas. She knew that some of her best staff members had young children, so she expected helpful feed back.

- The president of Scheid, a grandfather himself, wanted this program to be run in a professional manner, so he personally contacted the local state university and made an appointment with the head of its Human Growth and Development Department. He wanted to know about successful programs, the kinds of credentials the child care staff should have, the dangers and liabilities to look out for, and how much it would all cost.

- The director of human resources put a notice in each employee's paycheck envelope. Those who had their pay electronically deposited in their bank got the note in the mail. The note informed them that this service would be available if enough employees would be willing to participate.

- Employees with children were asked for input on the features the new facility should have. Some suggestions—individual cubicles for nap time, for instance—were ruled out as being too expensive. Others were considered and implemented.

After a year of problems and good intentions, the child care center was established and everyone agreed that it was an idea long overdue. The sounds of happy three-year-olds were mingling with the, workday bustle. Managers felt the company had made a good choice. The center was good for employees' families, and it was good for business.

## Analyzing the Case

Can you see why the decision made by Scheid Packaging was a business decision, not simply an act of kindness or social responsibility? As you read a case like this, you should put yourself into an active frame of mind. This means that you are asking questions, raising doubts, noticing your own feelings, whether you have children of your own or not.

Don't fall into an easy, passive frame of mind. When you analyze a case, you have to get yourself into it actively. Paint pictures in your mind. Cast the players in the drama, using recognizable faces of famous people if it helps. You have to convince yourself that in such a situation people will act in predictable ways, and—most importantly—if they have to write, they will write in predictable ways.

## Key Terms

accreditation
child care
early childhood
early learning
fringe benefit
infant
interest center
professionalism
supervision
toddler

Explore the meaning of these terms, using your dictionary where possible. Discuss them with your teacher and classmates. Do any of them have current meanings that differ from their dictionary definitions?

## Exercise 9-1: Questions for Discussion

1. Do employers have an obligation to care for the well-being of their employees and their families? Would it be right for a local government to require employers to have child care centers? What about state governments? Or the federal government?
2. Is it possible for children who spend large amounts of time in child care to grow up "normally"? Do such children have any advantages over other children?
3. If you are employed, can you picture what a child care facility would be like at your workplace? Could it be a good one?
4. What are some of the long-range implications if there is an increase in the number of workplace child care centers?
5. To be a child care professional, does a person have to like children more than most people do, or is it simply another profession like teaching, lawyering, or banking? ◆

## Role Playing

In this case, the people who have very little power are gaining a benefit from people who have a lot of power. The reverse commuters consider themselves fortunate simply to have good jobs and are willing to make sacrifices to keep them. Within this chain are different levels of people who depend on each other. Try to identify with some of them and get inside their minds and hearts. For example:

- Corporation President Scheid, a tough, self-made-man, has done a lot of thinking about this problem. He has also discussed it with his wife and their four children.

- Zack Dixon is a young father living in the inner city and looking for a better job. He sees an advertisement for Scheid Packaging in the Sunday newspaper. His wife also works, and their baby-sitting arrangement is not a good one. He is intrigued by the idea of commuting to a suburban job and bringing his daughter with him.

- Joe Haley is the chief building engineer at the Scheid plant. His job will be to oversee the creation of a safe place to locate the child care facility within the building. To do this he will have to move some people—and even some walls—around the plant and then worry about local, state, and federal regulations for licensing a child care facility. His own kids are in their thirties.

- Martha Shandling is a secretary in the vice president's office. She has taken two child development courses at a local community college, so she has some definite ideas about this subject, and she is a little worried about its long-term success.

## Exercise 9-2: Role Playing

Sit any three of these people down at a table and have them talk about their own experiences in child raising. Then have one of them bring up the subject of child care at the work site. Take the conversation wherever you think it might go. Try doing two separate role-playing sessions, one with a skeptical, somewhat pessimistic tone and one where everyone puts a positive spin on the project. ◆

## Exercise 9-3: Writing Assignments

1. Create an outline for a three-paragraph essay (introduction, larger body paragraph, conclusion), using one of these thesis statements:
   a. Working parents face serious challenges.
   b. The children of working parents face serious challenges.

c.    Corporations have responsibilities for the well-being of employees.

2.    Write the introduction and conclusion paragraphs for an imaginary essay based on one of these three thesis statements. ◆

# WRITING CONVENTION: SEMICOLONS AND COLONS

## Semicolons

As you saw in the section on commas (Chapter 7), punctuation marks attempt to do for writing what pauses, inflection, and timing do for speaking. They help an audience know what is important and what goes with what. Colons and semicolons fall into this same category. In some ways they are like commas, only stronger. In fact, a semicolon has been referred to as a supercomma or even a "comma on steroids." While those names may sound a bit unconventional, they are descriptive. When a comma isn't strong enough, you may want to use a semicolon. Look at these examples. Three of them (1–3) are OK. Number 4 is to be avoided at all costs.

1.    I was sure I had brought my credit *card. I* discovered that I hadn't.

**(period between two sentences)**

2.    I was sure I had brought my credit *card, but I* discovered that I hadn't.

**(comma + conjunction making one sentence)**

3.    I was sure I had brought my credit *card; I* discovered that I hadn't.

**(semicolon making one sentence)**

4.    I was sure I had brought my credit *card I* discovered that I hadn't.

**(nothing between them = a run-on sentence)**

These examples demonstrate options for handling related clauses:

Number 1 keeps the sentences separate and lets their closeness show their connection.

Number 2 uses a comma and a conjunction to join the sets of ideas together in what is called a **compound sentence.** This method can be used only if the conjunction is one of the following: *and, or, nor, but, for, so, yet*. These six conjunctions are called **coordinating conjunctions** because they join words together as equals. Another kind of conjunction, called a **subordinating conjunction,** includes words like *when, since, although, because, unless, after, until.* These are used to join words together in such a way that one idea is shown to be more or less significant than the other.

Number 3 uses a semicolon to form a compound sentence without the use of a conjunction. The semicolon allows you to take two sentences and show the close connection between them in a strong way. Because the effect gained in using semicolons is strong and dramatic, they should be used carefully. Don't overuse them.

Number 4 is incorrect. It is a **run-on sentence** because it makes no attempt to punctuate the point where the two sentences run together.

## Exercise 9-4: Semicolons

Here are some run-on sentences. Correct each of them by punctuating them in the three acceptable ways shown in the previous section. The first has been done for you.

1.  Children need expert care they don't always get it.
    Children need expert care. They don't always get it. (two sentences)
    Children need expert care, but they don't always get it. (compound sentence)
    Children need expert care; they don't always get it. (semicolon)

2.  Fringe benefits are not gifts they are earned.
    _____
    _____

3.  The employees deserved to be consulted they were.
    _____
    _____

4.  That bird has been singing beautifully it makes me feel happy.
    _____
    _____ ◆

## Colons

The colon is another powerful form of punctuation. Think of it as that impressive sounding person in the movies who stands at the ballroom door and announces each of the famous guests as they make their entrance. The main job of a colon is to let us know that something is coming next or about to take place in a sentence, paragraph, or essay. It also has some miscellaneous uses. Look at some examples.

1.   There are two common reactions to dull sermons: sleep and boredom.
2.   The designation of the last century's greatest American athlete was the correct one: Michael Jordan.
3.   The announcement posted on the door made it clear: "School will be closed tomorrow." (Introduction of a quotation)
4.   The final boat crossed the line at 3:51 P.M.

It's important to notice that in the first three uses of the colon, there must be a complete sentence in place before the colon. In other words it would be correct grammatically to put a period where the colon is if you chose to do so. The colon in sentence 4 is a conventional use to indicate time. In addition, a colon is also used rather than a comma in formal letters following the name or title of the person being addressed. (To review letter format, see Chapter 6.)

Dear Admiral Smith:

Dear Mom,

Dear Madam or Sir, (or Dear Madam or Sir:)

To Whom It May Concern:

## Exercise 9-5: Semicolons and Colons

Place colons and semicolons where they belong in the following.

1.   He cleared his throat and made the following announcement "Elvis has left the building."
2.   I've learned a few things about life I wish I had learned them sooner.
3.   Many corporations base decisions on only one thing the bottom line.

4.   A single shot rang out the prime minister fell forward into the punch-
     bowl.
5.   The stadium clock showed 106 remaining in the game.
6.   At that point fate dealt her the best possible card the Ace of Spades. ◆

# METHOD OF DEVELOPMENT: DEFINITION

The use of definition to develop your written ideas can range from simple to complicated, depending on your subject matter. In either case, the principle is the same: to
make sure that you and your audience are talking about the same thing. For example,
this chapter's case refers to *reverse commuters.* For that term to make sense, the
reader must first know what a commuter is. Then, with additional information, the
reader will also understand the term *reverse commuter.* Reread the first paragraph of
the case and see if you find at least informal definitions of these two terms.

A definition can be provided for readers in various ways. They range from a full-
fledged technical definition, complete with complex distinctions, down to a few simple words for clarification. Compare the following.

1.   Now, when I say "big," I mean bigger than a chocolate chip cookie.

2.   "Merchant" means a person who deals in goods of the kind or other-
     wise by his occupation holds himself out as having knowledge or skill
     peculiar to the practices or goods involved in the transaction or to
     whom such knowledge or skill may be attributed by his employment
     of an agent or broker or other intermediary who by his occupation
     holds himself out as having such knowledge or skill. (from the *Uni-
     form Commercial Code*)

Number 1 is in a discussion of rocks suitable for skipping along a lakeshore. Number 2 is in a law school textbook on the nature of legal contracts. Even though they
are very different, they are both definitions. Obviously, they differ a great deal in how
formal they are and their intended audience.

By now your efforts at role playing and getting inside the minds of various kinds
of audiences should be helping you see how to use a definition in a way that will help
you communicate your thoughts. You want to use definitions that will clarify ideas,
not make them more confusing. You also want to help your readers feel confident that
they are getting your point. Words can be "loaded" and not necessarily mean the same
thing to different people. Take terms like *liberal* and *conservative,* for instance, or

*radical* and *moderate.* Defining these words is a minefield because they have different meanings, depending on a person's politics. Still, it's important that you make the effort to clarify exactly what you are talking about, especially if there is a chance you might be misunderstood.

Finally, use whatever method of definition works best for your writing. Some possible methods:

- By using comparison and contrast, you can say what it is you mean to say and clarify what you do not mean to say.

- You can refer to an authority of some kind, such as a dictionary definition, or the way something is commonly understood.

- You can use the scientific method, which defines something by telling what general category it falls into and then pointing out how it is different from the other members of that category.

## Exercise 9-6: Definitions

Give definitions of the following. Note the writer and intended audience.

1. A young woman has been away at college for two semesters. She is defining for her parents what she means when she says she is "serious" about a young man she has been seeing.
2. A coach is defining for the women's basketball team what it means to be "dedicated" to winning.
3. The president of a small company is explaining to his managers what he means by the term "belt tightening."
4. Two students are collaborating on a science research project . After having some disputes, one of them wants to put in writing what she considers "my share" of the work. ◆

**Visit the Longman Englishpages!**

For additional readings, practice exercises, Internet links, and activities, visit us online at
**http://www.ablongman.com/englishpages**

# CHAPTER 10

# QUOTATIONS/
# EXPLAINING A PROCESS

 ## CASE: TRANSFER TO ANOTHER COLLEGE

Over the last two years, 27-year-old Daryl Turner has accumulated 36 credit hours at Cesar Chavez Community College in downtown Houston. He has done this while working full time at the local branch of a national computer supply chain and doing his part to help support his daughter Keisha.

Now he is at a crossroads.

Mr. Turner knows he can continue to accumulate credits at Chavez and eventually receive an associate's degree (A.A., A.S., or A.G.S.). At that point, he may be able to transfer to a four-year college and work toward his bachelor's degree. On one hand, he asks himself whether or not the A.A. is important enough to delay his transferring right now. He knows he might lose some of his credit hours in the process, but he would be closer to his ultimate goal, a degree in business. On the other hand, he also knows that he might not finish the B.A. requirements, and then he would be without any degree at all.

Fortunately, Chavez Community College has a transfer center staffed by a director, a clerical staff member, and two student aides. Mr. Turner wonders if this office could really do him any good and decides to find out. As soon as he does, several things happen:

*(Continued)*

*(Continued from previous page)*

- He removes a Transfer Center notice from a bulletin board in the school's lobby, after first briefly looking over his shoulder to see if anyone has seen him doing it. He also picks up the center's brochure from a table outside the cafeteria.

- The Transfer Center is closed for the day, so he removes the coupon from the brochure, fills it out, and deposits it in the plastic box on the center's door. Within two days he receives a phone call from a staff member who arranges an appointment. Unknown to him, there is already a letter on its way to his home address outlining the services available to all students who might wish to transfer.

- Although it's a coincidence, two days later, an article in the current issue of the college's newspaper surprises him by praising the work of the Transfer Center and encouraging students to take advantage of it. As he reads the story, Mr. Turner has a sense of *deja vu.* He wonders where he has read these words, and then he realizes that the newspaper has lifted whole sentences from the same brochure that he had just received in the mail. He wonders to himself: "plagiarism?"

- This just happens to be the semester when financial support for the Transfer Center could be disappearing. It is partly funded by a grant from the state's community college board. The center's director at Chavez, Kristi Fagen, has been preparing the paperwork to reapply for grant money. She has accumulated statistics and filled out the many required forms, but now she needs to write a cover statement that pleads her case.

- At Ms. Fagen's request, a student who had transferred from Chavez to the University of Texas at Laredo writes a testimonial letter. In it he talks of his current success and says he might not have been able to transfer without the help of the Transfer Center. Ms. Fagen adds this letter to her application material.

- Mr. Turner keeps his appointment with the Transfer Center staff. It goes well. He gets answers to his questions and good advice without any pressure. After a second appointment and a meeting with one of his instructors, he decides to transfer in the fall of next year.

- Mr. Turner knows his job at the electronics store is not great, but it is pretty good, and he hates to lose it. He decides to write a letter to his boss and hand deliver it. In the letter he describes his past performance, discusses his dreams, and requests some assurance that he might continue his career with the company in the future. He revises the letter several times, wondering if he should simply talk it over with his boss and hope for the best. He decides that a letter sitting permanently in a file cabinet would be a good idea, so he rewrites it one last time.

- When the following September arrives, Daryl Turner has become a student at the University of Texas, Ft. Worth. He is a bit frightened, but he feels he has made an informed and wise decision.

Meanwhile, back in Houston, the president of Chavez Community College gets a letter from the state community college board informing her that there will be money for the Transfer Center for one more year. She passes it on to Ms. Fagen, along with a note of congratulations.

## Analyzing the Case

Mr. Turner thinks he is going to have to make a difficult decision on his own. What he discovers is that, although he does have to make the decision, there is a lot of help available to him if he looks for it. As this book frequently points out, one good way to find things out is to read what people have written for you. If you have dealt successfully with a large bureaucracy, such as a college, you know you have to protect yourself against the dangers of excessive paperwork and "human error." You have to look for good advisors early on in your bureaucratic adventure, people you can trust to treat you like a human and not simply a record in the database. Chavez Community College and its Transfer Center aim to provide this kind of advice and assistance. How does this compare with your own experience?

## Key Terms

academic reputation
advisor
articulation
credit hour
grade point average
job readiness
liberal arts
major
transferability
vocational

Explore the meaning of these terms, using your dictionary where possible. Discuss them with your teacher and classmates. Do any of them have current meanings that differ from their dictionary definitions?

## Exercise 10-1: Questions for Discussion

1.  Is the value of a college degree overrated? Does it, in fact, guarantee that you will make more money during your lifetime than someone who doesn't have one? Is financial reward the most important reason for pursuing a degree?
2.  Was the local paper committing plagiarism by using the exact words supplied by the college? Or might that have been a common and legitimate use of public relations material?

3.  Do people value something for which they have had to sacrifice more than something that was simply given to them? Why is this? Is this always the case?

4.  The state and this public college are spending money to show students how to transfer from one school to another. Is the college doing something for Mr. Turner that he ought to be able to do for himself? Is this an example of wasting the taxpayer's money on baby-sitting, as some might suggest, or is it a wise use of public funds?

5.  Can you think of ways that a school might involve itself in a student's decision making that might be inappropriate? Why not just let people "sink or swim"? ◆

## Role Playing

Colleges—at all levels—involve thousands of people and generate truckloads of printed material. All of the people mentioned in this case (including Mr. Turner's daughter Keisha) do some writing as part of their state in life. Written words make things happen. Get yourself inside the world of some of the people involved in this case and imagine the part that writing plays in their lives. Imagine yourself, for instance, as:

- Daryl Turner, who hopes that he has done the right thing in moving from an environment in which he felt comfortable to one that is much larger and less familiar.

- Philip Stavros, a student aide who works part time in the Transfer Center. He has had a chance to see firsthand how the center helps some people, and he wishes it could connect with more of them. He is making use of its database and collection of online college catalogs to do some planning for his own educational future.

- Joy Kelly, a mid-level official at the state's community college board headquarters. She is the first one to see the applications for money coming in from colleges all over the state, and she wishes there were more of it to go around.

- Marlene Wang, Ed.D., president of Chavez Community College. She would like to take the credit for the success of her school's Transfer Center, but she has learned to let others have the major share of the credit. So far, this has been a good practice for her.

## Exercise 10-2: Role Playing

Have two of these people sit down, introduce themselves to each other, and then talk about a third person on the list. Be sure to have something about writing be part of their conversation. ◆

## Exercise 10-3: Writing Assignments

1. Plan out and then write a three-paragraph essay on the advantages or disadvantages of attending a community college. Your audience is a group of juniors and seniors from your old high school. Give examples.
2. Repeat the previous assignment, but this time write about a couple of advantages and disadvantages, using comparison and contrast to help develop your ideas.
3. Colleges serve both traditional and nontraditional students, meaning either 18-year-old high school graduates or older, employed people who bring a different set of experiences with them to school. Write two paragraphs. In the first define the traditional college student, and in the second define the nontraditional. Use your own experience if it helps. ◆

# WRITING CONVENTION: QUOTATIONS

Not all the words you write for your audiences are your own. As you say in conversation, you will also write, "So then she said . . . " By using the exact words of someone else, you can strengthen your own argument, but you must follow certain conventional procedures. If not, you run the risk of confusing your audience. Also, if you use someone else's exact words and give the impression—intentionally or not—that they are your own, you commit the serious offense of plagiarism.

**Plagiarism** is intellectual theft. Original writing belongs to the person who writes it. It is dishonest and in some cases, illegal for others to attempt to pass it off as their own. This is certainly true in formal academic situations, such as reports, research or term papers, and speeches. Admittedly, there are fuzzy instances where a person may have become so familiar with another's ideas that he or she simply utters or writes them without even thinking about plagiarism. If you casually tell a joke you heard recently, it's your joke, and no one really expects you to give credit to its author. But if you deliberately try to mislead your audience into thinking that someone else's words have originated with you, you commit plagiarism.

**Quotation marks** are always used in pairs, one set at the beginning and one at the end of the quoted person's exact words. For example: "This college is wonderful." If the sentence also contains words that are your own and not exact quotations, they may be separated from the quoted material by commas. Look at these examples:

1. He said, "This college is wonderful."
2. "This college," he said, "is wonderful."
3. "This college is wonderful," he said.
4. "This college is wonderful. I am impressed," he said.

One way to remember this convention is the *66/99 rule.* Look closely at the quotations in a printed book (this one, for instance) and you will notice that the opening quotation marks look something like the number 66, while the closing marks resemble 99. Now look back at the previous examples and you will see the 66/99 rule in action:

Commas and periods go outside the 66 and inside the 99.

Of course, if the quoted material has its own internal commas, they follow the same rules described in Chapter 7. The same goes for periods, as example 4 illustrates.

Quotation marks are sometimes used to draw attention to a specialized or emphatic use of a word, even if it was not actually spoken by another person. For example:

The "normal" reaction to loud noise was missing in the concert's front row.

Be careful with this use of quotation marks. It's easy to overuse it and to sound like you're trying to be "cute" or "clever," if you "know" what I mean.

The final point to remember about quotation marks is that they function like an audiotape recording. If you indicate a **direct** quote, you are saying that these are the very words the person spoke or wrote. A much more common way of reporting another person's words is through **indirect** quotation. Look at these examples:

1. The librarian told the student that he would look into the matter.
2. The librarian told the student, "I'll look into the matter."
3. Fred said he was hungry.
4. Fred said he was so hungry he could "eat a horse."

Use quotations exactly. For instance, notice the inaccuracy of this one:

5.    Fred said, "He could eat a horse."

The first word out of *Fred's* mouth in this sentence would have been *I,* not *he.*

In some situations, you will quote the exact words of someone who is quoting the exact words of someone else. To do this, use single quotation marks (' . . .'). For example:

6.    The waiter asked, "Sir, did your wife say, 'This soup is an outrage,' or simply that she didn't like it?"

(Note: Suggestions on the use of quotations are also contained in Appendix B for English as a second language students.)

## Exercise 10-4: Quotations

Add quotation marks wherever they belong in the following examples. Don't use them where they are not required.

1.    President Roosevelt said that America should be afraid of fear.
2.    President Roosevelt said, The only thing we have to fear is fear itself.
3.    What in the world am I doing here? he asked.
4.    What in the world he asked am I doing here?
5.    He wondered what in the world he was doing there.  ◆

## Exercise 10-5: Correcting Quotations

If the following are correct, put *C* in the blank. If incorrect, put *I* and fix the sentence.

1.    _____ "No one was ever ruined by a book", he observed.
2.    _____ I'd like to know "why you said you were angry."
3.    _____ The loudspeaker announced, 'All aboard for Memphis.'

4. _____ "Don't lie to us," the lawyer said. "We're not stupid."
5. _____ "This is my final word." "I don't intend to say any more," he insisted. ◆

---

**Spoken vs. Written conventions.**

In the last decade or so, "She *said*" has often been replaced in speaking, particularly among some teenagers, by "She *goes*":

So then she goes, "I'm going to the mall. Want to come?"
And he goes, "Like, OK."

Avoid this informal language in your written expression, but realize that languages change and someday this may be an acceptable written use of "go."

---

# METHOD OF DEVELOPMENT: PROCESS

An excellent way to develop certain ideas in writing is to explain how things follow, step by step, through a process. Picture this movie scene: The good guys are surrounded on all sides by dangers and, of course, by bad guys. The hero gathers his group close to him and says, "Now listen carefully. Here's my plan. First, we . . .," as the screen fades to black. Sure, it's a cliché, but it's become a cliché because it's such a good idea. We want to know there's a plan, a process for getting the job done. Your audience wants this assurance, too.

Turn back to Chapter 2 which presents a process used by good writers. The writing process entails a number of steps in a logical sequence. It doesn't always work perfectly, but it does work, and it is a good process for most writers. After reading about this process, your own experience with it has enabled you to decide whether or not it is a good process for you.

What makes a process work is the fact that the series of steps on the page seem to the reader to be in order, logical, and realistic. What's wrong with the process in the accompanying box?

---

### How to replace a defective wall switch

1.    Remove the screws from the faceplate, and take it off.
2.    Remove the screws at top and bottom of the old switch and pull it out of the wall as far as the wires will allow.
3.    Loosen the screws on either side of the old switch and pull off the wires.
4.    Replace the wires on either side of the new switch and push it back into its receptacle.
5.    Find the fusebox or circuit breaker and turn off the electrical power.
6.    Replace the screws at the top and bottom of the new switch and replace the faceplate over it.
7.    Turn the electricity back on.

---

Any problem with this process? Right: You are probably dead before reaching step 5 because that step should have been number 1. A process is useful only if its steps are in order. Once again, the importance of putting yourself in your reader's place is apparent. Audiences know only what you tell them in writing, not what is inside your mind.

Here is another example of a process used to develop a paragraph:

Success in mastering a foreign language means being willing to go through several stages. First of all you must really want to learn the language and realize that it is a difficult, frustrating procedure. Then you must be willing to expose yourself to the new language in large doses, even though you understand almost nothing of what is being said. Gradually, you will find certain words and phrases becoming recognizable. Meanwhile, you are systematically working your way through beginning elements of grammar and vocabulary by using books, tapes, and, if you're lucky, a language lab. Eventually, after a great deal of effort, you are finding your way around in the language and even enjoying it. After continued effort, you become thoroughly comfortable with the sounds, the rules, the idioms (particular ways of saying something in a language), and the spirit of the language. You know the language as a culture and way of life, not just as a set of rules and expressions. You stop translating everything before speaking or writing. Finally, when you find yourself thinking and even dreaming in the language, you know that you have mastered it.

Notice how many transitional words were used in writing this paragraph. They are particularly valuable in helping your audience think their way through the process with you. Among the transitional expressions are *first of all, then,* and *gradually.*

## Exercise 10-6: Process

In addition to those already mentioned, make a list of other transitional expressions you find in the sample paragraph. ◆

## Exercise 10-7: Practice with Process

Write a three-paragraph essay on one of the following. Start with a brief introduction that tells your audience what you are going to explain and maybe a word or two about why this process is valuable or important. Then write a body paragraph similar to the one on learning a language. Follow this up with a brief conclusion that reminds the audience of what you were attempting to explain.

1.   Burglar-proofing a house or apartment
2.   Blowing a respectable bubble with bubblegum
3.   Growing prize-winning roses
4.   Converting someone to your point of view (use examples)
5.   Learning to play a musical instrument. ◆

**Visit the Longman Englishpages!**

For additional readings, practice exercises, Internet links, and activities, visit us online at
**http://www.ablongman.com/englishpages**

# CHAPTER 11

# CONSISTENT TENSE AND PERSON/CLASSIFICATION

 ## CASE: CENSORSHIP IN THE LIBRARY

The Wheeler County Public Library's main branch has a problem. Three weeks ago one of its patrons discovered what he considered to be an offensive book on the shelves in the children's section. The book *Who's Your Daddy?* offers a nonjudgmental portrayal of a family unit in which a child is raised by two gay men. The complaining library user, Charles Blake, expressed his initial concern by bringing the book to a clerk at the checkout counter. From there he was referred to the head of the children's department, and from there to the executive librarian, who assured him that she would look into the matter and get back to him.

Mr. Blake and his wife Norma were not satisfied with this answer. They wrote a letter to the president of the library's board of trustees, demanding that the library get rid of the book and noting that taxpayers paid the trustees' salary. (In fact, the trustees are elected, unpaid volunteers.) The board of trustees suggested to the executive librarian that the matter be put on the agenda for the next monthly meeting on the second Wednesday of the month. They also directed that a letter be drafted to be sent to the Blakes assuring them of the board's concern.

Meanwhile, Mr. Blake had contacted his pastor, his state legislative representative, and the editor of the local community newspaper. He received a short written reply from the first two. The newspaper printed his

*(Continued)*

*(Continued from previous page)*

letter in its next issue, but it also printed a one-paragraph editorial that commented on the professionalism of the library staff and warned against the dangers of censorship. This enraged the Blakes and convinced them that the next meeting of the library board, which was by law open to the public, would be the best place to tell their side of the story.

At the meeting, Mr. and Mrs. Blake were given time to speak and were listened to politely. However, after hearing them, the board's president announced that the matter would be considered by its Policy Committee, which consists of board members and library staff members. If this group determined that the book should not be on the shelves, it would be removed.

By now the two unhappy library patrons were ready for battle. They started calling their friends and mailing out a one-page summary of what had happened. They wrote another letter to the local paper, which again

was published, and they urged their fellow citizens to pack the next meeting of the library board. "It is imperative," they said, "that we stand up for our community's values and keep our library safe for our children."

Now the meeting was one week away, and a flurry of writing had been taking place. Internal memos and electronic mail were circulating among library staff and board members. The American Library Association, after being notified of the situation, offered to help and to advise if necessary. A local gay rights organization offered to send representatives to the meeting if the library staff thought it would be helpful. Quite a few letters of support and of condemnation were sent to the library and to the local paper. Several of them contained identical paragraphs, duplicating word for word the reasons for getting rid of the book or keeping it on the shelf.

What would happen at the meeting was anybody's guess.

## Analyzing the Case

Reread this case and see whether your initial reaction to it has changed at all. This is the kind of case where different perceptions of the truth are bound to raise issues. Depending on your thoughts on several of the questions that are raised, you will come down more on one side than the other. Can you assume that all of the people involved in this dispute are equally sincere? If you could, then it would be easier to analyze the kinds of things that they would write in such a situation. However, if you suspect some people's motives, it will be more difficult to sort things out. As librarians and others have discovered, censorship is an issue that gets people angry and agitated.

## Key Terms

censorship
community standards
discretion
diversity
family values
lifestyle
obscenity
professionalism
propriety
tolerance

Explore the meaning of these terms, using your dictionary where possible. Discuss them with your teacher and classmates. Do any of them have current meanings that differ from their dictionary definitions?

## Exercise 11-1: Questions for Discussion

1.  Is any kind of censorship justified, or is it always a denial of public rights? Does the fact that the book in question was in the children's section make a difference?
2.  Does it sound like the Blakes have been given their due, or were they given a bureaucratic runaround? On what do you base your opinion?
3.  Are there any situations in which you are willing to give up some of your freedom for a good reason? How about increased airport security measures that restrict your ability to board a plane quickly and conveniently —or even to make a dumb joke about packing a bomb in your suitcase?
4.  Should people, including children, be given more responsibility for their actions than they are, rather than less? For example, should children be allowed Internet access anywhere they wish on a library's computer? Cite some other specific examples to strengthen your point.
5.  Who should make the major decisions about what books and materials are suitable for a local public library? Is it a job for professional librarians, or the citizens who pay the library taxes and fees, or local government officials, or simply the free marketplace of published books and authors? All of the above? None of the above?

## Role Playing

Put yourself inside the library censorship case. Use your own personal experiences and memories. Knowing your audience, whether it consists of one person or many, means that you can make good judgments about word choice, about the kind of language you should use, and about what might work best in a particular case. Try once again to get inside some of the characters involved in this case.

For example:

•   Mr. Blake, who feels that as a taxpayer he is the one of the people who should decide how his tax dollars are spent, and he certainly doesn't want them spent on "trash" like *Who's Your Daddy?*

- Mrs. Blake, who first learned of this case when her outraged husband came home from the library and told her of his discovery. Since that day she has wondered, frequently, whether they should be taking this action, but she has continued to stand by her husband.

- A local community leader who received a copy of the Blakes' letter. He is not gay, but he was raised by two lesbian women. With his background, should he get involved in this dispute?

- The head of the children's department at the Wheeler County Public Library. She feels caught in the middle, but she feels that there are professional ways of handling problems like this one.

- A part-time library employee. He was putting books back on some nearby shelves when Mr. Blake made his discovery.

- A library board member who shares some of Mr. Blake's sentiments but also feels obligated to support the library staff. Since he serves as a volunteer on the board, he felt defensive when Mr. Blake said, "Remember, we're the ones who pay your salary!"

## Exercise 11-2: Role Playing

1. Pick two of the people listed here and stage a conversation between them. If necessary, give them names and make up a realistic background for them. Have them ask each other questions about their reactions to the library situation and to the larger questions it raises. It's all right to have some pauses and silences in the conversation while people's imaginations are working. Have at least one observer take notes and ask questions of the participants to keep the conversation going.

2. Interview Mr. and Mrs. Blake. Try to determine their motivation. Are they in total agreement on everything? Use your detective skills by asking indirect questions. For example, don't ask, "Why do you hate homosexuals?" Instead, ask, "Do you think most people would have reacted the way you did?"

3. Stage a conversation between the executive librarian and a library patron who has heard about the controversy and wants to know more about it before getting involved. When another patron comes along, the first one tries to tell the second one what the librarian has just said. Would the second version sound much different?

4.  Stage a conversation between two fourth-graders who were browsing in the children's section when Mr. Blake began demanding that action be taken. One of the children is a bit wiser than the other. How are the words they use different from the ones an adult might use, especially in writing? ◆

## Exercise 11-3: Writing Assignments

1.  Mr. Blake's original letter to the library board got things moving. Write his opening and closing paragraphs. Refer to Chapter 6 for ideas on letter writing.

2.  The president of the library board has asked the executive librarian to draft a letter to send to the editor of the local paper. What does the letter say about such things as censorship, trusting the judgment of professionals, and tolerating various viewpoints? Write some sentences she could use.

3.  At the local high school, seniors are taking a course on the U.S. Constitution. Their teacher, Mr. Dodge, wants them to write something about the controversy at the local library. He prepares an assignment sheet that gives a brief background and then tells the students what he wants them to try to convey in their papers. Can you write part of his assignment sheet for him?

4.  One of the seniors in Mr. Dodge's class wants to write a letter to the American Library Association, asking for background material and policy statements that might be useful in doing this assignment. Write the letter, addressing it to:

    The American Library Association
    50 East Huron Street
    Chicago, IL 60611

5.  Make up your own writing assignment. Invent a role and a situation related to this case that call for a particular piece of writing, and then write it. Use your imagination and explore some of the less obvious persons who have been touched by the censorship case. ◆

# WRITING CONVENTION: CONSISTENCY IN TENSE AND PERSON

Suppose you're writing the third paragraph of an essay on the things you saw and heard at the library board's big meeting. You're describing the events—the shouting, name calling, pounding on the table—in your paper, and suddenly your phone rings. After answering the phone, you're hungry and you have a snack. When you return to your keyboard, you forget that you have been writing in the *past* tense. Your next sentence begins, "And then Mr. and Mrs. Blake get up and angrily leave the meeting." It's a fine sentence, but it has shifted from past tense to present. Three sentences later, you shift back to past tense: "He stood outside the library and shouted at the small crowd that had gathered." Your readers will notice this inconsistency.

While it is not as great a violation of a writing convention as some others (sentence completeness, for example), inconsistency can distract your readers and possibly confuse them. If you wish to be taken seriously as a person who communicates in writing, you have to give your audience a consistent point of view. This means sticking with the present or the past except when the meaning of a particular sentence demands that you shift tenses. Careful reading of your own material will enable you to accomplish this. Most errors of this type are due to lack of attention or interruption. (Answer that phone.)

In addition to **tense** inconsistency, another possible distraction for your reader comes from inconsistency of **person.** The concept of person is an important one in English. It is based on the notion that three viewpoints are possible in a situation where communication is taking place: the person who is speaking, the person who is spoken to, and the person (or thing) who is being spoken about. Each of these persons can be singular or plural.

| Person | Singular | Plural |
|--------|----------|--------|
| **First** | I | we |
| **Second** | you | you |
| **Third** | he, she, it | they |

Consider these sentences:

*I* insist on regular flossing. (first person, singular)

*We* dentists insist on regular flossing. (first person, plural)

*You,* my friend, must floss regularly. (second person, singular)

All of *you* must floss regularly. (second person, plural)

*My cousin* must floss regularly. (third person, singular)

*It* is important to floss regularly. (third person, singular)

*People* must floss regularly. (third person, plural)

All of these various points of view are useful, but you must take care not to mix them in a way that will distract and possibly confuse your audience.

## Exercise 11-4: Consistent Tense and Person

Rewrite the following paragraph. Choose one tense and one person and stick with them.

I always hated unplanned encounters. I'm standing on a street corner, minding my own business, and suddenly a raspy voice says, "Hey, Charley." I whirled around nervously. After all, you never know who might be after you. Well, who is it but my old grade school enemy Hector, walking a bit unsteadily towards me. He was the last person I wanted to see just then. In fact, you never want to see a person who always wants to borrow money. So, when I realized I couldn't get away, I start to walk slowly toward him. He just stands there, and he had that phony smile on his face, the one that seems to be saying you're too nice a person to turn me down. After a few minutes, you would have thought that the past bitterness had never happened. Soon I'm watching him as he strolled down the sidewalk, his hand clutching the money I give him. You don't feel good about the rest of the day when it started off like this, but tomorrow is bound to be better. ◆

# METHOD OF DEVELOPMENT: CLASSIFICATION

The Wheeler County Library, like all libraries, is founded on the idea that words, ideas, and expressions can be classified. Someone had to decide on what shelf *Who's*

*Your Daddy?* would be placed. Using either the Dewey Decimal System or the Library of Congress system, librarians work hard at putting everything under its appropriate heading. Classification is another of those fundamental ways that humans think. Just as we look for causes and their effects, or comparisons and contrasts, we naturally classify the parts of our life into groups and categories. As a popular bumper sticker says, "There are two kinds of people in this world: Us and the (expletives)."

Careful classification can be difficult work, but our audience will profit from the effort we put into doing it. Classifying things requires that we use our imaginations to see the best way to divide them up into handy categories. Setting up a category or categories makes the difference in everything that happens afterwards. Think, for example, of the categories used for the Oscars, as opposed to those for the Golden Globes. The differences are considerable, but they are both attempting to classify the same kinds of achievements. By choosing how to set up the classifications, a writer determines what will go into those categories.

A good example of this challenge was shown in two attempts to identify the greatest African-Americans of the last century. One listing, by the influential web site BlackVoices.com, had only one category: the 100 most influential African-Americans ranked in order of importance. Another list, this one by Chicago's famous DuSable Museum of African-American History, also attempted to list the most influential people. However, the museum's list was divided into smaller classifications such as the arts, military, business, sports, entertainment, and politics and civil rights. Because of this, the two lists were different, even though many of the same people were on both. Thus, on the first list, Dr. Martin Luther King Jr., was listed as the most influential, while on the second list he was ranked as one of the most influential in the category "Politics and Civil Rights."

## Exercise 11-5: Classification

Name two possible categories for each of the following groups. The first one has been done for you.

1.  Mariners, clippers, packers, wizards: occupations, team names
2.  Optimistic, pessimistic, realistic, fatalistic

    _____

3.  Stewardess, actress, seamstress, baroness

    _____

4.  Grumpy, bashful, happy, sneezy

    _____

5.   Lynx, sable, beetle, cougar

_____

6.   Elm, pine, hawthorn, oak

_____ ◆

## Exercise 11-6: Classification Options

Find at least three ways to classify the following. The first one has been done for you.

1.   Salespersons: <u>uninterested, rude, helpful, unavailable, experienced</u>_____
2.   Wars: _____

_____

3.   Difficult decisions: _____

_____

4.   Outlooks on life: _____

_____

5.   Healthy foods:_____

_____

6.   Unhealthy foods: _____ ◆

## Exercise 11-7: Classification in Writing

Compose an essay on one of the following topics. Indicate who your intended audience is. Be sure to have a main idea (thesis) that you are trying to convey to the reader.

1.   Types of teachers
2.   Types of bosses
3.   Types of successful TV shows
4.   Ways to organize your time
5.   Types of inspiration ◆

# CHAPTER 12

# TYPES OF COLLEGE WRITING

For the last three chapters, you have practiced writing essays. Before that you concentrated on individual paragraphs. For both jobs you used various methods of development and followed standard writing conventions. You have done this because you know your college writing career will extend far beyond this course, and your writing skills will be of greatest value in the world outside the English classroom. Here is a preview of this world, along with some tips and advice.

## ACADEMIC ESSAYS

You will be expected to write essays, long or short, for many of the courses and projects you encounter in college. Sometimes these assignments will require you to write without warning, in the classroom, and within a definite time limit. You'll hear these sobering words or something like them:

> "All right, put your books and notes away. Write an essay on the chapter assigned today in your American history text. Be sure you have a clear main idea. Be specific and give details. Write on 8½″ by 11″ paper. Write on every other line and leave a one-inch margin around the page. Don't forget to put your names on the papers. I'll collect them at the end of the period. Have a nice day."

Assuming you have read the history text chapter, you are ready to meet this teacher's expectations and turn out a solid, readable essay. Here's why:

- You have a clear idea of who your audience is. By now you have some idea of how this teacher thinks and you have had a chance to do some role playing in which you carried on imaginary conversations with him or her from your seat in the next to last row.

- You have a sense of how readers think and of how important it is to keep them on the track by sticking to a clear main idea, by organizing your material according to some useful plan, by using specific details, and by using transitional words to clarify the connections between one idea and the next.

- You have a toolbox full of ways to get material down on the page. If it fits the situation, you can use the five *W*s or any of the other methods of development you've learned. Instead of panicking and looking at the clock on the wall, ask yourself whether this might be a good place to use cause and effect, description, comparison and contrast, examples, definition, or classification. If it helps, you can use more than one of these techniques to get your ideas flowing on to the paper.

There will be times when the assigned essay is due in a week or more. You still use the same skills and techniques you have been working on in this book. Even with a busy life, you have time to do some things a bit differently than you would do under the pressure of an in-class essay. For one thing, you can get an early start on making at least a rough outline. Base it on what you think your thesis statement is going to be. Maybe jot down a couple of ideas in a rough outline, even if you have to set them all aside for a couple days. The next time you look at your notes, you may be surprised to find that your subconscious mind has been working on them somehow in the meantime. You may find that you suddenly see a much better way of putting it all together. At any rate, you now have something to work with and you don't have to begin at the last minute.

Before doing your final polishing and proofreading, set it all aside again. For the final proofreading, try to imagine that it's someone else's paper so you won't be distracted by the content. Pretend you found it where someone had left it on a park bench and you only intend to see if it has misspellings, typos, inconsistent use of tense and person, and words left out. When you turn it in, you can feel confident that it was written with care and skill.

## Debate over the Five-Paragraph Essay

The famous "five-paragraph essay" has caused a controversy among English teachers during the last couple decades. In your college writing courses, you may become exposed to this battle, even outside of your English classroom. First, recall the definition of an essay:

> A piece of writing that makes use of a number of paragraphs that are joined together according to some kind of organizational plan. All of the paragraphs work together to express and explain a main point or thesis.

A five-paragraph essay consists of an introductory paragraph, three body paragraphs, and a concluding paragraph.

Here's the debate in a nutshell: Some teachers say that five-paragraph essay writing is a useless skill since people "in the real world" don't write them. You don't put "five-paragraph essay writer" on your resume. The form is artificial and phony, so why should students practice doing it? Other teachers disagree. They concede that it is not something an employer might ask you to write, but they are convinced that the skills you develop by practicing on five-paragraph essays will be useful in any kind of writing you may undertake outside the classroom. Pianists practice by playing "useless" scales; basketball players shoot hundreds of practice free throws. In real-life situations their practice pays off.

Your feelings on the merits of five-paragraph essays may have little to do with whether or not you wind up writing them in your English classes, but you should be aware of the debate and make up your own mind. Ask your teacher what she or he thinks about it.

## Exercise 12-1: Academic Essays

Write an essay with yourself as the audience. Base it on something you are studying in another course or in one that you hope to be taking. ◆

# RESEARCH PAPERS

This book has devoted little discussion to the techniques used in doing research. However, it is a skill you will be developing as you move through your college career.

Because of the ever changing nature of computers and the Internet, the traditional methods of research presented in English textbooks only a few years ago may seem out of date. The days of typing footnotes with a typewriter, using sheets of carbon paper, and looking things up in dog-eared research guides seem almost as old-fashioned as driving a horse and buggy. Fortunately, excellent publications, both printed and online, can lead you through the research process.

Depending on your audience, you will have to become familiar with the formats that are used by different groups of researchers. For example, if you are writing something for a humanities or literature course, you may be asked to use the Modern Language Association (MLA) rules for listing page numbers, giving references, and making bibliographies. If you are researching a subject in the social sciences (history, psychology, anthropology, etc.), you may use the American Psychological Association (APA) system to present your material. More recently, a system has been introduced to be used primarily with online sources instead of books. It's been endorsed by the Alliance for Computers and Writing (ACW), and it will probably undergo changes as the world of computers and the Internet evolves. Another example, developed by the Council of Biology Editors (CBE), is suitable for research papers done in the biological sciences (anatomy, microbiology, zoology, etc.). Whether you use MLA, APA, ACW, CBE, or any other system for presenting your material, you need to remember that the basic skills of writing for an audience are the same.

## Exercise 12-2: Research

Find some information on doing research/term papers. Look in the handbook you're using for this course. Visit the college library, ask to speak to a research librarian, and get some free advice. Browse in the college bookstore and find a textbook used in the English composition course that concentrates on research papers. ◆

# ESSAY EXAMINATIONS

It will be your fate to take examinations that include essay questions. Make the most of these opportunities by using the same skills you use in longer, full-scale essays. Teachers who grade essay exams love to find answers that start with a simple statement of what the answer will contain (a topic sentence or thesis). They are more likely to be impressed by an answer that sticks to the point than by those that seem to be the work of students who are simply writing anything until they can figure out what they really want to say. Teachers also love to find answers that contain facts, specific details, and sense imagery, such as sights and sounds.

Be sure to read the question carefully before writing a word. Do some imaginary role playing with the exam's author:

What exactly are you asking me here?

By asking me this question, what are you trying to learn about my mastery of this course?

Could I possibly say something that you would consider unimportant?

Then give the question your best shot, secure in knowing that you are well equipped to communicate with your instructor.

## Exercise 12-3: Essay Examinations

Do some role playing. You're the teacher of an undergraduate course in _____, and you need to make up an essay exam for midterm. What kinds of questions are you going to ask? Ask the questions in such a way that your students can give worthwhile answers and learn something in the process. ◆

# WRITING FOR OTHER COURSES ("WRITING ACROSS THE CURRICULUM")

Not all of your collegiate writing will be done in English classes. Most of it, unless you decide to major in English, will be done for other subjects. Here again, it is most important that you think about the way people within a particular field write for each other. Scientists want to be understood and appreciated by other scientists, and therefore they write in a certain way for each other. The same is true of historians, lawyers, businesspeople, artists, football coaches, and librarians. Naturally, in all of these assignments, the audience will expect you to use standard written English and to follow the conventions of accepted spelling, grammar, and usage. Fussy English teachers are not the only people who care about these conventions.

Notice the way your textbooks say things. Pick up on the kinds of issues that are important to people within the course or professional area that you are studying. Do they use terminology that is peculiar to them, and, if so, where can you find glossaries

or lists of these terms along with their definitions? Do they take certain ideas for granted? Do people in these fields demand different kinds of evidence from each other before accepting each other's ideas? Do they use the pronouns "I" and "we" (first person) when they write, or do they express ideas as being totally objective, not based on their personal judgments? Are figures of speech—metaphors, similes, personifications—part of the way they write? Remember that in each of these fields people are writing *words*. Sure, it's possible to "write" ideas musically or mathematically by using special notation and symbols. But most of the writing you will do is verbal; it is expressed in words, and these words are available to you. You can learn how they are used by the people who use them well, and you can model your writing on their examples.

## Exercise 12-4: Writing for Other Courses

Borrow a textbook from a classmate who is taking a subject you have not yet studied. Examine the table of contents, index, notes at the ends of chapters, acknowledgments, preface, and suggestions for further reading. Try to get a sense of how the book's author relates to other people in this particular field. Can you pick up any hints about the way you would write if you wanted to sound like an expert in this field? Write down a couple words you have never seen before and look them up in your dictionary. ◆

# WRITING ABOUT LITERATURE

One of the most commonly assigned forms of college writing asks you to analyze and discuss literary works: poems, plays, short stories, novels, and certain kinds of literary essays. For instance, your instructor may tell you to write about "The Real Meaning of Robert Frost's 'Mending Wall.'" Here's an area where your ability to relate to an audience is crucial. Literary analysis and discussion have their own rules, and your audience will expect a certain kind of writing from you. You may be expected to learn specific literary terms and even certain formats that you need to follow. Whether you're writing a book report, a poetry study, or a full-fledged term paper complete with notes and source listings, you need to keep reminding yourself that the assignment is still just writing. You still need to lead your readers to see the things you want seen.

## Exercise 12-5: Learning About Literary Analysis

Here is a typical syllabus or course description for a college introduction to literature. Use it as a preview of the various ways you can write about literature.

---

**Syllabus: Introduction to Literature**

**GENERAL OBJECTIVES:** The overall objective of the Introduction to Literature course is to help students gain competence in understanding and assessing representative works of literature in various genres and to express their knowledge using the methods and terminology appropriate to a college-level exploration of literature. In addition, they will deepen their appreciation and enjoyment of literature through reading, reflection, and discussion.

**SPECIFIC OBJECTIVES:** By the end of the semester, students will have demonstrated competence in the following skills through class discussion, quizzes and examinations, as well as evaluative and/or research papers.

*(Continued)*

*(Continued from previous page)*

### Drama
- The ability to describe and analyze a play's plot/structure, characterization, dialogue, and theme.
- The ability to appreciate and discuss the history of drama, dramatic irony, and basic elements of stagecraft as they relate to the literary value of a play.

### Poetry
- The ability to discuss poems, using, where relevant, appropriate terminology for metrical and verse forms, both traditional and nontraditional.
- The ability to recognize and discuss evidence of such features as symbolism, ambiguity, imagery, figurative language, and speaker's voice.

### Fiction
- The ability to compare and contrast the characteristics of novels and short stories.
- The ability to identify and discuss such features as plot, characterization, point of view, dialogue, and theme.

### Literary Prose
- The ability to identify and discuss the characteristics and features of essays and other prose compositions, using literary criteria and terminology.

### Other
- The ability to demonstrate a nominal understanding of the various main approaches to literary criticism.
- The ability to locate and understand literary works within their history and traditions.
- The ability to discuss the validity of such concepts as "good" and "great" literature, within the context of personal taste, subjectivity, objectivity, and historical milieu.

Now that you've read through this document, do the following:

1. Underline any words you don't know.
2. Put checkmarks next to four of the specific objectives that you think you would find most interesting.

3. Put an X next to the four specific objectives that you think you would find most difficult. (Were any of them also among the most interesting?)

4. Is there any way that this syllabus could be improved to make it more valuable to the course's incoming students?

_____

_____

_____◆

## Exercise 12-6: Writing About Literature

Here is a famous poem, one that is contained in many textbooks used for Introduction to Literature courses. Read it slowly and think about it as if it were one of the cases we have read in this book.

### Richard Cory
*by Edwin Arlington Robinson*

Whenever Richard Cory went downtown,
We people on the pavement looked at him:
He was a gentleman from sole to crown,
Clean favored and imperially slim.

And he was always quietly arrayed.
And he was always human when he talked.
But still he fluttered pulses when he said,
"Good morning," and he glittered when he walked.

And he was rich—yes, richer than a king—
And admirably schooled in every grace:
In fine, we thought that he was everything
To make us wish that we were in his place.

So on we worked and waited for the light,
And went without the meat, and cursed the bread;
And Richard Cory, one calm summer night,
Went home and put a bullet through his head.

1897

Based on your reading of "Richard Cory," do one or more of the following assignments.

1.  Treat Richard Cory as a case, like the other cases in this book. Analyze the situation it describes as if it were an actual set of occurrences, and list the kinds of writing that might have taken place. For instance, what would the opening paragraph of a newspaper story say about this famous citizen's death? Was there a suicide note, and, if so, what would someone as private as Richard Cory say about himself? Set up some role playing in a conversation that includes three of these people: Richard Cory's next door neighbor, his pastor, a distant relative, the mayor of the town, and—if by some miracle he is available for this exercise—Richard Cory himself.

2.  Write a five-paragraph essay on this poem. As with paragraphs and other essays, you should decide on a unifying main idea you want to get across and then try to stick to it. Write plainly and directly, but don't be afraid to model your writing on that of writers you enjoy reading. In fact, some of the things that poets, novelists, and playwrights do best can make their way into your writing. Don't be afraid to experiment with words. Poets surprise us with their ability to make words do new things. Authors of fiction and drama have an ability to see through the eyes of others. Isn't that what you have been attempting to do throughout this course as you took on different points of view in the cases?

3.  Pick another literary work—poem, play, novel, story—and write a five-paragraph essay on it. Your audience is your fellow classmates. In writing about literature, don't forget that it is meant to be enjoyed and appreciated, not dissected like a laboratory frog. Your ability to read for pleasure will help you give pleasure to your audience. ◆

---

**Visit the Longman Englishpages!**

For additional readings, practice exercises, Internet links, and activities, visit us online at
**http://www.ablongman.com/englishpages**

# ADDITIONAL RESOURCES FOR WRITERS

# APPENDIX A

# ADDITIONAL CASES FOR STUDY

These cases will help you sharpen your writing skills. Some focus on specific objectives. Use the skills you developed in Chapters 1, 2, 3, and 8. It might be a good idea to take another look at those chapters. Remember, the approach you have been using is the following:

1. Read the case and discuss the questions it raises.
2. Explore the key terms.
3. Examine the points of view of people involved in the case through role playing.
4. Develop models of the kind of documents that might be written by the people in the case.
5. Write paragraphs or essays based on the case or on the issues raised by the case. Revise, polish, proofread, and let your finished products make you feel that you've accomplished something worthwhile.
6. Demonstrate your skill in using the writing conventions and methods of developments you have been studying.

 ## Case I: CREDIT CARD PROBLEMS

You stand at the checkout counter of a large department store. Your purchases (two gallons of latex interior wall paint, two paint roller replacements, and a roll of one-inch masking tape) sit on the counter in front of

*(Continued)*

(*Continued from previous page*)

you. As you daydream about how long it will take you to paint your bed-room, you realize that your purchase still hasn't been approved. You've been standing there for a while now, and the people in line behind you are getting restless. You look back at them and they stare at you.

Finally, the clerk turns from the computer screen and says, "I'm sorry. Do you have any other way to pay?"

You don't. This is how you expected to pay. You left your checkbook at home, and now you're starting to feel very uncomfortable. One of the peo-ple waiting behind you giggles softly. This time when you look back at them, they look away.

Exactly what happens next will be hard for you to recall when you try to tell the story to your family and friends. You have a confused, angry rec-ollection of arguing briefly with the clerk, snatching your credit card back, slamming one paint can against the other, and walking out of the store, pre-tending to be cool but feeling foolish.

You know for sure that you paid your charge account bill on time, so you stay angry. But, over the next few weeks, several events unfold:

- You send a letter to the store protesting this injustice.

- The store's credit manager sends a form letter suggesting that you are at fault but assuring you that everything can be "taken care of." There is a toll-free phone number you can call to discuss your account if you wish.

- Instead, you send the store an angrier (or firmer?) letter. At the bot-tom of the letter you indicate that you have sent a copy of it to a law firm (whose name you may have just invented).

- You receive a personal letter from the store's credit manager, J. H. Randall, admitting that a "human error" resulted in "the misunder-standing." Attached to this letter is a form letter that identifies you as a "special customer," and attached to the form letter is a small gift certificate as a token of appreciation for your continued patronage.

- You write the store a polite letter informing the management that you are taking your business elsewhere. It feels very good at the time, but you know you may be tempted to go back sometime in the future.

Your bedroom could still use a fresh coat of paint.

## Analyzing the Case

Depending on your personal history, you might find this case harder than some others to consider objectively. If you have never done battle with a large computerized database or credit bureau, consider yourself lucky and try to put yourself in the position of the would-be paint purchaser. If you have been on the receiving end of "Second Notices" or even bill collectors, you can identify with the victim and still realize that this is a fairly harmless case. Either way, you have to analyze a situation that may have some right and wrong on both sides. Does the customer overreact? Does the store treat the customer like a faceless number? What happens to the store's credit manager when he goes home and finds an erroneous second notice from the phone company? Does the customer's version of this episode become an exaggerated dragon slaying when it is told to friends and relatives? What would you have done? What *have* you done?

## Key Terms

computer error
customer loyalty
customer relations
customer service
human error
impersonal operation
justifiable resentment
overreaction
public relations
revolving charge

Explore the meaning of these terms, using your dictionary where possible. Discuss them with your teacher and classmates. Do any of them have current meanings that differ from their dictionary definitions?

## Questions for In-Class Writing or Discussion

1. It's obvious that automation has streamlined and improved every part of merchandising. Are there also disadvantages to this kind of record keeping and purchasing that people tend to overlook? Which people?
2. What is going through the minds of the people in line behind the victim? Do their thoughts and attitudes change as they see this mini-drama play

itself out? Would you have giggled? Would you have felt superior? Sympathetic? Annoyed? Compassionate? All of the above?

3.   Who is at fault? Should the customer have had the common sense to carry a checkbook or a major credit card? Are there "power games" going on here—maybe on both sides of the dispute?

4.   Are computerized buying and transacting business basically impersonal? If so, should customers who feel offended ever make it personal? Is the possibility of gaining revenge on a large agency—store, corporation, government agency, etc.—something to be relished? Or is this a childish impulse?

5.   Are there certain kinds of people who should not use credit cards and charge accounts? Are you one of those people? What about the fact that online transactions make it almost essential that you have a credit card? Is that an entirely good thing?

## Role Playing

Put yourself inside the credit card problems case. If your own personal experiences help you, use them. Remember that writing effectively always means writing for someone and having a clear image of who that audience is. Knowing your audience, whether it consists of one person or many, means that you can make good judgments about word choice, about the kind of language you should use, and about what might work best in a particular case. Try once again to get inside some of the characters involved in this case.

To understand this case, put yourself into the shoes—and minds—of some of the people listed here. If you have time, take another look at the material on audiences in Chapter 1 and on role playing in Chapter 2.

- The clerk at the paint counter. This person, who is probably paid only a modest salary, is in a difficult spot. Definite procedures are spelled out for situations like the one described in this case, but the possibility of messing things up always exists. How much exercise of authority is just right, without seeming to insult the customer? What happens if the customer protests loudly or insists on a specific resolution?

- The store's credit manager. This mid-level manager has to enforce policy but be ready to make exceptions. How difficult is it for a person in such a job to remain impersonal? Should it be considered a "defeat" if a customer merits an apology? Can such decisions ever become personal?

- The customer. How angry should someone get in a situation like this? Would it be more realistic and mature to simply say, "Oh, sorry," walk away from the counter, and assume that the store will work it all out fairly? Should the customer resent the fact that people waiting in line seemed to be amused by the embarrassing situation? Was it really amusement or just nervous laughter?

- A first-year college student who also shops at this store. She has recently received four separate offers from credit card companies. Each of them is willing to grant up to $2,000 credit with no co-signer and no questions asked. This student is not sure what to do.

## Exercises

1. Stage an imaginary conversation between two of the people listed previously. Give them names and make up a believable background for them. Have them ask each other about their own reactions to the particular case and to the larger questions it raises. Try to be as specific and detailed as possible. Be imaginative; don't be afraid of the humorous, embarrassing, and possibly unexpected details that may come out in such a conversation. Have at least one observer take notes and ask questions of one or the other to keep the conversation going.

2. Interview the unlucky customer. Try to determine the person's motivation. Was it a simple desire for justice, or was it a response to being embarrassed? Use your detective skills by asking indirect questions. For example, don't ask, "How did you feel when your charge was refused?" Instead, ask, "Do you think most people would have reacted the way you did?" Don't be afraid to fumble around a bit, and be willing to keep your sense of humor handy. There is plenty of time to be serious when you finally start carefully putting words on paper.

3. Stage a conversation between a checkout clerk trainee and a floor supervisor. Try to anticipate the kinds of problems that may arise because of unhappy customers. Reassure each other.

4. The credit manager from the store in question and another one from a store the first one used to work at are having lunch together. They start trading "war stories" about problem customers they have dealt with in the past. Use your imagination, even if some of the examples start putting a strain on reality.

## Writing Assignments

1.  This store's employee manual has a section (*Section G*) on dealing with customers whose credit is refused. Section G gives the sales staff some guidelines on being firm but courteous, even if a customer becomes abusive, but it's written in a wordy, bureaucratic tone. Without reading Section G, write three or four sentences in which you give employees some basic advice on dealing with problem customers. Write something that you might find useful if you were a salesperson. For instance, when should a manager or supervisor be asked to step in to handle a situation?

2.  Here is a letter from the store's *former* sales manager to another customer.

Not surprisingly, Mr. McNabb has been replaced. Rewrite his letter, saving any parts that you think are acceptable.

3.  The new credit manager, J. H. Diaz, has developed a form letter to handle cases like the one we're following. In it, he tries to be polite but to leave no doubt about the customer's obligation. Write the letter Mr. Diaz sent to our unhappy victim.

4.  Another letter, a form letter, apologizes to customers who have mistakenly been inconvenienced. It assures them that they are special and that the store wants their continued patronage. Write at least the opening paragraph of this letter.

5.  Invent a role and a situation related to this case that call for a particular piece of writing, and then write it. Use your imagination and explore some of the less obvious persons who have been touched by the credit card adventures. How about a letter to the Office of Consumer Affairs of the state's Attorney General, complaining about the store's shabby service? Is there enough evidence to make an accusation?

 ## CASE II: EMPLOYEE PERFORMANCE REVIEW

It began as a "mom and pop" company in 1956, but J&T Manufacturing Company has certainly grown. It started out in a storefront on 19th Street and grew to occupy three-quarters of the block. Recently, ground was

*(Continued)*

## *Clark's Department Store*

*1000 N. State Street, Boise ID, Phone: 555-CLARK*

October 23, 2001

Mr. Robert Wise
467 Glenwood Blvd.
Boise, ID 34567

Account No. 73 GT 400076

Dear Mr. Wise:

As we have informed you, more than once, your payment record is terrible. Why are you so irresponsible? Maybe you think we'll get tired of reminding you. Well, think again.

Our records show that you still have an outstanding balance of $119.76. We expect you to pay up. We are enclosing duplicate copies of your last three billing statements. If you have any questions, don't hesitate to call my office.

Cordially,

Arthur "Art" McNabb

enc.
cc: Georgette Brown
     Norton Pape

AM/jt

(*Continued from page 160*)

broken for a brand new building half a mile away that will contain administrative offices, research and development, and improved warehouse space. The company is now run by the children of the founding partners, and it employs 134 people, of whom 92 are full-timers.

There have been many changes from "the good old days." This is no longer a company where everybody knows everybody else. Therefore, J&T's Human Resources Department, which used to be called Personnel, decided to institute a more organized system of performance review. Every employee, from the vice presidents on down, would be evaluated according to a new, systematic method. Everyone was assured that this would result in an even better J&T Manufacturing. However, rumors began to float around, and some lower-ranking employees were nervous. So were some of the people in the Human Resources Department.

To start the process, a memo was sent to supervisors informing them that they would be expected to review their subordinates and that the supervisors themselves would also be subject to review. A consulting firm, Interhuman Resources, Ltd., was hired to advise the company on its new project. At the first meeting with J&T executives, Lola Chen, Interhuman's representative, informed her audience that this new process would result in increased productivity and a happier workforce. They wanted to hear more.

Interhuman gave J&T a set of ready-made forms to use for the evaluation process. J&T's president, Fred Torque, Jr., thanked the consultant but insisted that supervisors would be allowed to have some input on changing these forms if they wished.

Meanwhile, rumors continued to circulate in the shop and on the loading docks about what these new procedures might mean. There was some talk of organizing a union, but not much came of it.

Finally, the first attempt at implementing the procedure began. Within four months, every employee of J&T—not counting Mr. Torque and his partner, of course—had been evaluated. Some bugs needed to be worked out of the system, but most people had to admit that it had gone pretty well. The vice president of Human Resources, Jack Trikonis, wrote a memo to his staff congratulating them on a good start. Mr. Torque's assistant was given the job of putting out a desktop-publishing, no-frills company newsletter.

The front page of the first issue carried the hopeful headline "Employees Praise New HR Review."

. . . . . . .

One year later, the new procedure had directly affected every level of the company in the form of raises, pay cuts, promotions, demotions, firings, increased bonuses, decreased bonuses, and an overflowing suggestion box near the snack bar/kitchenette. Some of the suggestions were constructive; some were not. All were anonymous.

## Analyzing the Case

Change may be unavoidable, and it is often painful. What someone calls progress may look like a step backward to another. How would you see the changing face of J&T Manufacturing Co.'s management if you were an employee? Does this look like a reasonable approach to handling a growing operation, or do you see it as an attempt by impersonal bosses to be demanding and over-controlling? Notice how much the perception of written words depends on the relationship between a particular audience and the person writing for it.

## Key Terms

accountability
compensation
feedback
goals and objectives
human resources
measurable objective
merit
performance appraisal
performance rating
professional growth
seniority

Explore the meaning of these terms, using your dictionary where possible. Discuss them with your teacher and classmates. Do any of them have current meanings that differ from their dictionary definitions?

## Questions for In-Class Writing or Discussion

1. Is it possible for a "superior" to fairly judge an "inferior," or is such a concept unfair by its very nature? Some definitions are needed to discuss this, wouldn't you say?

2. List some qualities of a good manager and match them up with the appropriate qualities of a good subordinate. For example, is the approach to leading and following used by the military a good one for businesses to model themselves on? Why or why not?

3. How have you been affected by performance review in your working life? Was it handled formally or informally? Was it fair?

4. How does performance review in the workplace compare with the idea of giving grades to students? Are there basic differences or do both systems attempt to accomplish the same objectives?

5. When should performance review be a two-way street? For example, should students review the performance of their teachers? How about employees reviewing their bosses? How about children reviewing their parents? Should moviemakers get to review the movie critics?

## Role Playing

Put yourself inside the employee performance review case. Have you been officially evaluated by a boss, or have you been asked to evaluate someone yourself? Did you (or your boss) choose your words carefully? Try once again to get inside some of the characters involved in this case.

- Mr. Torque, the company's president, who has been around long enough to be convinced that this new system is a worthwhile gamble for the growing company.

- A 15-year employee who was one of the few minority workers at the time of his hiring. He is convinced that his supervisor is prejudiced and will use the performance review unfairly.

- A mid-level employee in the Human Resources Department who worked previously at another company where this kind of change was instituted. She thinks the new system will work out better at J&T than it did at her previous job.

- A shop foreperson, who has a pretty good feeling for the sentiments and reactions of people on the assembly line.

- An employee who is aware that she has been just getting by without much effort or initiative. She starts to think about updating her resume and looking for another job.

- The bartender at Mimi's Tap, across the street from the company's parking lot. Over the years she has learned a great deal about the feelings and opinions of J&T's workers, especially on paydays.

Has practice in role playing made you any more perceptive about other people's actions and reactions in your daily life?

## Exercises

1. Stage an imaginary conversation between two of the people listed previously. Try to be as specific and detailed as possible. Be imaginative; don't be afraid of the humorous, embarrassing, and possibly unexpected details that may come out in such a conversation. Have at least one observer take notes and ask questions of one or the other to keep the conversation going.

2. Interview one of the workers who was most fearful of this new system before it was put into place. Start with questions that are more indirect than direct, such as, "What do you think most of your fellow workers expected when they first heard about this?" Try to get at some real issues and find out whether or not the interviewee's fears were justified. Keep your sense of humor handy.

3. Stage a conversation between a husband and wife. One of them is an employee of J&T. The other is employed by a company that recently had its employee evaluation process revamped; this person tries to reassure the J&T spouse—or to warn about the terrible things that might happen. Use your imagination.

4. It's 5:30 P.M. on a Friday, payday. Two employees have been at Mimi's Bar since about 4:45, discussing the new evaluation procedures with the bartender. What might the employees and bartender be saying?

## Writing Assignments

1. Early in the process of switching to this new system, a brief notice was put into the pay envelopes of J&T employees, informing them about it. Write the notice. What kind of tone was the company trying to get across to its workers?

2.  Your supervisor has asked you to write a short statement listing your strengths and weaknesses. Make up some of each, but be careful about listing your weaknesses. They may come back to haunt you. Think carefully of your audience as you make this list.

3.  As an assistant to President Torque, one of your new duties is to put out a company newsletter. Write the first paragraph of the article that shows how much the employees love this new system. Remember, you've got to get your story approved by Mr. Torque; what does he want it to say? How truthful can you be in choosing your details?

4.  You're the supervisor of a "difficult" employee in the truck dispatching office. This is the kind of person who has always turned fellow employees into enemies. As you fill out the form, you put checkmarks in the unsatisfactory column for quite a few categories. At the end of the form, you are to write a paragraph that sums up your evaluation. You and the employee will both read this paragraph, discuss it, and then sign the form. What does the paragraph say?

5.  Write a short composition that takes a stand, pro or con, on this statement: "When people go to work for a company, they agree to do things the 'company's way,' whether or not they completely agree with it."

 ## CASE III: HELPING THE TEACHERS

Oliphant Elementary School recently changed its name to Rosa Parks Elementary School. Located in the inner city of a large metropolitan area, the school has had its problems, but now a feeling of optimism accompanies the name change. This spirit comes, in part, from the formation of a new school council of local parents, teachers, and community activists. The council has vowed to help make the school a good one and has informed the principal, Dr. Thigpen, that it expects improvements in tests scores over the next few years.

One of the major parts of the council's plan is a group of volunteer teacher aides who will do much more than babysit. Not surprisingly, the teachers are happy to hear this, although they are concerned that they will continue to control what goes on in their classrooms. Some council members say they will hold the teachers "accountable to the community" and make sure they understand "whose school it is." The teachers, for their part, have decided to wait and see whether or not their new helpers really help.

The school board "downtown" has decided to observe closely, both officially and unofficially, and not to interfere, at least for the time being. If this program turns out to produce positive results, the board will seek to expand it to other schools. If it fails—well, it wasn't their idea anyway.

As the group of helpers (called "classroom associates," or CAs) continues to be organized and the council works out its plan of operation, everyone associated with the school runs into some problems and experiences some successes. For example:

- As in many groups, people's egos begin to get in the way. One school council member in particular, Vice President Tyrone Anthony, has decided that he will personally oversee the organizing and supervising of the CAs. With a bachelor's degree from a local college, he is better educated than many of the local neighborhood residents, and he says his experience has taught him "most of the mistakes that teachers make." He expects to pass this wisdom on to the CAs.

- Another council member, Laverne Bledsoe, is not so sure. She argues with Anthony and insists that the teachers know what kind of help they need and what will be most helpful for the children. Other council members and would-be CAs find themselves falling somewhere in between these two viewpoints.

- Position papers are written by the council. The children will take these documents home to their parents in preparation for a community meeting in the school auditorium.

- Principal Thigpen attaches her own letter to this packet and thanks the parents for their interest in the work of the administration and faculty. She assures them that their children are "the most important people involved in this great effort."

- At the meeting, parents and others are asked to volunteer for CA duty. Those who are interested are to write a statement (no more than 300 words) that sets forth their qualifications and their

*(Continued)*

*(Continued from previous page)*

reasons for wanting to be trained as classroom associates. By the end of the two-week deadline, the council has received 16 letters.

- When the council has assembled all the applications, it is clear that some hard choices must be made. Council President Sandra Parker prepares a memo in which she tries to focus the problem. She realizes that, based on the written statements, it will be difficult to choose the best candidates for the 12 positions they hope to fill. For instance, the persons with the best educational qualifications don't always come across in their statements as well as some who clearly have educational shortcomings but good ideas. Careful interviewing is needed before the final choices are made.

- Another memo, this one to the teachers, asks for their input and requests that they supply one or two people to participate on the interview committee.

Finally, just before Labor Day, all the work has been done for the first full school year of the new program. The CAs have been given their final instructions and assignments. They have met with the faculty members they will assist and even helped to get the bulletin boards ready and decorated for opening day. The big clock on the classroom wall is ticking, and all is ready for the beginning of school.

How it will turn out depends on luck, hard work, and lots of honesty and goodwill.

## Analyzing the Case

Some people who volunteer for public service have motives that are not completely unselfish. Sure, they want to do good and to help others, but they also want to push their own agendas. This case is a good example of a situation where different motives result in a lot of words being written and reacted to. For example, if you're a teacher who might suddenly be given a helper who is much better than you at dealing with children, would you welcome this person with open arms? Or might you feel a bit threatened? When professionals and paraprofessionals work together, the result should be mutual respect, but it can be tension. Local schools, especially, are places that raise strong emotions because they serve the community's most valuable commodity, its children. The emotional power that elementary school generates in all of us as first graders carries over into our lives as adults. We hope it's balanced by adult doses of maturity and goodwill.

## Key Terms

curriculum
extracurricular
idealism
interaction
lesson plan
oversight
paraprofessional
partnership
professional
shared governance

Explore the meaning of these terms, using your dictionary where possible. Discuss them with your teacher and classmates. Do any of them have current meanings that differ from their dictionary definitions?

## Questions for In-Class Writing or Discussion

1. You've heard the expression, "Politics is too important to be left to the politicians." Could it also be said that education is too important to be left to the educators? Does your own experience explain your answer to this question?

2. Should educational responsibility belong to the lowest, grassroots level of the community, or should it be reserved for an overall organization, such as a municipal school board that has the wisdom of professionals at its disposal? Does this question deserve more than a simple, either/or answer?

3. Should teachers, including college teachers, share the responsibility for what goes on in the classroom by asking their students to help plan and develop the course and its materials?

4.  Is the emphasis on standardized tests in elementary school a good thing? Is it fair to compare all local schools on the basis of their students' performance on these tests?

5.  Politicians are fond of saying that "nothing is more important than the education of our children." Are they right? Do they mean what they say?

## Role Playing

Put yourself inside this case and find what the people involved in it are thinking as they prepare to write and talk about it. Do some role playing using these characters:

- Charles Jones, whose son Lyle is in the second grade. Mr. Jones has a high school education and works the night shift in a factory, but he wants to make a contribution, so he is going to apply to be a CA.

- Tyrone Anthony, vice president of the school council, who is pretty sure he knows what it will take "to get even the laziest teachers to do their jobs."

- Principal Thigpen, who hopes she can keep this experiment "under control" without offending anyone. What does she mean by control?

- Inez McGee, who is Lyle Jones second grade teacher. She hopes the CA assigned to her class will help her do her job and not get in the way.

- Laverne Bledsoe, another council member, who is helping Principal Thigpen develop the material that is being sent home with the children.

- Dorothy Clark, a college junior and a graduate of Rosa Parks Elementary School when it was named Oliphant. She's hoping to get a degree in education and maybe even wind up teaching at her old school.

## Exercise

1.  Stage an imaginary conversation between any two of the people listed above. They have met by the complimentary coffee pot in the area outside Principal Thigpen's office.

2.  Mr. Anthony and Ms. McGee recognize each other in the school hallway and begin to talk. Their conversation starts out politely. Does it continue that way?

3.  Mr. Jones is explaining to his wife why he wants to become a CA. She does not wish to be one herself. What do they say to each other?

4.  Ms. Bledsoe and Principal Thigpen are trying to decide what goes into the packet of materials to be sent home with the children explaining this new program.

## Writing Assignments

1.  Charles Jones is filling out his application to be a CA. After several questions about his qualifications, he is asked to write a paragraph. "In your own words," it says, "tell us why you think you would be able to help the children of Rosa Parks Elementary School." What does he say?
2.  Imagine that you are applying to be a CA at your own elementary school. How would you respond to the question asked in number 1?
3.  An assistant superintendent at the "downtown" office of the school district sends Principal Thigpen a memo, asking her to keep them posted on the progress and success of this experiment. Ms. Thigpen is a bit annoyed by the tone of the memo. What does it say?
4.  A woman who has been a CA for a year sends a letter to her sister in Youngstown. Two paragraphs of her letter are devoted to this new adventure. What does she say?
5.  Write an essay on one of the issues raised by this case. The audience is your fellow classmates.

 ## CASE IV: TWENTIETH REUNION

Nineteen years have passed since the class of 1982 graduated from Fred R. Remmy High School, a class that considered itself one of the school's finest. While it may be true that every class sees itself as worthy of this title, this one has some good reasons to celebrate itself. Many of its 297 graduating seniors went on to lead interesting, valuable lives, and a few of them achieved a bit of fame—a fairly successful rock musician, a congresswoman, and an NBA sixth-man who retired after five years in the league.

Now, as they see their 40s approaching, some of the graduates want finally to have a reunion worthy of their illustrious class. Previous attempts have been flops, although few like to admit it. Their tenth, for example, was

*(Continued)*

*(Continued from previous page)*

memorable only because the decorations fell from the rafters of the gymnasium, wounding their class president as he was introducing some favorite teachers.

The main problem, however, has been lack of turnout and even lack of response to mailings and promotional materials. The organizers hope that this year—their twentieth—they'll have the reunion they deserve.

Remmy has no formal alumni office, and the board of education is not much help either, so it's up to each class to arrange its own reunions. Here are some of the things that can make it happen:

- Early in the spring of 2001, a group of the most active alumni get together. A few of them have settled in the school's neighborhood, and many of them live close enough that they have stayed in touch over the years. Ward Lackowski, their class president (now bearing only a tiny scar on his forehead), contacts a number of his friends by phone and suggests that they meet at a local sports bar. There, a dozen people (seven men, five women) draw up a list of tasks and who should do them. They settle on a date and work out a schedule of events that will begin with a Friday night party at this very sports bar and end with a Sunday afternoon golf outing. The high point will be a Saturday night dance and buffet at the school.

- A letter is sent to the current principal of Remmy asking her permission to hold the reunion once again in the gym. (This time decorations will be held with double-strength duct tape.)

- A small group contacts the local and neighborhood newspapers to publicize the affair. One of the graduates writes to a cousin in Chicago who works in public relations, asking advice on how to handle the local media.

- One subgroup of alumni works on plans for a commemorative program booklet. They make a list of information to be included in the booklet, and they work on a letter to ask local business-people to buy advertising space in it. One of the business owners, a local Chevrolet dealer whose wife went to Remmy, composes a message that will take up a full page in the booklet. He realizes that he has mixed motives for buying the space.

- A letter is sent to as many of the class of '81 as possible. Recipients are asked to supply data on themselves (spouses, children, accomplishments, etc.) and addresses of any classmates the committee has been unable to track down. This letter seeks to set a happy, positive tone for the whole reunion. It promises "a great time for all."

- As graduates receive their invitations, they respond in various ways. Some immediately throw theirs into the wastebasket with the junk mail. Some read it over several times, sigh to themselves, stare out the window a few minutes—and then throw it out. Many, however, start thinking about how to respond. A few will volunteer to help with the preparations and even suggest tasks they might do to be useful. Others write cautious, uncomfortable letters, feeling that they are communicating with people they barely remember and never really liked anyway. A good number of respondents are truly happy that this event is in the works. They look forward to seeing their old friends and reminiscing about the good times at Remmy.

Finally the festive weekend arrives. The reunion is a great success. At Principal Ellington's request, Congresswoman Martinez reads a short, positive statement that spreads the thanks and the glory around to include everyone in the class of '81. Those who stick around for the golf outing say they don't want to go home.

Afterwards, one of the attendees writes a bright, funny letter to a friend who was unable to make it. The letter contains separate paragraphs on the high and low points of the celebration. It concludes with some reflections on the next reunion, the twenty-fifth.

## Analyzing the Case

If you've entered college straight out of high school, you may have some trouble identifying with these people. The kinds of things they are writing, however, are typical of anyone who is trying to solve problems or motivate someone else to do something. You can certainly identify with that.

The class of '81 is like other groups in its individuality and its sameness. Certain people tend to take charge, whether they are best qualified to do so or not. People's memories are selective; they remember the good times as being very good and the bad ones as awful. Twenty years beyond high school seems an eternity to some and a blip to others, especially to those who've been busy and involved during the interval. Now all of these classmates, or at least as many as can be tracked down, have a chance to reflect on who they once were and who they've become. They're bound to react differently, and their written expression will be different. Reunions are a good time for honesty and realism, if possible. The things that seemed extremely important back then—who sat with whom in the cafeteria—are now seen as trifling. The formerly cool may now be beer-bellied and ordinary, but they may be better than cool because they have come to terms with their lives and their futures. As you analyze this case, you should find yourself hoping that a group like this will have a worthwhile reunion and handle it like the solid adults they have become.

## Key Terms

accomplishment
alumnae
alumni
commemorative
clique
peer group
perspective
recollection
reminiscence
school spirit

Explore the meaning of these terms, using your dictionary where possible. Discuss them with your teacher and classmates. Do any of them have current meanings that differ from their dictionary definitions?

## Questions for In-Class Writing or Discussion

1.  Do adults basically continue to be what they were as high school seniors, or do they usually grow to be someone very different? How do you know?
2.  Is success in high school a good indication of how a person's life will turn out? How would you define *success?* Does your definition change as you age? What things stay the same?

3.  Why might it be more difficult to plan a school reunion than a good-sized regional sales meeting of a corporation? What are the differences and similarities?

4.  How would a high school reunion have a different "flavor" than that of, for instance, a college reunion or even a reunion of old military service buddies?

5.  Many people coming back for a high school reunion are more nervous and self-conscious than they would be for a college reunion. Why do you think this is?

## Role Playing

Regardless of your age, put yourself inside this reunion case. If your own personal experiences help you, use them. As you've discovered by now, writing effectively always means writing for someone and having a clear image of who that audience is. Knowing your audience, whether it consists of one person or many, means that you can make good judgments about word choice, about the kind of language you should use, and about what might work best in a particular case. Try once again to get inside some of the characters involved in this case. You're getting better at this, aren't you?

- A member of the small group that spearheads this reunion. He realizes that there is a lot of work to do, but he feels a sense of responsibility. He still cares about his school and his classmates, even after 20 years.

- A 64-year-old chemistry teacher who has been asked to show up and be recognized by the students he taught in the 1980s. He spends half an hour looking through old yearbooks in the school library and finds some familiar faces. What will he say to them?

- A graduate who has since moved halfway across the country. She gets the mailing and wishes she could attend the reunion. She wonders whether her husband, who is not a Remmy graduate, would accompany her.

- A local business owner who discusses with his partner whether or not to spend the $250 for a full-page ad in the commemorative booklet. He decides not to do it.

- Someone, accompanied by a spouse, who runs into a high school sweetheart. It seems that the old flame is newly divorced and the meeting starts to bring back a lot of memories. What happens next? Who says what to whom?

## Exercises

1.  Stage an imaginary conversation between two of the people listed previously. Give them names and make up a believable background for them. Have them ask each other about their own reactions to the particular case and to the larger questions it raises. Try to be as specific and detailed as possible. Be imaginative; don't be afraid of the humorous, embarrassing, and possibly unexpected details that may come out in such a conversation. Have at least one observer take notes and ask questions of one or the other to keep the conversation going.

2.  Interview the student who wins one of the prizes handed out at the gymnasium dance, maybe the one for "least changed" or "longest distance traveled."

3.  Stage a conversation between two graduates. One of them thinks that he or she will be embarrassed or uncomfortable at the reunion because of (choose one): appearance, current income level, marital status, or educational level. The other grad tries to persuade the classmate to come anyway.

4.  During the dance there is a ceremony honoring various people, awarding semi-serious prizes, and recalling the good old days. Someone gets up and gives a short speech that turns out to be inappropriate and embarrassing. People laugh, but it's nervous laughter. What does the person say?

## Writing Assignments

1.  The chemistry teacher is asked to give a brief speech accepting his award as "favorite teacher." He writes it out in longhand. He tries to write it in such a way that he might be able to use parts of it in similar situations if they should arise. That means he uses general ideas. Write a paragraph of his speech and then, if it sounds dull, spice it up a bit by adding some details about one or more of the graduates he remembers best or maybe how he felt at his own twentieth reunion in 1972.

2.  Remmy's principal, Dr. Ellington, has a form letter she has used in the past in corresponding with reunion groups. She finds it in her file and tells her secretary to make the appropriate changes ("class of '81," etc.). What does it say? What commitments does she make concerning her own time and the school's resources?

3.  Write the letter that the organizing group sends to local businesses asking them to buy advertising space in the commemorative booklet. What can they say that will be most effective?

4.    The student in another part of the country writes the organizers a letter of regret. It is so honest and open that parts of it are read at the awards ceremony. Write at least the opening and closing paragraphs.

5.    Invent a role and a situation related to this case that call for a particular piece of writing, and then write it. Use your imagination and explore some of the less obvious persons who have been touched by the twentieth reunion.

---

 # Case V: The Hometown Champs

After many years of fielding mediocre teams, South Summit High amazes the town's fans by sending its Ground Squirrels to the state Class B football finals. What's even more amazing is that they win. They become the state champions in their division. Now what? One successful season is not enough to prepare the citizens of South Summit for all the good and bad consequences of success. But they learn fast.

Because of this championship season, many things happen. Here are some of them:

- The local government, in cooperation with the school administration, makes plans for an "Honor Your Ground Squirrels Day." The festivities come off with only a few minor glitches, and the townspeople are pleased.

- Local politicians and civic leaders attempt to take their share of the credit for the team's success and to do what they can to guarantee its future glory—and theirs.

- South Summit merchants discover that profiting from the success of a local team is possible but not always predictable.

- The nine-member marching band and its director decide that they should recruit new members and buy new uniforms.

- Middle-aged former high school athletes find themselves remembering how their teams compared with the new champs. Their memories aren't completely accurate.

*(Continued)*

(*Continued from previous page*)

- School officials are pressured by a number of alumni and parents to guarantee another winning season, "no matter what it takes."

- The South Summit High Department of English and Speech suggests to the principal that its debate and forensics team ought to have an increase in travel funds so that they too can bring glory to the town.

- The football coach receives mail from many sources; some of them are unexpected.

Unfortunately, a year later South Summit loses in the final minutes of its local league championship game. After that it doesn't make it to the state tournament again. There are still some "Go Squirrels" sweatshirts on the shelves in Parker's Department Store on Main Street.

## Analyzing the Case

This case is complex because it involves many different groups who feel that they are united but who have different self-interests. Their motives may be good ones, but they are definitely not the same. Because of this variety, you must figure out the differing motivations for the target audiences for written communication. For example, which residents of South Summit are happier than others because of the team's success? Which ones will find it hardest to accept defeat, having once tasted victory? Who will handle the whole situation with the most common sense?

## Key Terms

athleticism
booster/boosterism
civic pride
commercialism
competition
educational priorities
exploitation
fan loyalty
identification
sportsmanship

Explore the meaning of these terms, using your dictionary where possible. Discuss them with your teacher and classmates. Do any of them have current meanings that differ from their dictionary definitions?

## Questions for In-Class Writing or Discussion

1.  What are the rewards of being a loyal fan? Do these benefits differ for people of different ages?
2.  An old saying warns, "Be careful what you ask for. You might get it." Could this warning have been useful for some of the hopeful fans of South Summit or for any community that pins its civic hopes on its local teams?
3.  Can fan loyalty be abused or taken too far?
4.  Will all the memories of the championship season carried into adulthood by these students of South Summit High be good ones? Will they change as the students get older?
5.  How does "school spirit" change as a person goes through different stages of life?
6.  Is fan loyalty to a team similar to the loyalty and team spirit one has toward an employer? What are the major differences?

## Role Playing

Remember that writing effectively means writing for someone and having a clear image of who that audience is. Knowing your audience, whether it consists of one person or many, means that you can make good judgments about word choice, about the kind of language you should use, and about what might work best in a particular case. Try once again to get inside some of the characters involved in this case. As in athletics, you get better at this with practice.

*   A South Summit football player. He is not a star, but he has made his contribution to the team's success, including a third quarter interception in the championship game. He will consider this achievement one of his greatest, no matter what the rest of his life may bring.

*   The president of the South Summit Chamber of Commerce. She wants to use the championship to benefit the town's business community, and she is looking for ways to accomplish this without seeming to be too mercenary.

*   The mother of one of the team's better players. Nineteen years ago she married his father, the quarterback of another one of South Summit's

successful football teams. Since then she has heard more than once about what happened that year and what might have happened with "just a few more breaks."

- The mayor of South Summit. He intends to have the team's cocaptains speak at a town council meeting and to ride down Main Street with them in an open convertible (no matter what the weather) on their way to a rally in the high school stadium. He is, incidentally, running for reelection.

- The reporter from the *South Summit Sentinel* who covers high school sports, along with births, deaths, and marriages. This has been the best year of his young life.

- The coach of the Ground Squirrels. He knows that his best players are graduating and that this may have been the most rewarding season he will ever have. He wonders if he will have any worthwhile job offers as a result of his efforts, but he also feels strongly loyal to South Summit.

- The manager of Parker's Department Store. Her sportswear department has a large stock of Ground Squirrel paraphernalia, including T-shirts, sweatshirts, posters, and bumper stickers that say "Squirrels Rule!"

- A counselor at the high school who has had more than her share of sessions with juniors and seniors who are wondering if maybe the football team gets too much attention. She tries to help them make up their own minds.

## Exercises

1. Stage a conversation between two of the people listed previously. Give them names and figure out a realistic background for them. Have them ask each other about their own reactions to the success of the local team. Try to be as specific and detailed as possible; be imaginative; don't be afraid of the humorous and possibly unexpected details that may come out in such a conversation. Have at least one observer take notes and ask questions of one or the other to keep the conversation going.

2. Interview a senior member of the football team. Find out where the person goes from here. What effect has playing on a state championship team had on the player's outlook on the future. Try to be a detective. Ask indirect questions. For instance, don't ask, "What are you going to do with the rest of your life?" Instead, maybe ask, "At your tenth South Summit reunion will you show any effect from having been a member of this team?" Again,

don't be afraid to fumble around a bit, and be willing to keep a light touch in the conversation. There is plenty of time to be serious when you finally start carefully putting words on paper.

3.   Become the worst kind of booster, one who identifies so closely with the fortunes of the team that he or she would be willing to bend the rules if it meant that South Summit might beat its rivals. This includes treatment of referees, recruitment of eighth-grade athletes, and unsportsmanlike dealings with people from other communities. Show what a good villain you can be.

## Writing Assignments

1.   You are the assistant to the mayor of South Summit. He has asked you to write the introduction to the speech he will give at the big rally. He also wants you to include a couple of points he should touch on as he goes along. Remember that he is running for reelection, so his success means your job.

2.   You are a social studies teacher at South Summit High. You are composing an in-class writing assignment (one or two paragraphs) for your students. Do it in such a way that they will have to think about what this means to the town. Assure them that they can say whatever they want, provided they support their opinions.

3.   You are the sports writer for the *South Summit Sentinel,* published weekly. The paper's editor has asked you to help her write an editorial for the issue that coincides with the big celebration. Your friends and fellow workers are going to know that you were the brains behind this editorial, even if your name doesn't appear with it, so come up with a strong opening paragraph. Avoid the usual sports page clichés.

4.   You are a retired lawyer who, years ago, played football for South Summit. Write a letter to the editor of the *Sentinel* about how happy you are. Keep it brief so that it may get printed without too much editorial cutting.

5.   You are the president of the local chamber of commerce. Write a memo to your staff and members asking them to take advantage of the town's "school spirit" and suggesting ways that they might do this. Use your imagination. Would a "Champion Burger" be a likely seller at the town's busiest cafe? How about half-price admission at the local movie theater to patrons wearing something with the Ground Squirrels logo on it?

6.   Invent a role and a situation related to this case that call for a particular piece of writing, and then write it. Use your imagination and explore some of the less obvious persons who have been touched by the town's triumph.

# Case VI: The College Job Fair

For the past five years, Malone College has staged a job fair during the spring semester. This year more than 50 local and national businesses and corporations will be sending representatives to set up booths and displays. Others will be sending brochures and literature to be placed on display tables. Some exhibit areas will be staffed continuously; others will have videotape and computer graphics displays running when their representatives cannot be on duty.

In a nearby area, experts give workshops and seminars on job readiness and employment trends. Federal agencies send materials on workers' rights, equal employment opportunities, and on-the-job safety. Recruiters from the Army, Navy, Marines, National Guard, and service organizations send representatives. All of them jockey for the best booth locations, and they notice where their competitors are located. Free snacks and beverages are available. Up to now, employers and other exhibitors have been allowed to participate at no cost, but, if the fair continues to become more successful, an exhibit fee may be charged.

At first the work of organizing and producing the fair was done mainly by college staff members, working under the dean of student activities. Gradually, however, more and more of the college community, including students, have gotten involved. This cooperation has resulted in a successful fair.

But "success" means different things to different players in this effort:

- To the college administration, it means that alumni, community business people, college staff, faculty, students, and neighboring colleges recognize it as something worth doing because of its results and because it enhances the college's image.

- To the students who work on its organization, it means a sense of accomplishment. They know they have performed a valuable service for their fellow students, and they also know they are a real part of the college.

- To the students who take advantage of the fair's exhibits and contacts, it means learning about the job market, getting in touch with potential employers, and getting some good practice in selling themselves to others.

* To the local business and corporate representatives, it means showcasing themselves as concerned members of the community, getting a chance for some inexpensive exposure, and making contact with some well-educated, potential employees.

For the fair to be successful, a lot of planning must be done well in advance of April 10, the date of the activity. For example, reservations must be made for a large enough facility (college auditorium, gymnasium, community meeting hall, municipal building, etc.). Advance publicity is also important. This means posters, flyers distributed wherever students gather, stories in the school newspaper, press releases to the local papers, and free public service announcements (PSAs) on local radio and television stations.

Finally, on the day of the fair, many student volunteers and college staff members are needed to act as guides, mentors, envelope stuffers, equipment movers, trouble shooters, and gofers.

As is true with most worthwhile activities, the sixth annual Malone College Job Fair will require that a lot of people write a lot of words. As you work your way through the possibilities of this case, try to imagine what these words should be and prove to yourself that you could write them.

## Analyzing the Case

This case is complicated because it involves several different groups who are working together but who may have different motives in wanting the activity to succeed. Their motives are good ones, but they are not the same. Because of this diversity, you must figure out their varied motivations. For example, do college administrators write the same things to students that they write to their staff members? Do students want to hear what business and corporate sponsors are hearing? Finally, what's in it for the local sponsors, and how do they become convinced that it's worth committing their time and money? How does the college convince national corporations to send representatives? Will local media be convinced that this event is worth covering?

## Key Terms

benefit package
career path
community outreach
corporate responsibility
employability
employment trend
human resources
internship
mentor
personnel
resume

Explore the meaning of these terms, using your dictionary where possible. Discuss them with your teacher and classmates. Do any of them have current meanings that differ from their dictionary definitions?

## Questions for In-Class Writing or Discussion

1. Compare a job fair with other kinds of fairs. At a county or state fair, for example, what is exhibited? Why do exhibitors go to the trouble of fattening their prize hogs, canning their prize currant jellies, and competing for blue ribbons?
2. There may be an element of politics, both open and unspoken, at both kinds of fairs. Explore this idea, giving examples of the similarities or differences.
3. Does the fairgoer's ability to wander from one attraction to another add to the fair's attractiveness? Is this also one of its drawbacks? Explain your answer.
4. What might the job fair's planners learn from other kinds of fairs, such as state fairs, antique fairs, or baseball card fairs?

## Role Playing

As you have seen, writing effectively means writing for someone and having a clear image of who that audience is. Knowing your audience, whether it consists of one person or many, means that you can make good judgments about word choice, about the kind of language you should use, and about what might work best in this particular case. Consider these key people:

- A college president, who is too busy to take much part in the actual work of organizing and running a job fair but who wants to encourage his administrative staff to do their best for the college and the community.

- An overworked dean of student activities who knows that the buck stops at her desk as far as this project is concerned and who, therefore, must convince her staff (counselors, assistant deans, and program directors) that it must be successful.

- The career development director, who knows that the dean is counting on her to make it all come together.

- The students, many of them business majors, who want to make a difference in their lives and the lives of others, but who also want to get some credit for what they do.

- A local business owner (department store, gas/electric company, bank, insurance company) who remembers coming in previous years and not finding anyone who would wind up working for him.

- The human resources executive of a national corporation who must decide whether or not to commit part of her limited resources to this one of many requests from around the country.

- Most important of all, the Malone College student who wants to find a good job and maybe even a career.

## Exercises

1. Stage a conversation between two of the people listed previously. Their discussion takes place a week before the job fair. Give them names and sketch out a realistic background for them. Have them ask each other about their own employment history and how they got the jobs they have today (including the job of student). Try to be as specific and detailed as possible; be imaginative; don't be afraid of the humorous and possibly ridiculous details that may emerge from such a conversation. Have at least one observer take notes and ask questions of one or the other to keep the conversation going.

2. Interview a member of the class and then, based on the answers you get, try to tell this person what you think their ideal job would be. Try to be a detective. Ask indirect questions that will give you an idea of the field in which this person might succeed; don't simply ask what their preferences might be. For example, "Is making a lot of money important to most people?"

might get a more honest answer than "Is making a lot of money important *to you?*" Again, don't be afraid to fumble around a bit, and try to keep a light touch in the conversation. There is plenty of time to be serious when you finally start carefully putting words on paper.

## Writing Assignments

1. Write about how well last year's job fair went. You are the president of Malone College and you are writing a memo to your administrators and staff one week after last year's fair. List some of the comments people made to you when you put in an appearance at the fair. Tell your people that you are counting on them to make next year's fair even better and explain why this continued success is important, giving at least three reasons. Conclude by thanking them.

2. Write a short press release. You are the college's career development director. You need to give some details about the upcoming fair in such a way that the college newspaper and the local newspapers will pay attention to you. Stress the value of this activity to the community and to the college.

3. Write a negative letter to the career development director. You are a local businessperson who went to some trouble to take part in last year's fair for the first time and who has no intention of participating this year. What's more, you intend to tell your fellow employers to do the same. Why is this? Was it the turnout, the physical setup, the staff support? Use concrete details. Use your imagination, but include your high hopes based on what you had heard from other participants and your disappointment at what actually happened. In composing your letter, decide whether you really mean to close the door or whether you might be hoping that the college will plead with you to reconsider.

4. You guessed it. Now you are the career development director. Plead with the businessperson in the previous assignment. Promise him or her whatever you think you can. Put yourself inside the mind of your audience and try to determine how serious the threat might be. Apologize without whining, but make it clear that continued participation is something the college really wants.

5. You are a student who worked as a guide and mentor last year. Write a note to the career development director, making some suggestions for this year's fair. Pay particular attention to how the student volunteers were used, treated, rewarded, exploited, and valued. Was this a good experience for

you? Were you able to help people who attended? What new techniques might the college use to make the fair more interesting and effective? Are there technological developments that could be put to use? Do you have some practical, nitty-gritty suggestions to make about any aspect of the fair? If you were the recipient of this letter, what kind of advice would you like to be getting from someone like you? What kind of advice might you not appreciate?

6.    Invent a role and a situation related to this fair that call for a particular piece of writing, and then write it.

 ## CASE VII: A SUPERMARKET CLOSES

Phenom Foods, a large supermarket chain, announces that it is going to close one of its stores in a "declining neighborhood." A brief press release, reprinted in the local newspaper, expresses regret but assures the store's patrons that they will be welcomed at the chain's other locations. It also states that responsibility to the company's stockholders has forced this unfortunate action. The same announcement is taped to the inside of the store's front windows and doors.

In a series of internal memos, the company's management discusses the effects of the closing:

- how many employees will be laid off
- what the closing will mean to suppliers (dairy, produce, paper products, etc.)
- which employees can be shifted to other stores
- what public relations problems can be expected

Appropriate memos are sent from the company's main office to the local employees who will be carrying out the activities involved in closing the store.

A handout is prepared for distribution to customers at the checkout counter, explaining the company's position and asking for the community's understanding.

*(Continued)*

*(Continued from previous page)*

Meanwhile, a community organization decides to try to fight the closing. A handout is distributed inviting neighborhood residents to a meeting in the local elementary school auditorium. There they will decide how to respond to Phenom Foods. At the meeting another handout is distributed. It questions the motivation of the supermarket chain, and it hints that there might be a call for a citywide boycott of the chain. An appeal is made to suppliers and vendors that work with the chain. During and after the meeting, a letter of protest is prepared for delivery to the management of Phenom Foods. A copy is also hand-delivered to the local newspaper. A young reporter, covering the neighborhood beat, takes notes at the meeting and writes a 150-word article, giving only the basic facts about the situation.

Inside the supermarket chain, the personnel department is sending a letter to local employees, announcing the shutdown and explaining what their options are within the company. The assistant manager of the doomed store receives his copy and prepares a letter explaining why he deserves continued employment with the company. Others write similar letters.

Down the street from Phenom Foods, a small mom-and-pop store is already passing out copies of a letter to the community. The handout, written by the owners' 25-year-old daughter, pledges loyalty to the community and announces a sale.

A local community developer, after asking around a bit, sends a letter to Phenom asking whether the company has any plans for the vacant property. A return letter from the chain's legal department says that there are no immediate plans.

The organizer of the neighborhood meeting sends a follow-up letter to the editor of the local newspaper, but it does not get printed. The organizer does, however, receive a polite form letter from the editor thanking the author for writing it.

Four months after the first announcement, the store is closed.

## Analyzing the Case

This situation is complicated, isn't it? Notice how many of the actions require written words for their completion. Also notice that nobody writes simply to be writing. Once more, review the case and count the different pieces of writing that were generated. How many did you find?

## Key Terms

bottom line
community activism
grass roots
opportunism
political pressure
practicality
prioritizing
regionalism
social responsibility
top-down management

Explore the meaning of these terms, using your dictionary where possible. Discuss them with your teacher and classmates. Do any of them have current meanings that differ from their dictionary definitions?

## Questions for In-Class Writing or Discussion

1. The neighborhood consists of people. If you, as a member of the Phenom Foods public relations department, are writing a message to them, is your audience the same people that the mom-and-pop store down the street will address with their homemade advertising handout? If not, what's the difference?
2. Employees within the Phenom Foods organization get their information on a need-to-know basis, as determined by people higher up in the organization. That means that the store manager will be told more details than the person who rounds up shopping carts in the parking lot. Will they both get essentially the same message about the store's closing?
3. Why does the local newspaper run a story about the store closing and community meeting but decline to print the community organizer's letter to the editor? What might the organizer do to draw continued attention to the store closing?

## Role Playing

As you review the case, picture these people and answer the following questions.

A. A young mother who works at the checkout counter of Phenom Foods.
B. A longtime neighborhood resident who attended the community meeting at the elementary school.
C. The editor of the neighborhood newspaper.

*Questions*

1. What do these people have in common?
2. Which of the three might have the most trouble communicating with the other two? Why? (Beware of stereotypes.)
3. Which of the three would you find the easiest to communicate with?

Imagine how you would react if the written words were directed at you. Then by putting yourself in someone else's place you can sharpen your ability to pick just the right words and tone. You will be yourself, but you will also become other people through your imagination.

*Sample Dialogue*

Phenom Foods' late shift supervisor is discussing the store's closing with a reporter from the neighborhood newspaper. Take one of these parts and act it out with a partner. When you reach the last words, keep the dialogue going. Try to get into each other's minds by really listening to each others' words.

| | |
|---|---|
| **Supervisor** | I don't know if I should be talking to you. What do you want? |
| **Reporter** | Relax, I just want to ask you a couple of questions. When were you told that your store would be closing? |
| **Supervisor** | I was told the same time as everybody else. Why did you ask me that? |
| **Reporter** | I just wondered if people in positions of authority, like you, got any advance notice about it. Did your people find out about when you did, or did you have to tell them about it? |
| **Supervisor** | No, we all had it dropped on us at the same time. So what? |
| **Reporter** | Tell me what happened, please. I won't print anything you don't want me to. Go on. In your own words. |
| **Supervisor** | Well . . . |

You take it from here. Try to explore each other's motivation. Are you both just doing your job? How much do you trust each other, and how does this show up in the words you use with each other?

During the actions of the supermarket case, many pieces of writing are produced. Part of the role-playing activity is to imagine what the characters in the case would write and then to imagine how their audiences would receive them. Do the authors have an accurate sense of the people for whom they are writing? Do they misjudge or miscalculate?

To help you decide, you can examine this sample documents. Take a look at this letter from the manager of the local store's produce department who hopes she will not be out of a job.

---

*Daphne McGuire*
*2300 E. Touhy Ave, #4*
*Chicago, IL 60699*

July 30, 2001

Mr. Fred Figg
Manager
Phenom Foods
3000 E. Farwell Ave.
Chicago IL 60698

Dear Mr. Figg,

I have learned that our store is going to be closed. I wish to request that I be given special consideration when the layoffs start. As you know, I have been a loyal employee for eight years now. I come to work on time and I have received good evaluations from my supervisors, including you, Mr. Figg, sir. And I do know my produce.

I hope that for these and other reasons, you will make every effort to ensure that I continue to have a job with our beloved Phenom Foods. I care about this company more than most people do, and I know you do too.

Sincerely yours,


Daphne McGuire
Coordinator of Produce

What can be said about Ms. McGuire? How well does she know her manager, Mr. Figg? Would you have written this letter? Why or why not? Could this letter be salvaged if it were to be rewritten, assuming Ms. McGuire hadn't already sent it? Put yourself in Mr. Figg's place, and then imagine his reaction when he receives this letter. Do some role playing. Based on what you can presume about the store manager and his troubled state of mind, how would you have addressed him?

## Exercise

Revise Ms. McGuire's letter to Mr. Figg. Think of the right tone to use. Mr. Figg has 75 employees who need to be dealt with during this crisis. What is he likely to want to hear in a letter from any one of them? What one point do you think would be the most persuasive for Ms. McGuire to include in her letter in order to obtain another position at another Phenom store? Don't say too much.

 ## CASE VIII: FINDING A JOB THROUGH THE INTERNET

Kathy Hughes needs a job. She's halfway through her senior year as a marketing major at a southern state university, and she's getting worried. She sits in the student lounge, slumping down in one of the lumpy couches, trying again to make some plans and to consider her options. Near her on the wall are huge bulletin boards, containing notes that say things like "Need a ride to Montgomery over Christmas break," or "Will tutor in calculus. Reasonable." There are also some job listings, but none of them strikes her as leading to her dream career, whatever that is.

She stares at the lined yellow pad on which she's been writing and doodling. It contains a list titled "Job Search Possibilities." On the list are "Placement Office, networking with friends, Sunday paper job listings, employment agency, job fair, on-campus recruiters, divine intervention, Internet/online search, unemployment, Peace Corps, army, grad school, a life of crime, win the lottery." She and her friends had shared much laughter last night as they compiled the list. Now Kathy is not laughing. She's concerned that the secure world of college is coming to an end, and she wonders what comes next. After a while, she underlines "Internet," draws circles around it, draws arrows coming at it from different directions, tucks the notepad in her bookbag, and leaves the lounge.

In her three and a half years at the university, Kathy has spent a lot of time using computers, especially to access the Internet. Although she does not consider herself an expert, she knows how technology can both enrich and complicate her life. She has taken several web-based courses and numerous online exams for other courses, researched term papers through general and specialized databases, and even set up her own no-frills web site to share photos and messages with her family back in Mississippi. But she has never sat down at a keyboard to try to get a job.

Nevertheless, from what she has learned, she is becoming convinced that her best tool for job hunting may be the Internet. This is where she'll concentrate her efforts, even though she won't rule out other avenues, such as the Business Department's placement office and even the want ads in the Sunday newspapers.

So Kathy Hughes takes her future into her own hands and does the following:

- She finally joins the on-campus chapter of the association for people in her chosen profession of marketing. She has attended a couple of the group's meetings but never actually joined and paid the $75 annual dues. She is contacted almost immediately and asked if she would be interested in helping to recruit others into the group.

- She asks two of her marketing professors if they would be willing to be listed as references on her resume. Since Kathy has been a pretty good student, they both agree. They know from experience that they probably won't be contacted by potential employers anyway.

- She pays for her own subscription to one of the major journals in the field of marketing, knowing that the subscription list will be sold to others in the field. She knows this will bring her even more mail (including junk mail and spam) from people in her profession. It will also help her to feel more like a professional.

*(Continued)*

*(Continued from previous page)*

- She goes to an online job search site, humongousjobs.com, and downloads information on preparing an electronic resume and writing effective e-mail application letters. She learns, for instance, that electronic search engines look for nouns rather than verbs, so she should write things like "*member* of college's marketing association," rather than "*joined* college's marketing association." She also finds that some of the format features she likes to use ("bullets," typefaces with serifs, and multiple indentations) don't work well in electronic resumes, so she will be careful to avoid them. She gets the impression that there are certain buzzwords and terminology that people in her field—like any field—expect to hear. She'll include some marketing jargon and list the software packages she knows how to use.

- She opens a personal account on this site and is amazed to learn that it doesn't cost her any money, but she's a little worried about the security of the personal information she is putting out in cyberspace. She asks humongousjobs.com to pull up only available jobs in marketing within the states of Alabama and Mississippi, which pay $40,000 or more, which have been advertised for less than two months, and which will be available with a starting date after her June graduation. Even with these limitations, she expects to receive a lot of information to sort through. She is right.

- Once the job descriptions start coming in (53 in the first week), she chooses 19 of the most attractive ones and submits her resume along with a carefully written application letter. She is careful to use words that have a "marketing sound" to them. She researches the companies by looking up their web sites. She hopes to impress the recruiters by including selected details about their companies in her application letters. This calls for a different letter for each company, although she includes certain "boilerplate" sections in all of them.

- By March 1, she has scheduled six interviews. Two of them will be conducted by on-campus recruiters from the larger companies, and the other four will require her to do some unexpected traveling during her spring break. She decides she's getting too old for that annual trip to the Florida beach anyway.

The results are everything she had hoped they would be. She accepts a job offer from one of the three she most wanted.

At the June graduation ceremony, Kathy Hughes is a happy woman. Crossing the auditorium stage to accept her diploma, she knows she will walk down the stairs on the other side and into a waiting job. If it turns out to be her "career position," that's great, but it is a good job and, thanks to her Internet job search, she's on her way. As she cleans out her room and packs to go home, she sees that list sticking out of her bookbag. She smiles and then throws it into the rapidly filling dumpster.

## Key Terms

career path
cyberspace
employability
entry-level
human resources (HR)
job market
marketing
professional jargon
resume
search engine

Explore the meaning of these terms, using your dictionary where possible. Discuss them with your teacher and classmates. Do any of them have current meanings that differ from their dictionary definitions?

## Analyzing the Case

Is there anything that can't happen online? It seems sometimes that the world of the Internet is becoming the world, period. Do you recall in 1999 when a media-conscious person had his name changed to "DotCom.Guy" and proceeded to live entirely through the 'net? For one year, he never left his apartment and, according to his publicist, everything he needed or wanted could be obtained with a keyboard, a mouse, and a credit card. Few of us would doubt this, although we probably wouldn't want to put it to the test. The cyber revolution has obviously made a major change in just about everything everybody does. The life and college education of Kathy Hughes is drastically different from that of her parents and grandparents. Most of the changes related to computers are positive, and job searching seems to fall into this category. The whole profession of human resources has undergone so many changes that old-time personnel managers have to adapt or to shake their heads and get out of the way. Change is happening so rapidly that in a few years, Kathy Hughes's nieces and nephews may find her job search experience to be quaint and old-fashioned.

## Questions for In-Class Writing or Discussion

1.  The changes brought about by the Internet revolution are not all positive, are they? For instance, has something been lost by the fact that so many operations (like sending job applications) can be done in seconds when they used to take hours and days of monotonous work? Or is that the same argument that people used when it became possible to send a letter from New York to San Francisco in only three weeks? In other words, is progress always good? For more background on this question, take a look at "Claim Your Domain Name Before Internet Winter Hits" in Appendix C.

2.  Is "information overload" finally occurring? That is, will we all become bombarded with so much information and complexity that we will have to slow down as a nation and simplify our lives? Is the example of Thoreau, living by Walden Pond, a useful one? Or would Thoreau today have a modem, to say nothing of a cell phone?

3.  How has the Internet made the world a global village? And what are the implications of the peoples of the world being divided into computer haves and have-nots?

## Role Playing

Take on the identities of some of the people involved in this case and see how their interaction would affect the kind of writing they would do. Maybe for this set of role-playing exercises it would be appropriate to do some interacting online in a computer lab, rather than seated together in a classroom. Send an e-mail to the person at the next terminal. If you do, don't forget that the principles of communicating with an audience aren't changed because they're reading e-mail rather than pieces of paper. Get inside the minds and viewpoints of some of these people:

- Roger Conley, a professor of advertising and marketing, who has taught Kathy Hughes two of her major courses. He gave her a B+ in both of them.

- Candy Jackson, placement counselor in the Department of Business (which includes advertising and marketing), who has advised Kathy on choosing the most promising job offers.

- Kathy's father Langston, who was also a business major at the university in the 1970s. He is fascinated and impressed by his daughter's success in taking advantage of the Internet.

- Terry and Chris, two of Kathy's friends, who share an apartment with her two blocks from campus. They were sharing a pizza at the time Kathy's list of future possibilities was being composed.

- Martina Blanc, human resources recruiter for a large chain of department stores in the Montgomery, Alabama, area. She was impressed with Kathy's letter and resume, and she scheduled an interview with her during spring break.

- Henry David Thoreau (1817–1862), author of *Walden* (1854). He went to the woods near Walden Pond in Massachusetts to see if he could live a simpler life and become a better person doing it. He's extremely bright, but some technical applications may need to be explained to him rather simply.

- Kathy Hughes.

## Exercise

Get three or more of these people together and have them explore the questions raised by this case. Concentrate especially on how they need to use language to communicate with each other online, on paper, or in person. Have them ask each other about their own reactions to the particular case and to the larger questions it raises. Add details to make up believable backgrounds for them. Try to be as specific and detailed as possible. Be imaginative; don't be afraid of the humorous, embarrassing, and possibly unexpected details that may come out in such a conversation.

## Writing Assignments

1.  Professor Conley may be asked by some of Kathy's prospective employers for a letter of recommendation. Since this happens regularly, he has a file in his computer containing paragraphs he can drop into letters when he needs them. Some of these are all-purpose but very positive. Some are not so positive for the times when he has to tactfully warn someone about his students' shortcomings. Try to write one of each for him to use in the future.

2.  Martina Blanc needs to tell Kathy how glad her store is that she will be working there. What sorts of things does she tell Kathy to expect in her new job?

3.  Pick your dream company to work for and write a letter to the director of human resources explaining why you would be very good for the company. If General Motors needs you as an executive, say so.

4.  Check your handbook for guidelines on preparing a resume, including an electronic one, and begin to prepare yours. See if the word processing program you are using has templates for resume preparation.

5.  Write a five-paragraph essay on some of the most important effects the Internet has had on your life. Be as specific as you can. The audience is your classmates.

# CASE IX: THE ALL NEW AND IMPROVED COLLEGE

Cadbury College needs a makeover. The 1990s were not good to this small, liberal arts college, and so far the new century has been no more promising. Isolated just outside the quiet town of Cadbury in central Kansas, the school is fighting for its life. Enrollment is down for the seventh straight year. Many of the buildings are in need of repair. Appeals to the alumni have failed to bring in much money, and the incoming freshmen are facing an increase in tuition, the fourth since 1998. The president, after 27 mediocre years in office, finally announces his plans to retire, move to Atlanta, and learn to play golf with his grandchildren.

Cadbury's board of trustees, anxious to keep the college from going over a cliff, conducts a nationwide search for a new president, but they aren't impressed by the applicants. Then one of the trustees has an idea. He remembers that Arthur Burnett, a graduate of Cadbury's class of '85, has gone on to achieve some success as an academic administrator. He's been a registrar, a dean of admissions, and, most recently, vice president of a medium-sized, state-supported college in Arkansas. He's never been a president. "Maybe we should contact him about the job," says the trustee, who graduated with him. The rest of the trustees agree, thinking, "What do we have to lose?"

To their amazement, their offer is accepted. After very little negotiating, the new president arrives July 20, relocating with his wife and nine-year-old daughter. He moves into the on-campus mansion, which is as run-down as the rest of the neighboring buildings. By Labor Day, Cadbury College's most exciting and controversial year in its 89-year history has begun. Faculty members are angry because they had no say in President Burnett's hiring, but, along with the students and the townspeople of Cadbury, they are waiting to see what this hometown product is going to do with their lives. If he can figure out how to save Cadbury College, he will have everyone's support.

President Burnett decides to act fast. By midterm of his first semester, the new leader does the following:

- He announces the cancellation of his presidential inaugural celebration, saying that the money raised for the festivities could be better spent on a new roof for the athletic fieldhouse.

- He informs the head of the faculty senate that she will be attending the monthly meetings of the Cadbury Board of Trustees from now on. She will also have a regular place on the agenda and be encouraged to report on the faculty's concerns.

- He attempts to persuade the trustees that the student government president should also be given the same privileges. The new board president (his old classmate) informs him that "many of the board meetings are open to the public, so anyone, *even a student,* can ask to be heard."

- He hires a consulting firm to help create a new image and marketing plan for Cadbury College. He persuades the trustees to pay $104,000 to Nouveaucollege.com for its promotional services for one year. His old college in Arkansas used this company, and the

*(Continued)*

*(Continued from previous page)*

results were excellent, he says. Part of the plan includes a contest, open to everyone in the school and the town of Cadbury, to come up with a new marketing slogan and logo for the college. The prize of $300 may be too small to inspire many entries.

- He gets his hair cut at Nick's Barber Shop on Pine Street in downtown Cadbury, where as a small child he used to sit up on a board that Nick's father would put across the arms of the barber chair. Now he asks Nick Jr. and his other customers what he should do to improve Cadbury College. A reporter for the *Cadbury Clarion,* who is getting a haircut at the time, writes a feature story about it.

- He wonders out loud what might happen if Cadbury were to drop its intercollegiate athletic programs (Division III) and spend money instead on an improved intramural sports program. An immediate uproar of protest from some major alumni contributors, the editors of the school newspaper, 95 percent of Cadbury's athletes, and all of its coaches causing President Burnett to back off, at least temporarily.

- He institutes a crackdown on excessive drinking at fraternity and sorority parties and hires off-duty Cadbury police officers to work as part-time security along with the existing five-person campus security force. When he proposes a "no tolerance" policy, with expulsion as a possible penalty, he gets a letter from a group of tavern owners in downtown Cadbury, asking him to think twice about his plan. The Combined Greek Council, including members of the fraternity he belonged to in the 1980s, asks him to be "realistic."

- He proposes a new class-attendance policy. An instructor would be encouraged to withdraw any student who has six or more unexcused absences from a course. If the course were not made up within two semesters, the student would get an automatic failing grade. "If Cadbury is going to be taken seriously, we have to take ourselves seriously," says President Burnett. The student government backs the idea, but the school newspaper strongly opposes it in a front-page editorial. Burnett asks the dean of student activities to get him "some information" on the editor of the paper. The paper makes plans to support a new candidate for student government president in the spring semester elections.

As the college approaches its holiday break, everyone has formed a strong set of opinions about President Burnett. His supporters and his detractors are getting louder, while approximately a third of the Cadbury College community is saying, "Let's give him some more time and see what happens." Burnett says he has a lot more ideas and is anxious to try them out. Whatever may happen after January 1, it won't be dull.

## Analyzing the Case

Have you ever found yourself in a difficult situation where you were trying to do your best but finding that things were quickly spinning out of control? Your expectations were reasonable, but you come to realize that you didn't know about some important pieces of the situation. Is it possible that the Cadbury Board of Trustees acted too quickly in hiring the new president? Should they have known that he would be as controversial as he has become? Or did they do the right thing by trying to shake up their dying college? President Burnett wants to perform an academic Heimlich maneuver on his choking alma mater, trying to save its life. Should the trustees be afraid that he may become more powerful than they are? Who really runs a college like Cadbury? Is it the administrators? The faculty? The trustees? The students? Or is it the "market," the outside consultants, and "image makers"?

## Key Terms

academic community
alma mater
desperation
head hunting
image making
in loco parentis
micromanagement
serendipity
shared governance
trustee

Explore the meaning of these terms, using your dictionary where possible. Discuss them with your teacher and classmates. Do any of them have current meanings that differ from their dictionary definitions?

## Questions for In-Class Writing or Discussion

1. Is a college just like any other large organization that provides a product (courses, grades, and degrees) for its consumers (students)?
2. Is a college's reputation sometimes based on factors that are not really its most important characteristics? You may have seen the rankings of colleges in *U.S. News and World Report,* for instance, or even lists of the "best party schools." Do you think such lists are fair and accurate?
3. What gives Cadbury's students the right to think that they should have a say in how their college is run?
4. How much time should the new president be given to prove himself? Are there actions that he should not be allowed to take? Who decides what they are?
5. Is your college comparable to Cadbury in any way? What are the major differences between them?

## Role Playing

Put yourself inside the minds and hearts of some of the people involved in Cadbury College's great adventure. All of these participants have a stake in the school's survival, but they have different sets of priorities and goals.

- Susan Jackson, a junior and assistant editor of the school newspaper, is hoping for a career in journalism after she leaves Cadbury. She has already been an unpaid summer intern on the *Cadbury Clarion,* so she feels that she knows the town and the college pretty well.

- Marcia Jensen is an instructor in the Biology Department. She has kept a low profile so far in her five years at Cadbury, but she is beginning to think she should take a stand on the issues raised by President Burnett's actions. She is also hoping to receive tenure after her sixth year.

- Renata Juarez has a son attending Cadbury. She works hard to supplement the partial scholarship that her son Ramon receives. After attending the Parents Weekend in September and receiving quite a few letters and phone calls from Ramon, she is not sure she should let him stay past his freshman year. She fears that the college may not pull out of its slump and could even shut down.

- Norman Blakemore is the former president of Cadbury. From his home in Atlanta, he tries to figure out what is happening to the school he ran for almost three decades. He knows that it was time for him to go, but he's not sure his successor is the best leader for the college. He assured the new president that he would give him advice and support, but so far he has not received any requests, only a phone call asking for the combination to the empty safe in the president's office.

- Marty Givins, a political science major, is president of the junior class. He intends to run for student government president next year, and he intends to campaign against the programs of President Burnett.

- Myrna Navin is Cadbury's vice president for academic affairs. She was one of the two in-house applicants who were seriously considered for the president's job, but, in spite of her disappointment, she is trying her best to be a loyal and helpful "team player."

- Eugene Rainier, aged 62, is a longtime member of Cadbury's three-person groundskeeping crew. He likes the students, and they know him as one of the friendliest and wisest people on campus. He has mixed feelings about the way "his college" is going.

- Arthur Burnett has just finished his first semester as president of the college. He has a lot of plans he hopes to put into effect during the coming year.

## Exercises

1. Stage an imaginary conversation between two of the people listed previously. Have each of them ask the other about their reactions to the way things are going at Cadbury College. Try to be as specific and detailed as possible. Be imaginative; don't be afraid of the humorous, embarrassing, and possibly unexpected details that may come out in such a conversation. Have at least one observer take notes and ask questions of one or the other to keep the conversation going.

2. Have three of the people listed previously, other than President Burnett, write one practical suggestion for improving the college. Concentrate on such issues as increasing enrollment, building student morale, improving Cadbury's reputation, and bringing in more money for needed school

expenses. Each of the three role players may get assistance from other members of the class. Then present these ideas to the new president. It's his job to pick the best idea and explain why he thinks it is best. It is definitely not necessary to agree with him.

3. Conduct a roundtable discussion in which the moderator asks four of the people listed previously what they would do if they were president for a week. Don't be afraid to use your imagination and sense of humor. After all, you'll be out in a week.

## Writing Assignments

1. A reporter from the *Cadbury Chronicle* writes about what happened when he was in Nick's Barber Shop for a haircut at the same time as President Burnett. Start by making a list of details you want to include in the article. For example, describe the interior of the shop, the body language of the barber and other customers, the unexpected words that were spoken, the temporary silence in the shop after President Burnett left, and the discussion after his departure.

2. President Burnett asks his assistant to draft a letter for his signature. It will be addressed to the joint council of fraternities and sororities, and it will ask council members to help him control excessive drinking by students on campus and in the town of Cadbury. Write at least the first two paragraphs.

3. You're a consultant with Nouveaucollege.com, the image makeover firm hired by President Burnett. Write a memo to him outlining some ideas about a contest to come up with a new logo and slogan for the college. Show him that you're worth the big bucks the college is paying you by being enthusiastic and optimistic.

4. Write a letter from freshman Ramon Juarez to his mother and sister in Kansas City. Explain why you want to stay at Cadbury and reassure your family that things are going to be OK.

5. Write a five-paragraph essay on one of the ideas developed in this case. Be sure to have a clear main idea. The intended audience is your classmates.

# Appendix B

# English as a Second Language

America is a land of many languages. The one you are using in this course is English or, more exactly, American English. It has a long history, and it is a rich, flexible language, but as a language it is no better or worse than others. However, if you wish to succeed in communicating in this country (and much of the world), you must learn to use it. For millions of people living in North America, this means learning English as their second language, one to use along with their primary language. Learning *E*nglish as a *s*econd *l*anguage, or ESL, is not the major focus of this book, but here are some basic ideas, hints, and tips that can make it easier for you to use English effectively.

First let's consider a bit of general theory. Languages can be divided into many categories, but two useful ones are **inflected** languages and those that use a system based on **word order.** Look at these two examples. The first is in Latin, the second in English:

Vir vidit canem.
The man sees the dog.

They both mean exactly the same. Now look at these two:

Canem vidit vir.
The man sees the dog.

They still both mean the same. How can this be? In English, if we were to reverse the order of the words as we've done with the Latin, we'd get

The dog sees the man.

But in Latin we can put those three words in any order (even "Canem vir vidit") and they will still match our English sentence, "The man sees the dog." So, how does a user of Latin know what the words mean? Look closely at the end of the word can*em*. By using an ending (inflection) with an *m* in it (-*am* and -*um* are other possibilities), the Latin speaker or writer signals the audience that this canine creature is not just a dog, but *a dog which is having something done to it*. In this example, it's being *looked at/seen*.

Now, what if the Latin writer said this?

Virum vidit canis.

Did you get it? Right, now the sentence says, "The dog sees the man," and the tip-off is that the word for man, *vir*um, has an inflection ending in *m*. But, as we've seen, if we put our English words into this order, we'd get

The man sees the dog.

That's because English depends more than Latin does on its word order to convey information, while Latin depends more on its inflections. This is not to say that English doesn't use any inflections. Look, for instance, at the letter *s* which can turn dog into dog*s*. Or the -*ed* we put on the end of a verb (walk/walk*ed*) to show that the verb's action has already taken place. Likewise, in Latin a good writer can use different word order to change emphasis, but there is a definite difference in the ways that these two languages communicate. Latin depends much more on inflections, and English depends much more on word order.

Consider these six examples, each containing exactly the same words, but with a slight shift in word order. Placing the word "only" in different locations can move the meaning back and forth between a sweet Valentine card and a bitter soap opera.

> *Only* he said he loved her.
> He *only* said he loved her.
> He said *only* he loved her.
> He said he *only* loved her.
> He said he loved *only* her.
> He said he loved her *only.*

English used to have many more inflections than it does now. Old English (up to around 900 A.D.) had so many inflected endings on its words that it would look to modern English speakers like a foreign language. Over the centuries, as English has changed, it has dropped most of these inflections and come to depend more and more on its rules for word order. Think of the words Shakespeare used, such as "doth" and "dost." We've dropped the *th* and the *st,* and we get along fine with "do" and "does." "Did" works just as well as "didst." Most likely, that *m* inflection that we sometimes put on the end of "who" will also disappear from use. Even now, for instance, it sounds pompous to say "About who*m* are you talking?" Although this is strictly correct, most educated people might instead ask, "Who are you talking about?" Like all living languages, English is continuing to evolve into something new. Your own native language quite possibly emphasizes one or the other of these two features, inflection and word order.

Now that you've taken a general look at how English puts its words together, here are some more particular features for people who are learning the language. Based on the experience of ESL authorities, these are the areas that seem to cause nonnative speakers and writers the most difficulty.

## I.  Articles and Determiners

1.   Every noun that can be recognized as referring to an individual or something that can be counted must have an **article** (a/an, the) or a **determiner,** something that identifies it. Some examples:

     *Sally's* house (Sally's-determiner)
     *their* anniversary (their-determiner)
     *a* Big Mac (a-article)
     *the* greatest player in the NBA (the-article)

2.   Most plural nouns and nouns that refer to things that can't be counted do **not** have articles. Some examples:

     Life is worth living (not *The life is worth living*).
     She is studying mathematics (not *She is studying the mathematics*).
     A group's success requires teamwork (not the *teamwork*).

3.   If the reference to a particular individual, group, or quantity is clear to the audience, then use *the.* Otherwise, use *a/an,* a determiner (Sally's, their, MacDonald's), or nothing. Some examples:

*The* coffee at Starbuck's wakes you up (but *Coffee wakes you up*). She went to *a* small college (*The* college was 60 percent women. Note: after the first mention of something, it is assumed that the reader knows about it and *the* can be used.)

## II. Compound Tenses

1. Simple past tense is used only for single actions that happened at a particular time or for actions that happened during a specific period in the past. (I *went* to the store yesterday. DaVinci *lived* during the Italian Renaissance.) But actions that happened at an indefinite time in the past—sometime before "now"—are in the present perfect tense. (I *have seen* that movie. I *have* never *liked* olives. I *have given* up on the Chicago Cubs.)

2. Past perfect tense is used only for actions that happened before a specified time in the past—"before then" (He *had* already *given* up before he even started. The rain *had begun* to fall before I could find my umbrella.).

3. Past progressive (or continuous) tense is used only for actions that were going on when they were interrupted by another (simple past tense) action or while another continuing action was going on (I *was taking* a shower when the phone rang. My daughter *was talking* on the phone while I was fixing dinner.)

## III. Irregular Verbs

Fortunately, most English verbs are **regular.** That means they follow the same pattern. Take the word *walk,* for instance. It is a regular verb, and it has three main forms:

| | |
|---|---|
| Present: | *walk,* as in "I walk to the racetrack." |
| Past: | *walked,* as in "I walked to the racetrack." |
| Past Participle: | *walked,* as in "I have walked to the racetrack." or "I had walked to the racetrack." |

Now consider a common but **irregular** verb.

| | |
|---|---|
| Present: | drive, as in "I drive to school" |
| Past: | drove (not drived), as in "I drove to school." |
| Past Participle: | driven, as in "I have driven to school." or "I had driven to school." |

As in many concepts worth learning, it's the exceptions to the rules that make us work harder. It may sound cute, for example, to hear a two-year-old say, "I eated all my dinner." It would not be so cute to hear a 27-year old say the same (eat/ate/eaten, not eat/eated/ eated). Unfortunately, some of the most irregular of the verbs are also the most common, such as the different forms of *be* (is, am, are, was, were) or *have,* or *do.* Check the handbook you are using for this course. There is a good chance that it will contain a list of the most common irregular verbs in English. Study them and try to master a reasonable number at a time. Look for them when you read the newspaper or listen to the radio.

## IV.  Phrasal Verbs/Idioms

The most difficult part about learning any new language is mastering its **idioms.** These are the expressions that can't always be explained logically, except to say, "Well, that's just the way we say it in our language." Some verbs, especially, are used in combination with other words in ways that are highly idiomatic. Look, for example, at these expressions:

> I am *running to* the office building.
> I am *running for* the train.
> I am *running for* the office of president.
> I *am running up* a big bill on my credit card.
> I am *running down* this list of names.
> I have *been running around* all afternoon doing errands.
> I am *running through* my savings at an alarming rate.

A clear understanding of the precise meaning of these uses of *running* will not come easily. It will take patience and quite a bit of exposure to English speakers and writers. Or how about these uses of the common verb *get:*

> Let's *get down* to business.
> It's a difficult idea to *get across* to someone.
> I don't *get around* much anymore.
> Come on, Nancy, *get with* it.
> I hope to *get through to* my audience effectively.

These examples show how important it is to be conscious of idioms and idiomatic expressions. Be patient with yourself, and you will find yourself gradually building up your collection of these rich and useful treasures.

## V. Punctuation of Direct and Indirect Quotations

The Writing Convention section of Chapter 10 includes an explanation of this material. It can be a challenge for non-English speakers and writers, but, unlike idioms, this is one area where English is totally consistent and logical. Two tips:

1.  Remember to be conscious of tense changes in shifting from an indirect quotation to a direct one:

    Indirect: She said she *would be coming* to our party.
    Direct: She said, "I *will be coming* to your party."

2.  Remember to be conscious of pronoun changes in shifting from an indirect quotation to a direct one:

    Indirect: She said *she* would be coming to *our* party.
    Direct: She said, "*I* will be coming to *your* party."

## VI. Modal Auxiliaries

These are very useful words. Some of the most commonly used modal auxiliaries are *must, may, might, could, should, ought to,* and *had better.* They are not exactly verbs, but they are words that combine with verbs to enrich their meanings. Look at some examples. These first four tell the audience how certain the writer is about what is being said:

This *must be* Friday because I just got paid.
It *may be* Friday, but where's my check?
I *might buy* a raffle ticket if I feel lucky.
This *could be* my lucky day.

In the next set of examples, the modal auxiliaries help the verbs to make requests or suggestions, and they show how advisable or important the requests or suggestions are.

The doors *must be* locked before you leave the premises.
The windows *should be* closed in case of a rainstorm.
You *ought to have been* aware of these requirements.

Anyone who neglects them *had better* expect serious consequences.
You *could try* to be a little more considerate, *could*n't you?
If you have time, you *might want* to give these recent sales figures some attention.

## VII.  Adjective Clauses

We saw in Chapter 4 that groups of words can make up either clauses or phrases and that clauses can be either main clauses or subordinate clauses. Sometimes a subordinate clause can act like an adjective, a word that describes a noun in some way (what kind? how many? which?). These adjective clauses can be difficult for ESL students. Look at some examples:

1.   This is the Frisbee. It is ragged. (two sentences)
2.   This is the ragged Frisbee. (one sentence/one clause/*ragged* is an adjective that describes *Frisbee*)
3.   This is the Frisbee *that the dog chewed.* (one sentence/two clauses/the second clause acts like an adjective to describe the frisbee)

These are simple enough, but even a slightly more complicated sentence can be ruined by putting an adjective clause in the wrong place.

This Frisbee belongs to my daughter, which the dog chewed. (Poor construction: what did the dog chew?)
This Frisbee, which the dog chewed, belongs to my daughter. (The meaning is clear.)

So the rule is that adjective clauses must always be put directly after the word or words they describe.
Here's another common problem in using adjective clauses:

This is the web site. I warned you about it. (two sentences)
This is the web site which I warned you about it. (one sentence/two clauses; the second one is an adjective clause describing the dangerous web site.)

In the second example, the word *it* should be omitted:

This is the web site which I warned you about.
*not*
This is the web site which I warned you about it.

## VIII.  Conditional and Time Clauses

In sentences that discuss something likely to happen, these patterns are commonly used:

If taxes go up, businesses will hire fewer workers.
I will marry you when you get a steady job.

Notice that the main clause is usually in the future tense, and the subordinate clause is in the present tense.

Another possibility is a sentence that expresses an unlikely possibility:

If the Cubs won the World Series, Chicago would go crazy.
Business could hire more workers if taxes went down.
I could do the right thing if only I wanted.

In sentences like these, the main clause uses the past tense of will or can (would or should), and the subordinate clause usually uses the past tense.

. . . . . . . . .

What you've seen in this appendix is an overview of some of the most common difficulties encountered by people attempting to learn English as their second language. If you are one of these people, you will be able to find assistance and encouragement in various ways. In addition to your instructor and classmates, some helpful sources can be found in your handbook, in computer software, and on the Internet. Since you're an adult, learning a second language will never be as effortless as it is for children. You will analyze and try to figure things out, while a child will simply absorb it like sunshine on an August day. However, if you immerse yourself in the new language and try to avoid speaking in your more comfortable language whenever possible, you will find yourself becoming more skilled every day. And one day when you realize that you are beginning to think in your new language, your sense of accomplishment will be truly deserved.

# APPENDIX C

# PROFESSIONAL READINGS FOR STUDY

Here are two articles written by professionals, James Coates and Kerry Temple. These are people who expect other people to pay to read what they have written. As with other experts, you can learn much from examining their work. However, remind yourself of an important fact: What you have done during this course is exactly what they do—aside from the pay, of course. Like you, they recognize their audiences and then do what works best to communicate with them. They have no magic formulas or special powers. They sweat to do the same things you do. That means they make outlines, compose sentences, gather them into paragraphs, edit, polish, and proofread. Then they hand their writing over to others to see if their words worked the way they wanted. Isn't that what you are doing?

Take a look at the work of two good writers and see what they can teach you about your own writing. Some comments have been included, but make your own as you read. You may wish to ignore these comments the first time you read the articles. Simply cover them with a piece of paper. Underline parts that you like, and insert your own notes where you think they might add to your appreciation of the authors' works.

# Claim Your Domain Name Before the Internet Winter Hits

## By James Coates

*James Coates writes a weekly question-and-answer column on computers and the Internet in the* Chicago Tribune *and occasional articles like this one which appeared July 2, 2000.*

1   One of the really great things about working for newspapers is that adult supervision often gets overlooked. We get to do such things as work crossword puzzles, pursue our Erector Set-collecting hobbies on eBay.com and, of course, engage in what used to be called bull sessions.

[The author uses a relaxed, conversational tone to connect with his audience]

2   We even can use company time to set up our own Web sites, complete with custom addresses, using www.WhatEverYouWant.com.

[He gives us his thesis statement.]

3   It occurs to me that I can offer readers of this space a useful column by describing one recent bull session that ended up producing its own Web site. Talk turned to a column I had just written about my view that we may be on the verge of Internet Winter, a long-feared meltdown in the dot-com boom that has been gathering steam since 1996 and now seems to be slowing.

[He gives us a necessary definition.]

4   Internet Winter is based on the concept that the Web boom actually consists of a huge number of enterprises propping each other up by buying ad space on each other's sites. Amazon.com sells ads to Snap.com and then places ads of its own at the Snap site. Britannica.com runs ads for the New York Times Web site and the Times Web site runs ads for Britannica.com. The pattern repeats itself with wild abandon, as any surfing session will show you.

[Now come some specific names and details, not just generalities.]

5   As investors start to complain that none of these sites are making money, the operators have no choice but to economize and the most likely economies are to cut back on advertising.

[Newspapers typically use shorter paragraphs than we might in an essay. This is due in part to the paper's presentation of ideas in narrow, vertical columns.]

6   If Amazon stops buying ads on Snap.com, the operators of Snap must economize and will stop buying ads at

[Development through cause and effect]

Amazon. The result as other cash-strapped dot-coms follow that path: Internet Winter.

7   So in our bull session my immediate supervisor (make that unsupervisor) suggested that maybe instead of just writing about Internet Winter, I should check and see if anybody had staked out the www.InternetWinter.com Web address. If not, he suggested, I should reserve it myself. If the whole world ever starts talking about Internet Winter, lots of people will think to check out www.InternetWinter.com, and it just might become a hot property.

8   Maybe I could sell some banner ads.

[And now we, the readers, are in on the joke.]

9   We got to laughing at the delicious irony that a Web site devoted to the collapse of the Web might wind up being the only profitable Internet enterprise to emerge from Internet Winter.

10   As my boss talked, he logged on to www.register.com, which is the best way I know to check to see if somebody has registered a Web site name, which is called a domain.

[He gives us a definition of a possibly unfamiliar term.]

You just dream up a Web name and type it in a search box, and the software checks the 8 million or so names now registered in the domains ending in .com, .org, and .net.

11   With a thousand more claimed every hour, the pickings are getting slim. For example, Chase Manhattan Bank owns the .com domains Thatchase, Chasestinks, and Chasesucks. Charles Schwab & Co. owns, among other domains, screwschwab.com and schwabsucks.com.

[Note that he is discreet in not listing the offensive domain names here, although he was able to mention Chasestinks and others in the previous paragraph.]

12   The National Association for the Advancement of Colored People was smart enough to buy the rights to all of the hate words attacking African-Americans, and the Anti-Defamation League bought up virtually every conceivable anti-Semitic slur domain name.

[More insider terminology for a general newspaper audience]

13   This practice of looking for domain names and sitting on them is called cybersquatting. It has been going on ever since the first opportunist realized that one could buy a name like pepsi.com or burgerking.org and try to hold up those corporations for exorbitant fees to reclaim their own name.

[Why does he use this cliché? Have you seen IMHO (In My Humble Opinion) in an e-mail?]

14   In this writer's humble opinion, everybody should, at the very least, register a domain that is his or her own name.

[Not a complete sentence. Is that OK?]

If at all possible. You never know what the future might bring and, as today's column shows, it's very easy to claim at www.YourName.com.

15    I hit the jackpot with InternetWinter. It was wide open in .com, .org. and .net. All I had to do was hand over my credit card and some personal data (name, address, e-mail), and in a couple of mouse-clicks I became the proud owner of www.InternetWinter.com.

16    It costs $35 a year, and the holder can renew it as long as desired. Register.com is just one of many so-called Internet registrars that sells domain names, and I like it best because it lets you set up a minimalist Web site for each domain you own for free.

[Log on to his site and see what he considers "minimalist."]

17    It took me less than 30 minutes from the time that bull session started to dream up the idea, register the InternetWinter.com domain and use the FirstStepSite.com service to put up a down-and-dirty Web site.

[Notice the wordplay of "put *up*" with "*down*-and-dirty."]

18    If I choose, I can spend time developing this site from now on. And, if I ever got serious about it, I could call upon any one of hundreds of Web-hosting services to put up a far more sophisticated site than the free placeholder service at FirstStepSite.com.

[What tone does Coates get by using such expressions as "hire me [someone]" and "take my gig"?]

19    Who knows? Maybe I can set up my InternetWinter.com site and hire me an investment banker and take my gig public, even as the Amazon.coms and Yahoo.coms are curling up for Internet Winter.

## Exercises

1.    Reread the article and then do some role playing. Have someone interview James Coates. Has he revealed enough of his personality and background for someone to play his part in the dialogue? How important is the person James Coates in making this article effective? Would it be just as effective if he did nothing to inject his personality into it (for example, as a collector and seller of Erector Sets)? Ask him if he would have liked to have taken his college courses online.

2.  The author uses the following methods of development: examples, comparison/contrast, cause and effect, definition, and process. Does he use any others? Were you aware that he was using these techniques as you read the piece?

3.  Write a newspaper column, aimed at general readers, in which you attempt to use Coates's easygoing tone to explain something worthwhile. Think of a hobby or area of special knowledge that you could make interesting for a larger group of readers, and be as detailed as he is.

# Wood Ghost

## by Kerry Temple

### A Note on Vocabulary:

To fully appreciate this piece, you should know the words listed at the end of this box and highlighted in bold in the text. However, don't look them up yet. Rather, as you read, you should try to understand them from the context of the article. In many cases you can make an educated guess, and in others the author will add sufficient explanation to get you through. They are useful words, and on your second reading of "Wood Ghost," you should make them part of your vocabulary, either by looking them up in your dictionary, if necessary, or by seeing their meaning more clearly from the surrounding context of the article.

Here's the list in the order in which they occur. (You may also wish to underline and investigate others that are not included here.)

| | | |
|---|---|---|
| cobalt | wraith | societal |
| celestial | banshee | resiliency |
| nocturnal | caterwauling | belligerent |
| digresses | venery | reclusive |
| meanders | trachea | homo sapiens |
| carnivore | decimated | wantonly |
| predatory | habitat | bobbed |
| beguiling | mythology | copse |
| apparition | | |

*Kerry Temple is editor of* Notre Dame Magazine. *His article appeared in the Spring 1996 issue. This article might be studied in conjunction with the case on animal rights in Chapter 1.*

1     It is just before dawn. The damp air is cold—late-autumn-cold—with frost on the tall, brown grasses and ice and patches of crusty snow. Most of the stars have faded in the east, but a half-moon shines in the west and Venus and Jupiter twinkle like jewels against the **cobalt** sky. But there, beneath the **celestial** canopy, in the shadows of maple and birch and sycamore, the rabbit lies belly-open. Steam rises from the bloody mess.

[Note how the choice of words and images grabs our attention. At this point, he introduces the hero of the article.]

[He varies the length of his sentences, using long and short ones.]

2     The wildcat is eating, ripping apart his prey, leaving only skull and bone and scraps of fur. A black crow titters and caws in the tree nearby. The eastern sky is brightening.

3     The cat has been up all night. He has covered almost 10 miles, maybe more, on his **nocturnal** ramble through his home range, for he **digresses**—scouting for prey, investigating unusual signs and smells, nosing around, ambling about leaving his marks upon the territory he calls his own so his course **meanders,** delivering him finally to the swift, lean rabbit that provided the last nourishment he needed before the crack of day.

[Next he will create a complete change of scene and mood, but he knows that we have the image of the bobcat and the rabbit in our minds. He will return to it when he is ready.]

4     Now full and slow and sleepy, the cat recoils into a harbor of brush and licks the sticky blood from his whiskers and his paws.

[These four sentences are not complete. This technique can be used but must be employed carefully.]

5    As a boy growing up down South, I dreamed of seeing bobcats in the woods. In a land of squirrels, raccoons and opossums, they—not wolf, lion or bear—were the wild things. The solitary **carnivore.** Meateater and mystic. A deadly blend of elegance and cunning, tooth and claw, ferocity and grace. An animal whose shadowy presence loomed large in our landscape and in my imagination, informing both with the scent of elemental danger, **predatory** wildness, **beguiling apparition.**

[This accounts for the article's title]

6    Its **wraith**-like nature had prompted some old-timers to call it "wood ghost," for it is a reclusive, almost secretive animal, so rarely seen that many doubt that it prowls their neighborhood—until they hear its **banshee** cry. As a teenager backpacking in Texas or canoeing in Arkansas, I would lie awake at night listening for that other-worldly wailing, the **caterwauling** that Thackeray described as "a shriek and a yell like the devils of hell." But I never heard it, and in time I began to wonder if any such creatures were still out there in the few remaining wild spots east of the Rockies.

[British novelist, 1811–1863, author of *Vanity Fair*]

[Up to now he has hinted at his main idea or thesis. This paragraph makes it clear.]

7    It was important to me then, as it is now, to think that such elemental wildness still vitalized the countryside where I lived—however curbed, fenced or civilized. So I delighted in the occasional sightings of this pint-sized descendant of the saber-tooth tiger—though these were reports of something lurking in the shadows before dissolving from sight, glimpses of the haunting amber eyes blazing in the twilight. Still, the idea that this distant cousin of the panther, this wily remnant of untamed America might roam my boyhood's rolling, piney hills infected that landscape with a hint of joy and peril.

[Now that he's set a mood and helped us focus on his main idea, he can spend the next several paragraphs giving us the background we need to appreciate his hero, the mysterious bobcat.]

[Scientific name for the bobcat]

8    **Lynx rufus** traces its lineage to ancestral lynx that prowled the Asian high country 4 million years ago. About 200,000 years ago these cats crossed the Bering Straits eastward to give rise to the Canada lynx, the bobcat's closest relative but clear subordinate in territorial wargames.

9    The bobcat's reputation as a ferocious predator had an immediate impact on the Europeans who descended upon this continent 500 years ago. To colonists, who must have been fidgety about all the strange and fearsome

creatures lurking in the woods, the wildcat made a singular impression.

[For comparison purposes, reread the Writing Conventions section on spelling in Chapter 2.]

"The wilde cat," wrote William Wood in *New England's Prospect: A True, Lively, and Experimental Description of that Part of America,* "is more dangerous to bee met withall than any other creature." The chronicler also expressed admiration for the bobcat's hunting technique that it "useth to kill Deare": "Knowing the Deares tracts," he explained in 1634, "hee will lye lurking in long weedes, the Deare passing by he suddenly leapes upon his backe, from thence gets to his necke, and scratcheth out his throate."

10    Tales of bobcats bringing down 200-pound deer are passed down by those who marvel at the cat's bold **venery.** Aware of the same trails within its territory, the bobcat will climb a tree usually on the side away from the trail in order to conceal its claw marks and wait for a passing deer. Pouncing on its prey, it will go for the throat. The relentless snapping action of its jaws, which has been likened to the rapid firing of a sewing machine, enables an adult bobcat, wrote one naturalist, "to pulverize the throat, including the major blood vessels and **trachea,** in a matter of seconds."

[Powerful, vivid images and figures of speech]

11    Because of its fierce and independent nature, its wild and crafty ways, the bobcat rests prominently in the anthology of our national folklore, its snarling visage on the same pages as Daniel Boone, Davy Crockett and other pioneer heroes. Its reputation has prompted some observers to exaggerate the animal's size. As early as 1637, Thomas Morton wrote warily of bobcats and said they were as "bigg as a great Hound."

[The actual facts are as important as the legends.]

12    In truth, the bobcat is slightly larger than a housecat and usually weighs about 25 pounds. Although vicious when cornered, the wildcat's relatively small size makes its ability to prey upon deer all the more impressive.

13    More often the bobcat, who cannot supplement his diet with plants because his stomach physiology is specialized for meat, settles for smaller game—rabbits, mice, squirrels, chipmunks, gophers and such. But it is also admired for its ability to survive by taking third and fourth choice—snakes,

frogs, birds, porcupines (it apparently can pass the quills through the intestine), fish, cave bats, lizards . . . whatever it takes to get along.

14    Where humans have cultivated its territory, bobcats have shown an appetite for livestock, most notably poultry. In Ohio a farmer lost 35 domestic rabbits, 23 ducks, several chickens and one lamb to a sly bobcat he could not trap— but that he shot when it had made one trip too many into the barn. In Colorado one night a bobcat removed a rock from the foundation of a henhouse, feasted on 51 chickens, but was then too big to sneak back out his entry hole. Raids such as these put a price on the bobcat's head long before the American Revolution. And its notoriety as a bandit almost cost the bobcat its very existence.

* * * * *

[Contrast Temple's treatment of this absurd incident with the way it might appear in, say, a Disney film.]
[Now he follows the background information with some reflections on its significance.]

15    Americans have never really known what to do with the wild animals that flourished here before the European onslaught. Some were taken for their meat, some for their pelts, and others—like the wolf, the bear and the wild cats— were killed like outlaws. They were a nuisance; they threatened the safety of those carving a civilization out of the Great American Wilderness. But as was the case with the native peoples who were also in the way of westward expansion, their populations were more severely **decimated** by a reduction in **habitat.**

[He links mistreatment of native American animals with that of native American people.]

16    By the end of the 19th century, the bobcat had become more of a character in our cultural **mythology** than a main player in the territory once its own. Still, in 1915, reacting to the bobcats' threat to livestock, a government Predator and Control Agency was created within the U.S. Department of Agriculture. Over the next several decades literally thousands of bobcats, wolves and mountain lions were killed through a carefully orchestrated poisoning program. It was not until 1972, when President Nixon prohibited the use of toxic chemicals on federal lands, that **societal** forces slowed the wholesale slaughter of American wildlife. By then at least half a million bobcats had been killed.

17    And yet, although its habitats have been radically reduced by the encroaching civilization and it's still

[Refocusing on the bobcat's "heroism"]

hounded as a threat to livestock and trapped for its pelt, the bobcat has survived. Give credit for this hardy **resiliency** to the cat's **belligerent** nature, its knack for being there one moment and gone the next, and for its gritty adaptability. While the grizzlies, wolves and panthers have receded into the closets of America's frontier, the bobcat dug in its claws and hung on.

18    Though it prefers scrubby country and broken forests, the bobcat has made a niche for itself in each of the lower 48 states. The "wood ghost" has persisted because it has made a home in soggy swamplands, throughout the arid Southwest, even amid Midwestern farmland. It is, in essence, all around us—somewhere between 700,000 and 1.5 million of them, although its **reclusive** nature makes a census difficult. Even naturalists who study the creature may go a lifetime without spotting one. It has largely faded into the modern American landscape like a phantom prowler depositing signs of its sweet trespassings, somehow eluding the noose of **homo sapiens.**

[He switches now from objective explanation to more personal remembrances and observations.]

[Note the use of semicolons in a series of items which already contain commas.]

19    When I was younger, exploring the fields of my ever-widening universe, I was on the lookout for wildcats in the back country of Colorado and Utah, in New Mexico, Wyoming and the Adirondacks. I saw their claw marks near the bases of trees, which they use to sharpen their claws and mark their territory; their scat [dung], which is similar to a dog's but which they bury during summer to conceal their presence; and their tracks, which also resemble a dog's. But I found no bobcat on these travels.

20    And yet, as I sought the elusory wildcat and hiked its uncultured domain and read about its habits, I learned a lot about the cat and its country and my place in it. I learned, for example, that the cat places its hindfeet into the tracks of its forepaws, a practice biologists attribute to its instinct to stalk unnoticed.

[One interesting detail after another, adding to our overall picture of the bobcat.]

21    I learned, too, that the bobcat can spring eight feet into the air, that it makes its den in rocky ledges or caves, in abandoned fox dens, even hollow logs. Male and female find each other in early spring, spend some courting time together (howling **wantonly**) and mate. The male then wan-

ders freely off to continue his solitary existence. The kittens, usually three or four in a litter, appear about two months later and stay with the mother throughout the summer, learning bobcat ways. By late fall the young also will wander off, will first mate when they're about a year old, and will live about 15 years. Their isolated existence makes it easy for them to evaporate into the landscape, upholding their ancestral charm.

22    They are largely but not exclusively nocturnal. They get their name from their **bobbed** tail, and their ear tufts help them gather sounds. They use their whiskers as a navigational device when stalking, and females are much more combative than males when defending their territory. Their eyes glow in the dark because wildcats are eerie, phantom-like creatures—and also because light hits a reflective layer behind the retina, called the tapeturm, which bounces the light back, gives the eyes' rods a second chance to absorb the dim nighttime rays.

23    Except for man and his dogs, which really are no match for it, the bobcat has no serious enemies. If tracked, the cat may vault into a tree and wait in ambush. Or it may loop back, appearing behind its hunter, reversing the predator-prey relationship. Such is the stuff of myth and fact, fable and truth, both literal and figurative, which tell of bobcats.

[Summary of the previous paragraphs]

[Back again to the underlying importance of the bobcat as a symbol of strength, independence, and freedom.]

24    At some point I learned, as anyone does who studies animals long, a certain humility in the presence of wild things—the bobcat, or owl, or pronghorn antelope. They are so fast, their senses so keen, their genius so remarkable that humans, turned loose upon the land seem clumsy and dumb in comparison. To say nothing of their beauty and grace. Their power. Their rightness. Their capacity to slip into the landscape and to live there unencumbered. I envy them their intimacy with the earth. I have looked for bobcats every-where.

[Another way of stating main idea]

* * * * *

[It's time to bring us back to that powerful opening scene, knowing what we now know about the article's hero.]

25    I saw the bloody remains of rabbit first. My dog had sniffed it out in the woods where we walked religiously every day for seven years, rain or snow, midnight or dawn—a place along a river where we slipped easily, unobtrusively

into the countryside inhabited by deer and fox, hawks and coons. This was several years ago—at daybreak—but I recall it vividly. The dried blood, the tufts of hair, the ivory bone.

[He has skillfully left us in suspense. We know something important is about to happen, and we're ready for it.]

26    After a few moments I walked on, leaving the dog to scavenge the carrion. Emerging from a **copse** of trees, I was looking across a grassy clearing when an animal appeared some 30 yards in front of me, having stepped out of a hedgerow—as surprised to see me as I to see it. So we watched each other for a moment while I, stunned by its appearance, took inventory—and assured myself that it was indeed a bobcat staring back at me.

27    Although I stepped several paces closer to it, it did not appear threatened. In fact, I sensed that it was content to meet there like that, to stand face-to-face, to hold each other in a gaze, before moving on, easing into the thicket from which it had come, in no apparent hurry to get away.

[What this all means to the author and to us may still not be completely explainable, but it is all right for some things to remain mysterious.]

28    Since that morning I have thought of that encounter many times. It seems significant now, as I recall that meeting, that the bobcat came to that place, those woods, that intersection of my world and his.

## Exercises

1.  Imagine that your job is to trim 300 words from this article so that it will fit into the space alloted in another magazine. What would you cut? Would you cut whole paragraphs, or would you be more precise and "surgical" in removing individual clauses and phrases? Which parts could absolutely not be removed?

2.  Go back to the case on animal rights in Chapter 1. Now imagine this author, or someone similar to him, sitting in the auditorium as the two sides debate their views. Can you tell where his sympathies would lie? Are you sure? Since you don't know him personally, you must rely on his written words to draw *inferences* or conclusions about his

opinions. What does he write that might give you clues to his opinions?

3. Parts of this article are based on personal experience and parts appear to be based on research. Does his tone change when he switches from personal reflections to the more objective, factual sections? Can you point to individual words and phrases to illustrate this?

4. Some people object to what they call *anthropomorphizing* in the discussion of animals. This means presenting animals as human-like creatures. While it may be expected in popular films such as *The Lion King,* it causes controversy among scientists and philosophers when their discussion touches on the nature of animals and whether, for instance, they have "souls." Are animals "just like us only different," or do we do them an injustice when we attempt to humanize them? Does this article help you answer these questions?

5. Write a five-paragraph essay on one of the issues raised in this article. The audience is your fellow classmates.

# GLOSSARY

The definitions provided here apply to the terms as they are used in this book. In many cases, you will find other meanings for these terms in your dictionary. Words in **bold-face** refer to other entries in this glossary.

**abstract**   A quality of writing that emphasizes generalized, nonspecific ideas rather than particular subjects that can be seen, heard, and/or otherwise experienced via the senses. The opposite of **concrete.**

**academic writing**   Writing in college situations, primarily for college audiences, including examinations, essays, research papers, scholarly articles, and books.

**agreement**   In using pronouns, agreement means that a pronoun has the same number (singular or plural) and gender (masculine, feminine, neuter) as its **antecedent.** For example, in the sentence "Jill saw she had won," the word *she* is singular and feminine, just like Jill.

**antecedent**   In using pronouns, an antecedent is the person, place, or thing to which a pronoun refers. For example, in the sentence "Jill saw she had won," *Jill* is the antecedent of *she.*

**audience**   The intended reader or readers of a piece of writing. The writing may sometimes be read by people other than the intended audience but the author still must write with a particular reader or readers in mind.

**body paragraph**   One or more paragraphs that make up the main portion of an essay. These paragraphs develop the essay's **thesis.** See also **paragraph, introductory paragraph,** and **concluding paragraph.**

**case**   A situation or episode that presents information and/or narrates the events taking place at a particular time or in conjunction with a particular idea. This book contains 17 cases.

**casebook**   A textbook that makes use of situations that can be explored and studied to learn particular lessons or develop particular ideas. The book you are using is a casebook.

**cause/effect**   A **method of development** whereby a writer develops ideas by showing how certain results flow from a cause or by showing how a cause has certain results.

**chronological organization**   A method of writing an essay or paragraph by following a time sequence. The unfolding of a process, series of events, or history can give a plan of development to the piece of writing.

**classification**   A **method of development** in which a writer develops a main idea by organizing materials into categories and groups and showing how they relate to the point.

**clause** A group of words that contains a subject and a complete verb. See also **independent clause, dependent clause,** and **phrase.**

**cliché** An overused expression ("This team sure came to play") or situation (the car chase in the last reel of a movie). Clichés start out powerful, interesting, and original but become tired and worn from overuse.

**collaborate** Learning from fellow students through sharing of ideas, both written and spoken, and giving honest feedback and advice. **Role playing,** especially, requires collaboration in getting inside the minds and lives of people featured in the cases.

**colon** A punctuation mark [ : ] that usually signals that something significant is to follow. "The jury gave its verdict: innocent."

**comma** A punctuation mark [ , ] that has several functions, the most common of which is to indicate in writing the kinds of pauses a speaker makes to clarify the meaning of spoken words. Commas are also used to separate items in a series, to indicate nonrestrictive elements in a sentence, and to set off quoted material.

**comparison** A **method of development** in which a writer develops a paragraph or essay by showing the similarities among different elements of the subject matter. See **contrast.**

**compound sentence** A sentence containing two **independent clauses** which are joined together by a **coordinating conjunction** (and, or, nor, for, but, so, yet). Example: I was sure I had brought my credit card, *but* I discov-

ered that I hadn't. See **subordinating conjunction**

**coordinating conjunction** One of several words which can be used to join **independent clauses** together to form **compound sentences.** The coordinating conjunctions are *and, or, nor, for, but, so, yet.*

**concluding paragraph** The last **paragraph** in an essay or group of paragraphs. Generally, it summarizes what has gone before and strengthens the **thesis.**

**conclusion** See **concluding paragraph.**

**concrete** A quality of writing that emphasizes particular, individual, sensory details and features. The opposite of **abstract.**

**context** The situation in which a certain word or expression is found. In **vocabulary** study, the meaning of a word can often be figured out from its context and the way it appears to fit into its context.

**contrast** A **method of development** in which a writer develops a paragraph or essay by showing the differences among different elements of the subject matter. See **comparison.**

**definition** A **method of development** in which a writer gives a description or explanation of something in such a way that a reader can understand the defined object and see how it differs from other, perhaps similar, objects. As a method of development, definition enables a writer to explain individual parts or features of the subject, using separate sentences or paragraphs if necessary.

**dependent clause** Also called **subordinate clause.** A group of words that qualifies as a clause because it contains a subject and complete verb, but which cannot stand alone grammatically as a sentence. This is usually because it begins with a word such as *because, since, although, when, if, or after.* It needs to be connected to an **independent clause.**

**description** A **method of development** in which a writer uses physical description to develop a paragraph or essay by presenting images and sensory experiences that enrich the audience's appreciation of the subject matter.

**direct quotation** Presentation of someone's words, exactly as they are spoken or written. A direct quotation is set off by **quotation marks.** See also **indirect quotation.**

**emphatic organization** A method of writing a paragraph or essay that is based on the relative importance of the different ideas presented. It shares with an audience the sense of what is important, more important, and most important among various ideas. Generally speaking, it is good psychology to save the most important, strongest, most emphatic material for last. See also **organization, chronological organization, spatial organization.**

**English as a second language (ESL)** The use of the English language as spoken and written by a person whose birth language is something other than English. See Appendix B for an extended discussion of ESL.

**essay** A piece of writing consisting of a number of **paragraphs** joined together according to some kind of **organizational plan.** All the paragraphs work together to express and explain the **thesis.**

**euphemism** An expression used to make negative concepts sound less negative. Undertakers, for instance, refer to "the loved one" instead of "the body."

**examples, use of** A **method of development** that a writer can use to present ideas and materials to an audience. By giving examples of an idea, the author strengthens and supports the **topic sentence** or **thesis.**

**feedback** Commentary, criticism, praise, and suggestions an author receives from audience members and fellow writers.

**glossary** A list of words or terms gathered for a particular purpose. A typical glossary will be in alphabetical order and contain definitions of the terms.

**handbook** A systematic written guide to an area of knowledge. This textbook is intended to be used in conjunction with a writing handbook.

**idiom** A way of saying (or writing) something that is peculiar to a given language. To nonnative students of the language, an idiom may seem strange and/or illogical, but native speakers recognize it as being "just the way we say it in our language."

**indent** Beginning a paragraph a few spaces (usually five) from the left margin of a piece of writing.

**independent clause** A clause that can stand by itself as a grammatically complete sentence. It may be combined with other clauses and phrases. Also called **main clause.**

**indirect quotation** Paraphrasing the words and ideas of a speaker/writer instead of quoting them exactly as they were spoken or written. **Quotation marks** are not used in indirect quotation. Indirect quotation: Charley said that his lawn needed mowing. **Direct quotation:** Charley said, "My grass has gotten too long."

**inflection**    A change in the basic form of a word that adds meaning to the word. Some examples of inflections used in English are *-ed* (walk*ed*), *-s* (apple*s*), *-ing* (walk*ing*), *-m* (who*m*). Inflection and **word order** are two features by which a language communicates meaning.

**introductory paragraph**    The opening **paragraph** in an essay. It attempts to get the reader's attention, to state the essay's **thesis,** and, if possible, to give the reader a sense of how the essay will be developed.

**irregular verb**    Action word that significantly changes form to indicate a charge in tense. Example: do/did/ done. See also **regular verb.**

**letter**    A common form of written communication to a specific person or organization. Letters can be composed on paper and online. If they are intended for a formal situation, they have commonly accepted features, such as a date, address, salutation, body, closing, and signature.

**main clause**    See **independent clause.**

**main idea**    See **thesis.**

**metaphor**    An expression that compares one thing to another without using *like* or *as*. Example: "A life without love is cloudy and storm-filled." See **simile.**

**method of development**    A technique or device used by a writer to enrich and expand the subject matter. This book discusses the following methods of development: **description, examples, comparison/contrast, cause and effect, definition, process,** and **classification.**

**non-restrictive**    This refers to a group of words which are not essential to the basic meaning of a sentence but which are still contained in the sentence. Such a group of words is set off by commas. Example: Susan Montgomery, *who lives in the apartment next to ours,* has become a good friend of mine. **See restrictive.**

**noun**    A word that indicates a person, place, or thing. See **pronoun, agreement,** and **antecedent.**

**organization**    A plan for development of an essay or piece of writing. It may require use of an **outline.** Three methods of organization are **spatial, chronological,** and **emphatic.**

**outline**    A visual method of representing the **organization** of a piece of writing. Outlines may have varying degrees of formality. They can range from a scratch outline, consisting of a few hastily assembled headings in a list, to a formal outline that uses carefully indented headings and subheadings set off by numbers and letters.

**paragraph**    A collection of sentences grouped together for effective communication. Paragraphs are *visibly* separated from other paragraphs by spacing on the page and, often, because the first line is **indented.** Most importantly, the sentences are placed together, separate from other paragraphs, because they *belong* together. They make up a unit that expresses one basic part of what the author is trying to say to the audience.

**period**    A punctuation mark [ . ] that indicates the end of a complete sentence.

**person**    One of three possible viewpoints involved in the transfer of ideas through words: first person, the one who is doing the communicating, the author or speaker (I, we), second person, the person or persons to whom the communication is addressed, the audience or listener (you); and third person, anyone or anything else that is the subject of communication (he, she, they, it).

**phrase**    Words that are grouped together but don't make up a **clause** because they don't contain both a subject and a complete verb.

**plagiarism**    Theft of the ideas or, especially, the exact words of another without giving credit to the original author.

**point**    See **thesis.**

**polishing**    Making final adjustments to your words to get them the way you want them. Polishing for a writer is what using different grades of sandpaper is for a furniture maker.

**process**    A **method of development** in which a writer explains a process to clarify a **thesis.** Describing steps or phases also provides a logical framework for some or all of the work's outline.

**pronoun**    A word that takes the place of a noun. For example, *they* can take the place of *The Mets* in this sentence: "The Mets lost the series, but they played well." Pronouns must be in **agreement** with their **antecedents.**

**proofreading**    Careful and systematic examination of a finished piece of writing to find and correct such problems as misspellings, grammatical errors, unintentional repetitions, and typographical mistakes (typos).

**quotation**    Presenting the words or ideas of someone other than the author in a piece of writing. Quotation may be either **direct** or **indirect.**

**quotation mark**    A set of punctuation marks [" "] indicating that the words placed between them are the exact words spoken or written by the person other than the writer.

**regular verb**    A verb that uses **inflections** to indicate change in tense. Example: walk, walked, have walked. See also **irregular verb.**

**research**    Writing that relies on the work of other writers and authorities. Their words and ideas are gathered, evaluated, organized, and presented according to a careful outline in a format appropriate for the audience.

**restrictive**    This refers to a group of words within a sentence which are essential to the basic meaning of a sentence. Such a group of words is not set off by commas. Example: The woman *who lives in the apartment next to ours* has become a good friend of mine. See **non-restrictive.**

**role playing**    Putting yourself into the mind and situation of another. In this book, role playing is a central method of learning to improve your writing. By inserting yourself into the life of a character in a **case,** you learn how other people react to events and how they write about them.

**rough draft**    A preliminary version of a piece of writing. It may be done quickly to capture a set of ideas before going back over them to expand, reorganize, and polish. It may be developed along with a **rough outline.**

**rough outline** A preliminary scheme for organizing an essay. It may be somewhat incomplete and inconsistent, without the complete headings and development found in a finished outline.

**run-on sentence** A group of words consisting of two (or more) **independent clauses** which follow each other without any attempt to punctuate the point(s) where the clauses run together. Example: I was sure I had brought my credit card I discovered that I hadn't.

**semicolon** A punctuation mark [ ; ] that performs some of the functions of a **comma.** It is stronger and more emphatic than a comma.

**sentence** A group of words that contains at least one **independent clause.**

**simile** An expression that compares one thing to another by pointing out that they are similar. Example: "A life without love is like a day without sunshine." See **metaphor.**

**spatial organization** A method of **organization** used in writing a paragraph. Material is presented as it exists in physical space (left to right, front to back, top to bottom, etc.) Spatial organization works well when the subject material has physical dimensions of some kind, such as a battlefield, a piece of machinery, or a scenic view.

**stereotype** An oversimplified or overgeneralized image of something or someone. Stereotypes, such as those based on the supposed racial, ethnic, or lifestyle qualities of people, tend to be negative and are perceived as negative by readers.

**subordinate clause** See **dependent clause.**

**subordinating conjunction** A word used to form a sentence by joining an **independent clause** and a **dependent clause.** Example: I was confident *because* I had brought my credit card. Some other common subordinating conjunctions are *when, since, although, if,* and *after.*

**support** Use of details, examples, statistics, and other material to strengthen the basic ideas expressed in a **thesis** or **topic sentence.**

**tense** The way a language expresses the concept of relative time. Events written or spoken about are placed in the past, present, or future in ways that are meaningful to the audience. Tense in English requires appropriate **inflections** in the use of verbs (walk*s,* walk*ed,* walk*ing*), auxiliary words joined to the verbs (*is* walking, *has* walked, *must* walk), and other time indicators (yesterday, then, after, before).

**thesis** The **main idea** or **point** of an essay or paragraph.

**topic sentence** One sentence, frequently the first one, that sums up the overall idea of a paragraph. The rest of the paragraph's sentences work together to convey the topic sentence's idea effectively.

**transition** Words and expressions that indicate passage from one idea to another and the connections between ideas. Some common transitions are *in addition, finally, therefore, first, on the other hand,* and *consequently.*

**verb**    A word that indicates an action or a state of existence. See **tense, regular verb,** and **irregular verb.**

**vocabulary**    The accumulated stockpile of words a writer develops through reading, listening, and studying. Additions to a person's vocabulary come through encountering words in their surrounding **context** and figuring out their probable meanings and by more formal study through the use of dictionaries and glossaries.

**word order**    The feature of a language that places words in a particular sequence to convey meaning to an audience. Along with the use of **inflections,** it is one of the primary ways that a language works as a verbal system.

**writing across the curriculum**    Use of academic writing in different areas of study. A particular discipline or subject may have its own terminology and manner of expression accepted by others in the field, but academic writing still relies on the basic principles outlined in this book. In any field, a person communicates with an audience through use of **writing conventions, outlines, organization,** and **methods of development** to express a **thesis** in **paragraphs** and **essays.** In any area of the curriculum, the finished product is **polished** and carefully **proofread.**

**writing conventions**    The features of written communication that are accepted by the users of a language. Common spellings of words, logical use of punctuation, accepted meanings of words, and other conventions enable authors to convey concepts and tone to their audiences.

# CREDITS

# INDEX